LINKING VISIONS

Studies in Social, Political, and Legal Philosophy
Series Editor: James P. Sterba, University of Notre Dame

This series analyzes and evaluates critically the major political, social, and legal ideals, institutions, and practices of our time. The analysis may be historical or problem-centered; the evaluation may focus on theoretical underpinnings or practical implications. Among the recent titles in the series are:

LINKING VISIONS

Feminist Bioethics, Human Rights, and the Developing World

EDITED BY
ROSEMARIE TONG,
ANNE DONCHIN, AND
SUSAN DODDS

ROWMAN & LITTLEFIELD PUBLISHERS, INC.
Lanham • Boulder • New York • Toronto • Oxford

ROWMAN & LITTLEFIELD PUBLISHERS, INC.

Published in the United States of America
by Rowman & Littlefield Publishers, Inc.
A wholly owned subsidiary of The Rowman & Littlefield Publishing Group, Inc.
4501 Forbes Boulevard, Suite 200, Lanham, MD 20706
www.rowmanlittlefield.com

P.O. Box 317, Oxford OX2 9RU, UK

British Library Cataloguing in Publication Information Available

Library of Congress Cataloging-in-Publication Data

Linking visions : feminist bioethics, human rights, and the developing world /
    edited by Rosemarie Tong, Anne Donchin, and Susan Dodds.
        p. cm.— (Studies in social, political, and legal philosophy)
    Includes bibliographical references and index.
    ISBN 0-7425-3278-X (cloth : alk. paper) — ISBN 978-0-7425-3279-3
    I. Medical ethics. 2. Feminism—Moral and ethical aspects. 3.
Bioethics. 4. Women—Health and hygiene. I. Tong, Rosemarie. II.
Donchin, Anne. III. Dodds, Susan, 1962–
    R724.L55 2004
    174'.957—dc22

                                                                2004006788

Printed in the United States of America

♾™ The paper used in this publication meets the minimum requirements of American
National Standard for Information Sciences—Permanence of Paper for Printed Library
Materials, ANSI/NISO Z39.48-1992.

CONTENTS

Acknowledgments

WE WISH TO EXPRESS our heartfelt thanks to Lisa Singleton, the project manager and typist of this volume. She is an exceptional thinker, writer, wife, and mother who is rearing a thoroughly feminist daughter. We are deeply in her debt and view her as a major supporter of women's and girls' human rights in the United States and abroad.

In addition, we wish to thank Erin Cahill for her help preparing the manuscript and Fiona Borthwick for comments on sections of the collection. Our gratitude also extends to Eve DeVaro, Patricia MacDonald, and Jehanne Schweitzer. Throughout the years, Eve has consistently and strongly supported the publication of books that focus on feminist thinking, gender issues, and women's rights. Patricia's skills as a copyeditor are awesome, and Jehanne made the last stages of our book's production much easier than they would have been without her able assistance.

Finally, we would like to thank each of the uncredited reviewers who read drafts of chapters and then gave their invaluable reactions and input.

Introduction
Integrating Global and Local Perspectives

SUSAN DODDS

THE 2002 CONFERENCE of the International Network on Feminist Approaches to Bioethics (FAB), in Brasília, was an exciting and momentous occasion. Not only did the conference demonstrate the diversity and importance of feminist voices in bioethical debate, but it also celebrated the tenth anniversary of the organization. FAB has been active in promoting feminist bioethics, understood as an inclusive bioethical theory that draws on and affirms the standpoints and experiences of women and other oppressed groups. Through feminist approaches to bioethics, the presuppositions frequently unacknowledged as informing dominant bioethical debates can be uncovered, and their effects in privileging those with power can be challenged. More positively, once those assumptions are identified for what they are, new approaches and strategies can be developed that are responsive to the disparate conditions of women's lives across the globe (Holmes and Donchin 2002, 3–4).

It can no longer be said that feminist bioethics is on the periphery of bioethics: the International Network on Feminist Approaches to Bioethics has become the largest of the networks affiliated with the International Association of Bioethics (IAB). Indeed, the current president of the IAB, Dr. Florencia Luna, is a longtime FAB officer, and the board also includes past FAB co-coordinator Professor Rosemarie Tong. While it can no longer be said that feminist bioethics is overlooked in the bioethics literature, the issues that feminist bioethicists address concerning gender, oppression, and access to appropriate health care have not been so readily resolved. Being recognized as participants in debates about health care is not sufficient to make health care ethically adequate.

The contributions to this volume demonstrate the ways in which feminist bioethics has developed in recent years, showing how it has moved well beyond the debates that were common at FAB's start (Donchin and Purdy 1999). Today there is greater willingness to critically integrate and develop approaches previously criticized by feminists. In one sense these developments demonstrate both how feminist concerns have influenced mainstream debate in the bioethics literature (even the term *mainstream* sounds somewhat dated now) and the ways in which feminist theorizations and politics have shifted emphasis from critical responses to constructive contributions.

Greater diversity exists among feminist bioethicists' projects and concerns than ever before. One of the first collections on feminist approaches to bioethics, gleaned from articles in the feminist philosophy journal *Hypatia* by Holmes and Purdy (1992), emphasized "care" in medical ethics, reproductive ethics, and the use of women in clinical experimentation. Feminist work is no longer expected to be found dominantly in the areas of reproductive, sexual, or maternal ethics or on the role of women as patients: feminist work occurs on nearly every topic of current bioethics debate. The range of influences on feminist bioethics is also ever-expanding to include poststructuralism, developments in human rights theorizing, global ethics, development studies, feminist social theory, feminist anthropology, and myriad other areas of inquiry. One particular development is the ever-increasing presence of feminist voices from geographical regions and social groupings that were largely absent from bioethical debate just a few years ago. This development is reflected well in this collection.

Feminist Bioethics

Susan Sherwin recognizes the diversity of people who would describe themselves as feminists. There are common themes within this diversity:

> Generally, feminists share a recognition that women are oppressed in our society and an understanding that their oppression takes many different forms, compounded often by other forms of oppression based on features such as race, ethnicity, sexual orientation, and economic class. Because feminists believe that oppression is objectionable on both moral and political grounds, most are committed to transforming society in ways that will ensure the elimination of oppression in all its forms. (Sherwin 1996, 47)

The rich range of responses by feminist bioethicists to oppression in health and medicine can be readily found in the two earlier collections of papers drawn from FAB conferences, edited by Donchin and Purdy (1999) and by Tong, Anderson, and Santos (2001).

Feminist bioethicists raise concerns about oppression in the context of health care, medical research, and population health. In articulating the multiple forms

of oppression and feminist responses that challenge oppression, feminist bioethicists must inevitably employ a diverse range of approaches and discipline techniques. This diversity is needed to understand, analyze, and reconceptualize
bioethics through examination of the broader structural issues and networks of
power that frame both bioethics and health care (Sherwin 1996, 55). That
broader context includes global markets in health, medical technologies, and human tissues; recognition of the significant contribution to be made by distinct
ethical traditions and social contexts; access to health care for those living in
poverty; use of state authority to shape reproductive choices; global effects of
HIV/AIDS; and ideological commitments and their effects on women's and children's welfare.

We have produced this collection partly in response to the increased voice of
feminists whose work addresses cultures and countries too often perceived as on
the margin of mainstream bioethics. It is also a recognition of the significant conceptual contributions of feminists in a range of interrelated fields, especially as
they formulate appropriate responses to developments in medical technology,
global economics, population shifts, and poverty. In this collection, we have
brought together fourteen essays that address the themes of feminist bioethics,
human rights, and development. These are new works, several of which have been
drawn from papers presented at the Conference of the International Network on
Feminist Approaches to Bioethics (FAB) in Brasília in November 2002, as well as
others written for this collection.

Feminist bioethics encompasses a wide array of different feminist approaches.
The approaches that make up feminist bioethics, according to Tong, do not provide a complete alternative to other approaches to bioethics. Rather, "asking the
so-called woman question" in health care offers conceptual reinterpretations, provides grounds for reconsidering terminology, and, more important, reassesses the
focus on individuals as separate and independent, through its demonstration of
the array of human interdependencies and social relationships (Tong 1997,
243–44). In focusing attention on the significance of these connections, feminist
bioethicists also challenge the neat compartmentalization of the ethical issues,
power relations, and opportunities associated with health care as distinct from
those features as they arise in education, welfare, and people's status as citizens of
a particular state. Thus, when feminist bioethics addresses issues of human rights
and the circumstances of those living in, and negotiating health care within, developing nations, it refines the concepts employed in human rights and development discourses and also highlights the bioethical significance of the
interconnectedness of people's lives and its implications for social, political, and
legal institutions. The contributors to this collection share a commitment to feminist bioethics that informs their various investigations into the intersections, gaps,

and conflicts between discourses concerning feminist bioethics, human rights, and global development. Those themes are briefly introduced in the following sections, followed by an overview of the collection.

Human Rights

The human rights discourse of eighteenth-century revolutionary France and the American colonies emphasized the "rights of man" as articulated in the Declaration of the Rights of Man and of Citizens (National Assembly of France 1789) and Thomas Paine's *Rights of Man* (1915). Unlike legal or political rights that exist in virtue of their being promulgated by a state, the existence and significance of these rights were conceptually independent from their recognition by particular states. These rights are held simply in virtue of the individual's humanity and both generate responsibilities to the state for protection and limit the legitimate authority of the state to interfere with the exercise of those rights.

Mary Wollstonecraft, writing soon after the French Revolution, criticized the exclusion of women from the scope of the "rights of man" in the French Constitution and offered a corrective in her "Vindication of the Rights of Woman" (1792/1994). Indeed, Wollstonecraft was the first of a number of authors to write on the exclusive nature of human rights, including the articulation of them in the Universal Declaration of Human Rights (United Nations 1948), which grounds such rights in the "inherent dignity of human persons." Criticisms of human rights approaches are often similar to criticisms of the conception of rights frequently found in liberal political theory: they presuppose a conception of people as isolated, rational atoms; they privilege some groups over others; they mask the effects of race, class, gender, and cultural difference; and their articulation as negative rights (protections against interference) is thought to render these rights meaningless in a world in which a large portion of humanity lacks (positive) access to the material necessities of life.

The Universal Declaration of Human Rights was written in response to international postwar abhorrence of the treatment of Jews and other stigmatized groups by the government of Nazi Germany. The ideals expressed in the declaration did not have the force of international law, however, until the 1966 ratification of the International Covenant on Economic, Social and Cultural Rights and the International Covenant on Civil and Political Rights. The various UN declarations, conventions, protocols, and treaties developed over the past four decades have transformed the international understanding of human rights and their status such that they are less open to the criticisms of partiality and exclusion mentioned previously. Michael Ignatieff describes the effect of the international human rights conventions, with their capacity to enforce international norms by punishing violators, as part of a postwar juridical and advocacy revolution (Ignatieff 2001).

Appeals to "human rights" can thus be seen as making two different kinds of claim. For some writers, an appeal to human rights arises when the author makes a claim based on some preconventional ethical entitlement to recognition of an individual's or group's rights. These authors often recognize the appeal of the natural rights tradition but wish to avoid the metaphysical or epistemic limitations of natural rights approaches. For others, "human rights talk" occurs against the backdrop of the UN declarations and conventions. To claim a human right, for these commentators, is to appeal to a potentially enforceable international standard in the face of policies and practices seen to violate those international norms.

For Ignatieff, the purpose of appeals to human rights is to protect and enhance individual agency, while recognizing the diversity of ways in which that agency is expressed within different cultures and communities (Ignatieff 2001, 18). The international human rights conventions are valuable insofar as they can encourage, shame, or punish states so as to enhance the exercise of human rights. Ignatieff's approach to human rights is pragmatic: he is not concerned about establishing the foundations of human rights; rather, he is interested in the significance of being able to make claims of human rights for the lives of people.

> Such a grounding as modern human rights requires, I would argue, is based on what history tells us: that human beings are at risk of their lives if they lack a basic measure of free agency; that agency itself requires protection through internationally agreed standards; that these standards should entitle individuals to oppose and resist unjust laws and orders within their own states; and, finally that when all other remedies have been exhausted, that these individuals have the right to appeal to other peoples, nations, and international organizations for assistance in defending their rights. (Ignatieff 2001, 55)

Ignatieff's minimalist approach to human rights, a "thin universalism," still leaves open some questions about the degree to which "human rights talk" can address the specific concerns of gender, interdependence, and significant cultural and ethical difference. Although Ignatieff's approach emphasizes freedom and human agency, and their realization through membership in collectivities and communities, the approach does not offer a conceptual or pragmatic basis for critically examining gender and other hierarchies that oppress groups of individuals within collectivities (see Donchin in this volume). It is not clear, therefore, that his view can address the oppressive features of institutions and traditions within which women's agency may be limited. Some of the contributions to this collection articulate further the extent to which human rights discourse can be used to address these concerns.

Economic Development, Global Ethics, and Globalization

Ingatieff's focus on human rights grounded in "thin universalism" and as protecting human agency is closely related to issues of poverty and development and to the question of global ethics. An individual's "free agency" is clearly dependent on at least minimal material resources through which to secure life, relative health, and absence of crushing need. Human rights approaches need accounts informed by development studies to begin to address embodied human agency. At the same time, any human rights approach must grapple with the charge of false universalism that would accompany those understandings of the content of human rights that did not genuinely recognize and respect the diversity of ethical ways of life and traditions.

The developing literature in global ethics can be viewed as having at least two aims: to develop appropriate ethical standards that can be applied to international interactions, trade, policy, or social movements; or to identify the ethical impacts of globalization and seek to develop arguments responding to those effects. Both of these aims require attention to both local and global factors and their interaction.

Approaches to feminist bioethics that wish to draw on and extend human rights discourse and to make a significant contribution to debate about global ethics are faced with a number of considerations that are infrequently attended to in the bioethics literature. The two key interrelated issues are, first, the economic, social, and political effects of globalized capitalism and, second, the need to negotiate the tensions between charges of cultural imperialism and cultural relativism. The interrelationships between the two issues are evidenced by those commentators who argue that the advance of capitalism is a necessary precondition for democratic governance and protection of human rights and those who argue, to the contrary, that the globalization of markets frequently undermines the human rights of those living in developing nations (especially rights of cultural membership) or that markets support only those human rights that are market-friendly and frequently suppress local democratic movements (Brysk 2002; Shapiro and Hacker-Cordón 1999).

One effect of global markets is the extensive movement of people around the globe pursuing work as local economies are undermined by global competition. In the mass migration from poorer regions to industrial centers, cultural traditions are also transported and reconstructed. Global migration literally dislocates communities, so that it is no longer possible to assume that cultural traditions are either unaffected by global events, nor that cultural traditions are geographically specific. Therefore, discussions about human rights, cultural difference, and development must maintain a double focus—on local or regional differences between peoples and on the global movements of people holding cultural expectations, understandings, and values.

Feminists concerned about challenging oppression, while recognizing the oppressive effects of the false universalism that may accompany uncritical adoption of simplistic approaches to human rights, need to take particular care in negotiating these issues. Women's lives are affected by oppressive forces within both local traditions and global institutions. Uma Narayan has been particularly articulate in her rejection of the political quietism that can accompany cultural pluralist or standpoint approaches while, simultaneously, demanding that Western feminists listen to particular demands of justice made by non-Western feminists (Narayan 1990). Feminist opposition to oppression throughout the world demands articulation through the particular circumstances of women in their local and globalized contexts.

Martha Nussbaum, in *Women and Human Development* (2000), has recently examined the development needs of women trying to construct meaningful lives in local communities increasingly affected by economic globalization. Nussbaum does not use the language of human rights. Rather, she draws on the capabilities approach to welfare and development initially articulated by economist Amartya Sen (1982). In Nussbaum's capabilities approach, it is the role of states to provide their citizenry with the array of central human capabilities. Therefore, appropriate economic reform must attend to the effects of such reform on the capabilities of individuals to pursue embodied human agency. Nussbaum's response to the global expansion of capitalism is to argue for a set of ethical norms or basic principals that can serve as "constraints on the utility-enhancing choices nations may make" (Nussbaum 2000, 32). The emphasis on individual capabilities as separable from collective values or contexts and claims of universal human nature has caused some feminists to question whether Nussbaum's approach can adequately explain human agency as significantly constituted within social relationships (see, for example, Donchin in this volume). It is arguable that an adequate understanding of the impediments to women's agency and capabilities requires a critical understanding of the relationships between those capabilities and the complex social relationships that shape the lives of gendered members of particular cultures (Donchin 2000; Freedman 1999).

Taking the Theoretical and Practical Debates Forward

This collection is divided into four parts, each of which address the interrelationships of the previously outlined themes. The contributions in part I take the theoretical issues and critically respond to or integrate the relationships among feminist bioethics, human rights, and globalization. Dickenson's and Donchin's contributions specifically rise to the challenge of showing the significance of feminist approaches to bioethics as providing responses and refinements to the theoretical work on development and human rights. They demonstrate the capacity for explicitly feminist approaches to resolve the essentialist/relativism dichotomy in demanding human rights (especially women's rights) in diverse cultures. Both seek to draw out the feminist implications and limitations of Nussbaum's approach (among others), while demonstrating the need for feminists to attend to the development needs of women globally. These works critically engage with the literature while extending and revising feminist arguments.

Quinn likewise critically engages with Nussbaum but seeks a relational approach to development and support for human health needs. Quinn's objective is to enhance the capacity of those in poorer nations to articulate their needs and also to make those in positions of relative power recognize their interrelations with, and obligations toward, those who are relatively powerless. She draws on examples from Chile to illustrate how a carefully articulated conception of empathetic concern for those whose needs are not met can motivate appropriate responses to support those who urge changes from within Chile and demand international assistance from without.

Salles's contribution focuses on the risks to women's human rights associated with uncritical or stereotyped cultural or ethnic respect, using the example of cultural differences attributed to Hispanic patients in U.S. health care institutions. According to Salles, uncritical steps taken to recognize cultural or ethnic difference (for example, acting on assumptions that health care decisions are made collectively in a particular culture) can undermine patients' rights, particularly the rights of women who are members of patriarchal cultural or ethnic groups. Salles argues for the nonstereotyped recognition of ethnic or cultural difference only where that recognition is consistent with respect for patients' rights.

Nie and Tong both focus on the need to develop a common language of bioethics so that the debates about ethical issues in health care can be addressed as they arise around the world, drawing on diverse approaches and traditions. In doing so, Tong and Nie each engage in a critical dialogue of shared understandings, discursively demonstrating the points of contact, difference, and refinement between different traditions and conceptual approaches. Nie demonstrates the potential for communication between Chinese ethical traditions and a properly modified approach to human rights. Nie also demonstrates the particular social and traditional features of the lives of women in China that demand a critical response on human rights grounds, as well as within Chinese ethical traditions. Tong identifies why feminist bioethicists have been reluctant to use the language of human rights in making demands on behalf of women and also demonstrates the significance of adapting feminist arguments to gain the international normative force of demands grounded in human rights.

Part II examines reproduction and the ways in which national policy, development of reproductive therapies, international trade, and foreign policy shape women's reproductive choices and alternatives. Several of the contributions in this part demonstrate the importance of evaluating individual reproductive decision making against the backdrop of local contexts and government policies and use this to critically challenge assumptions that when women make reproductive choices, their choices are not mediated by (oppressive) social circumstances. Unlike contributions in other feminist bioethics collections addressing reproduction, these chapters specifically focus on the global context of reproductive decision making and the relationship between reproductive health and human rights.

Shanthi examines the complex relationships among government policy, public health campaigns, and cultural values to identify the features shaping the reproductive choices of women in India, where population growth poses a significant challenge to attempts by the state to reduce poverty and improve health. Zilberberg's contribution compares reproductive decision making in India and the United States, by comparing the context and ethical salience of reproductive sex selection in the two countries, where sex selection is sought in different contexts and using different techniques. Baird demonstrates the effects of U.S. foreign policy on women's health and access to health care and health education through its refusal to provide family planning funding to those nongovernmental organizations outside the United States that provide abortion counseling and abortion services or participate in debate about abortion in their own countries. Baird argues that the existence of this "global gag rule" harms women's health and human rights in developing countries, thereby demonstrating the limits of the U.S. government's commitment to universal protection of human rights. Finally, Tao examines the social factors shaping Chinese attitudes toward contracted or surrogate motherhood and uses Confucian ethics to demonstrate the potential to develop a Confucian feminist ethic that can provide an argument against the ethical acceptability of surrogacy in China.

Part III of this collection includes two contributions that explore the possibilities and risks of developments in genetic research. Bertomeu and Sommer critically assess the effects of extending private property rights in the form of patents over human genetic material. They argue that such exclusive rights benefit private corporations and remove some people's access to the benefits of our common genetic inheritance. They show how people, especially those in developing nations, will be excluded from access to health benefits (such as the diagnostic benefits available since the identification and isolation of the breast cancer gene BRCA1) and argue against the extension of these property rights. Hocking and Harvey-Blankenship, however, see positive opportunities arising from the development of DNA identification. They argue that the human rights of people in countries that have suffered civil war or military dictatorships can be promoted through provision of DNA identification services as a form of foreign aid. Where oppressive regimes have abducted women and children and have raised children separated from their biological kin, access to DNA identification can, they argue, assist families to reunite and allow children to know their genetic identity, thereby supporting their human rights.

Finally, part IV addresses the human rights challenges facing health policy makers in the face of HIV/AIDS. O'Keefe and Chinouya examine the difficulties in realizing public health goals for black African women who have migrated to the United Kingdom, given that public health initiatives frequently lack proper grounding in, or sensitivity to, the tenuous social and political situation of the migrant communities or the gendered nature of the traditional cultures that influence those communities. O'Keefe and Chinouya attempt to show how globalization influences the health care and human rights of black African women in Western and non-Western developing nations and how drawing on specific cultural practices can resolve some of these impediments. Kaplan takes a more general look at the relationship between international HIV/AIDS policies and strategies and the human rights of women and children in the various states. She specifically shows that where nations are selective in their approach to HIV prevention or HIV/AIDS treatment, women's and children's human rights are frequently abused.

Finally, a note on terminology: in this work, we recognize the contestable nature of terms such as *developing world*, *third world*, and *less-developed nations*, with their tacit acceptance that those countries are inferior or less "civilized" than the nations of the developed first world, or that the citizenry of the global South or those in non-Western states invariably suffer worse conditions (education, welfare, health, housing, etc.) than those who are privileged to live in the North or industrialized West. We are well aware of the rich cultural resources of many societies that fall within the economic category of developing nations, the immense wealth (for example, in oil reserves) held by a few in some third world states, the squalor of the slums of Europe and North America, and the abject poverty of indigenous peoples living within the wealthy nations of the world. Recognizing that writers from these states also find themselves using contestable language, we take courage from writers such as Uma Narayan, who uses the terms *Western*, *non-Western*, and *third world* in her work on cultural identities and traditions (Narayan 1997). These terms are used in this collection to loosely distinguish those states sharing either a Western-European cultural tradition or relative national wealth built on industrial production from those states that do not share that tradition or that source of wealth; however, we acknowledge that they are imprecise tools that may obscure as much as they illuminate. Wherever possible, the authors of the contributions to this work have been prompted by the editors to explain their usage of these terms, so as to more self-consciously consider the assumptions underlying their usage.

References

Brysk, Alison, ed. 2002. *Globalization and Human Rights.* Berkeley: University of California Press.

Donchin, Anne. 2000. "Autonomy and Interdependence: Quandaries in Genetic Decisionmaking." In *Relational Autonomy: Feminist Perspectives on Autonomy, Agency and the Social Self,* edited by Catriona Mackenzie and Natalie Stoljar, 236–58. New York: Oxford University Press.

Donchin, Anne, and Purdy, Laura, eds. 1999. *Embodying Bioethics: Recent Feminist Advances.* Lanham, Md.: Rowman & Littlefield.

Freedman, Lynn P. 1999. "Reflections on Emerging Frameworks of Health and Human Rights." In *Health and Human Rights: A Reader,* edited by Jonathan M. Mann, Sofia Grushkin, Michael A. Grodin, and George A. Annas, 227–52. London: Routledge.

Holmes, Helen Bequaert, and Donchin, Anne. 2002. *History of the International Network on Feminist Approaches to Bioethics (FAB).* Brasília, Brazil: Letras Livres.

Holmes, Helen Bequaert, and Purdy, Laura, eds. 1992. *Feminist Perspectives in Medical Ethics.* Bloomington: Indiana University Press.

Ignatieff, Michael. 2001. "Human Rights as Politics." In *Human Rights as Politics and Idolatry,* edited by Amy Gutman, 3–52. Princeton, N.J.: Princeton University Press.

Narayan, Uma. 1990. "The Project of Feminist Epistemology: Perspectives from a Non-Western Feminist." In *Gender/Body/Knowledge: Feminist Reconstructions of Being and Knowing,* edited by Alison Jagger and Susan Bordo, 256–69. New Brunswick, N.J.: Rutgers University Press.

———. 1997. *Dislocating Cultures: Identities, Traditions and Third-World Feminism.* New York: Routledge.

National Assembly of France. 1789/1915. Declaration of the Rights of Man and of Citizens. In *Rights of Man,* translated by Thomas Paine, 94–97. London: J. M. Dent & Sons.

Nussbaum, Martha. 2000. *Women and Human Development: The Capabilities Approach.* Cambridge, UK: Cambridge University Press.

Paine, Thomas. 1915. *Rights of Man.* London: J. M. Dent & Sons.

Sen, Amartya. 1982. *Choice, Welfare and Measurement.* Oxford: MIT Press.

Shapiro, Ian, and Hacker-Cordón, Casiano, eds. 1999. *Democracy's Edges.* New York: Cambridge University Press.

Sherwin, Susan. 1996. "Feminism and Bioethics." In *Feminism and Bioethics: Beyond Reproduction,* edited by Susan M. Wolf, 47–66. New York: Oxford University Press.

Tong, Rosemarie. 1997. *Feminist Approaches to Bioethics: Theoretical Reflections and Practical Applications.* Boulder, Colo.: Westview.

Tong, Rosemarie, Gwen Anderson, and Aida Santos, eds. 2001. *Globalizing Feminist Bioethics: Crosscultural Perspectives.* Boulder, Colo.: Westview.

United Nations. 1948. Universal Declaration of Human Rights. Paris: United Nations General Assembly.

Wollstonecraft, Mary. 1792/1994. "A Vindication of the Rights of Woman." In *Political Writings,* edited by Janet Todd, 63–283. Oxford, UK: Oxford University Press.

EXPLORING AFFINITIES BETWEEN FEMINIST BIOETHICS AND HUMAN RIGHTS

I

What Feminism Can Teach Global Ethics I

DONNA L. DICKENSON

FOR AT LEAST TWENTY YEARS, feminist scholars have been wrestling with questions about difference and essentialism, similar to those that underpin current debates in global ethics. Yet mainstream philosophy and political theory rarely mention their contribution, seem to have learned little from them, and often appear to think that no one else has dealt with these problems before. Second-wave feminism has overcome its inward-looking psychoanalytical fixation on difference to reaffirm the possibility of struggle against injustice, enhanced by a realistic incorporation of difference where it really is something more than an excuse for maintaining the status quo. Particularly in practical areas such as bioethics, feminism's version of difference is not quietist but reformist: it does not view all identities and norms as equally valid, nor does it seek to return to a communitarian golden age.

I will qualify these strong assertions with some cautionary notes: to start with, we cannot just tack on postcolonial, multicultural, or global feminisms to mainstream feminism, any more than canonical writers can legitimately tack on feminism to their variant of philosophy by claiming that everything said applies equally to men and women (Narayan and Harding 2000, vii; Dickenson 1997b, 17). Rather, these feminisms make us examine underpinning analytical assumptions and concepts, just as feminism does with the supposedly universal concepts of canonical philosophy and political theory. Essentially, however, I argue that feminism can teach global ethics a counsel of action rather than despair. I do so in three stages:

I. By analyzing aspects of progress and sticking points in recent canonical ethics and political theory concerning questions of difference, particularism, and justice, particularly relating to the *possibility of ethical universals*, which I call *global ethics in the first sense*

2. By arguing that on this *metatheoretical* level constituting the first strand of global ethics, feminist theory has confronted the tension between essentialism and difference in an instructive manner

3. By illustrating how feminism has been working to reconstruct canonical concepts that have failed to take difference adequately into account, with potential impact for *practical policy questions* arising in the context of economic globalization, which I shall call *global ethics in the second sense*

Canonical Ethics and Political Theory: Difference, Universalism, and Justice

There are several possible starting points from which canonical ethics and political theory may be said to have launched their renewed interest in the possibility and limitations of ethical universals. One is the attack in canonical theory on universal human rights and liberal models of justice mounted by Alasdair MacIntyre. Against the notion of ethical universals, MacIntyre depicts a current disastrous state of radical value pluralism in the substance of our moral beliefs, despite our superficial acceptance of unifying liberal rationality as applied to the procedures by which we adjudicate among them. "We thus inhabit a culture in which an inability to arrive at agreed rationally justifiable conclusions on the nature of justice and practical rationality coexists with appeals by contending social groups to sets of rival and conflicting convictions unsupported by rational justification" (MacIntyre 1988, 5–6). This dark picture will not seem implausible in the aftermath of September 11, 2001, and the Iraq War of 2003.

What MacIntyre advocates instead is something to which the Enlightenment, in his view, has ironically blinded us: "a conception of rational enquiry as embodied in a tradition, a conception according to which the standards of rational justification emerge from and are part of a history in which they are vindicated by the way in which they transcend the limitations of and provide remedies for the defects of their predecessors within the history of that same tradition" (MacIntyre 1988, 7). This assertion entails the inescapable conclusion that no moral system can be criticized except from within the framework of its own culture, its own historical time, and its particular assumptions. That may appear uncontentious to many readers, but in fact it entails deep paradoxes. The claim that nothing can be judged except from within its own culture is presented as being impervious itself to judgment from outside its culture; supposedly it holds for all time. Yet of course many cultures, particularly religious systems, would entirely reject the claim that their truth is relative. Relativism's incoherence lies in the absolute status of truth that it claims for itself, despite its skepticism about all such absolute standards.

A tension remains within MacIntyre's thought: he wants to reject the possibility of ethical universals—perhaps exactly because the detested liberalism posits them—but he cannot come up with an alternative that avoids the problem of infinite regress. The claim that there is instead only the practical-rationality-of-this-or-that-tradition and the justice-of-this-or-that-tradition is internally incoherent: there is no reason for anyone from outside MacIntyre's own virtue-centered, Thomist, or Aristotelian preferred traditions to accept that very statement. However, MacIntyre's presentation of traditions as open to challenge from within does chime with much practical and theoretical work by non-Western feminists. For example, Western and non-Western feminists meeting at the 1995 Beijing conference agreed on a final policy document including this phrase: "Any harmful aspect of certain traditional customary or modern practices that violates the rights of women should be prohibited and eliminated" (para. 112, cited in Okin 2000, 40). I return to this point in the final section.

Although MacIntyre does not frame his critique in such terms, other canonical theorists have presented the dilemma primarily in terms of the current conflict in many Western cultures between liberal democracy and multiculturalism (Kymlicka 1989, 1995; Parekh 2000; Barry 2001). The demand for recognition of ethnic or religious identity seems to enshrine a particular, substantive view of "a good life" and to go beyond the minimum required for (and indeed the maximum possible in) a liberal democracy, that is, procedural agreement (Dworkin 1978). What unites a liberal society is strong commitment to equal respect for all views and to the procedures established by laws and constitutions to mediate between these views, rather than agreement on what constitutes a virtuous or worthwhile life—which the liberal state cannot and should not determine. But without its own substantive "thick" account of the good for humanity, as opposed to its "thin" notion of procedural justice, modern-day liberalism is poorly armored against the demands of contending social groups who do possess such notions, even if unsupported by rational justification.

A bridge between MacIntyre's concerns and those of the multiculturalism debate is provided by Onora O'Neill's *Towards Justice and Virtue* (1996), which can be read as an effort to maintain some form of ethical universalism in the face of multiculturalism and relativism. A global theory of global justice is the eventual aim, although she says this book only tends toward such an account. (Here some caution is called for: the debate about multiculturalism is not quite the same as that about universalism. For example, liberal political theories agree that the state must be neutral between various conceptions of good life, admitting a certain degree of multiculturalism, but certain virtues such as toleration can still be required of all, and some account of universal morality can still be given).

Particularists such as virtue theorists wrongly pass up the chance to say something universal about justice, in O'Neill's s view; conversely, universalists such as John Rawls (1971) and Ronald Dworkin (2000) unnecessarily deny themselves the opportunity to say something about the virtues. Why, apart from the logical incoherence of full-fledged ethical relativism, should we say something universal about justice? O'Neill argues that we actually have little choice: "virtually any agent in the contemporary world takes the *scope of ethical consideration* to be more-or-less cosmopolitan for some matters; . . . those whose ethical consideration must be more-or-less cosmopolitan for some matters cannot express it *solely* by means of a mosaic of restricted ethical principles and commitments for dealing with restricted domains of life, but rather must adopt at least some basic ethical principles whose scope is much more inclusive, perhaps more-or-less cosmopolitan." (O'Neill 1996, 55, original emphasis)

Particularism is inadequate in the contemporary world. One way of rephrasing this point might be to note that particularism erects no barrier against economic globalization (McGrew 1997; Held and McGrew 2001). O'Neill's preferred formulation, however, is that complex modern states must be universal within their boundaries, and indeed across national boundaries, because international economic systems are also complex. Particularism by itself is therefore hopelessly nostalgic. Far from being sensitive to the ethical pluralism of modernity, particularists are largely blind to it, since they see ethical life as encapsulated in distinct domains by rigid grids of categories and sensibilities. Furthermore, one might add, particularisms that claim to be universalisms are particularly blind. For example, many canonical theories of property and justice typically exhibit just that fault, although they may contain concepts that are potentially appropriate to women's liberation if developed into genuinely universal notions counting women in (Dickenson 1997b).

Even if particularist principles could resolve conflict, there is still no reason for thinking them ethically authoritative. Something more basic *is* available, although particularists insist that there is no way for an individual or community to "go behind" justification in terms of identity or traditional practice. We have seen, however, at least in MacIntyre's formulation, that the most we can expect is for individual traditions to put their own houses in order, making them internally coherent. There is no reason for proponents of any particular value system to accept external principles inconsistent with its own logical grounding.

So far we have been examining O'Neill's claim that ethical particularism, in particular virtue theory, wrongly passes up the chance to say something that must be said about universal justice. The other half of O'Neill's assertion, however, is that universalists unnecessarily deny all of particularism, depriving themselves of the opportunity to use the virtues of the virtues. In O'Neill's partial compromise with particularism, some practical reasoning must have universal scope, although some can be permitted to have particularistic scope, provided that it is "followable" by all within the relevant wider community. Special pleading by particular communities can be allowed on a procedural basis, rather than a substantive one, so long as all, including outsiders, can follow the rationale. (Note the contrast to MacIntyre's emphasis, which lays stress on improving the coherence of an ethical tradition's narrative as read by its followers but which, despite the elaborate linguistic metaphors of translation, does not include any such specific requirement as O'Neill's demand that outsiders to the tradition be capable of following its rationale.)

"Followable" means both intelligible to a wider audience, in the Kantian sense that the particular principle's adoption by the wider community would not be logically incoherent, and more stringently, capable of being acted on, offering real possibilities for living in this world. Although O'Neill does not make this claim, I interpret her formulation as ruling out an ethic that offers women no scope for action, nothing to act on, no status as moral agents: such an ethic is therefore ruled out, even if it is intelligible to them as part of a traditional set of norms. For example, conventional theories on property fail to see how women, in what has traditionally been their "no-property world," could be motivated by the desire to amass property and thereby gain security (Dickenson 1997b).

Although O'Neill does not specifically mention feminist concerns, an applied example of similar thinking can be seen in the work of Israeli feminist Ayelet Shachar (2001). As Shachar points out, the logic of both communitarian and feminist arguments is the same: supposed universalism fails to do justice to difference. Like O'Neill, but in a more concrete legal context, Shachar attempts to reconcile justice at the community and gender levels through concepts of "embedded citizenship" and "joint governance." Taking as her starting point the notion that individual women belong to the community of their gender as well as to their ethnic and religious community, Shachar has tried to develop a scheme of priorities and "trumps" that acknowledges difference but stops well short of total relativism.

Martha Nussbaum's *Women and Human Development* (2000) contains similar applied examples drawn from feminist activism, although it shows little awareness of the theoretical contribution that feminism can make to global ethics. Nussbaum's capabilities approach provides the philosophical justification for global ethics in distributive justice, "a bare minimum of what respect for human dignity requires" (Nussbaum 2000, 5). Nussbaum's project is to "identify a list of central human capabilities, setting them in the context of a type of political liberalism that makes them specifically political goals and presents them in a manner free of any specific metaphysical grounding" (Nussbaum 2000, 5). The list of capabilities is of course open to question, and indeed Nussbaum herself has altered it from earlier versions, giving greater importance to property rights (Nussbaum 2000, 78, 80).

(She does not develop her arguments about property at any length, however, and in this she implicitly accepts the usual stereotype, common even among feminists, that women can only be objects of property rather than subjects.) The question for her is whether it is possible to develop a universally agreed-upon set of capabilities, "free of any specific metaphysical grounding" and immune to problems of philosophical relativism.

Nussbaum presents these capabilities in an Aristotelian manner, as those essential to human flourishing. Far from avoiding questions of relativism, of course, an Aristotelian approach invites it, insofar as the qualities or virtues appropriate to flourishing are culture-specific. Nussbaum needs an account of what it is to be human that overcomes such cultural relativism, but too much rests on rhetorical terms such as dignity, human, and flourishing. This becomes clear if we substitute *dog* for *person* and *canine* for *human* in this sentence: "Beneath a certain level of capability, in each area, a person has not been enabled to live in a truly human way" (Nussbaum 2000, 74).

To say that such-and-such capability is "human" means little in normative terms: the capability for violence is also human, although most of us think it should not be encouraged but rather fettered. Nussbaum might counter that she has further specified that these capabilities must be "informed by an intuitive idea of a life that is worthy of the dignity of the human being" (Nussbaum 2000, 83). But, of course, many warrior cultures, including the ancient Greeks, viewed violence in war as the very essence of the dignity of the (male) human being. Nussbaum admits that her notion of dignity is intuitive, but intuitions are largely culture-specific. We cannot get there—the idea of a global ethic, particularly one respecting women—from here, a naturalistic argument. Nussbaum is good at deconstructing arguments rooted in cultural relativism, but she is less successful in providing a universalistic alternative to limit what she terms "the intolerance of cultures" (Nussbaum 2000, 49).

Nussbaum also argues that the capabilities approach has the edge on human rights because it is not uniquely identified with the individualistic Western liberal tradition. Distancing herself from Aristotle, she characterizes her own proposal as "(clearly, unlike Aristotle's) . . . a partial, not comprehensive, conception of the good life, a moral conception selected for political purposes only" (Nussbaum 2000, 77). Here, perhaps, we simply come down to questions of strategy. Nussbaum does recognize that other non-Western cultures also hold conceptions of human rights (Nussbaum 2000, 89), and there I think she is correct. Zimbabwean academic lawyer Charles Ngwena and his South African colleague Michelle Engelbrecht, for example, have described something that sounds very much like human rights in traditional South African law, the concept of *ubuntu*, which they explicitly identify as being compatible with a Kantian, deontological ethical system. "*Ubuntu* signifies the recognition of the human worth and respect for the dignity of every person" (Preamble to the Constitution of the Republic of South Africa, Act no. 108, 1996, in Ngwena and Engelbrecht 2001, 4). In *S v. Makwanyane*, Mokgoro J said this about the meaning and concept of *ubuntu*:

> Generally, *ubuntu* translates as humaneness. In its fundamental sense, it translates as *personhood* and morality. Metaphorically, it expresses itself in *umuntu ngumuntu ngabantu*, describing the significance of group solidarity on survival issues so central to the survival of communities. While it envelops the key values of group solidarity, compassion, respect, human dignity, conformity to basic norms and collective unity, in its fundamental sense it denotes humanity and morality. Its spirit emphasizes respect for human dignity. (*Hoffmann v. South African Airways*, 11 BCLR 1211, CC [2000], para. 38)

Might it not be a better strategy to appeal to such existing concepts of rights in non-Western cultures, rather than play into the hands of antifeminists whose intuitions are rather different from Nussbaum's own? Why concede ground to what Nussbaum describes as a mistaken belief? That would be the political argument against Nussbaum's capabilities approach; the philosophical one is that a *description* of human capabilities cannot generate *normative* rules without appealing to some prior ethic, probably either a Kantian or a rights-based one. Nussbaum implicitly concedes this point when she notes: "Not all actual human abilities exert a moral claim, only the ones that have been evaluated as valuable from an ethical viewpoint" (Nussbaum 2000, 83). Clearly there is a risk of infinite regress here. Can more specifically feminist theories teach canonical theorists a way out of these and the other dilemmas identified in this section?

What Feminism Can Teach Global Ethics I: Theory

Nussbaum is leading us in the right direction by suggesting that we look to feminism to resolve the question of whether a global ethic is possible, but she is right for something less than the right reasons. Certainly the oppression of women matters, and it matters whether a relativist ethic cannot find the right weapons against that oppression. But it is within the theoretical debates in feminism, with which Nussbaum appears unfamiliar, that we can find some glimmerings of a larger answer to that question. If we remain within the boundaries of philosophical analysis but turn instead to feminist theory, something strange yet eminently predictable occurs. The debates that now exercise mainstream philosophy, international relations, and political theory so vigorously, concerning universalism, particularism, cosmopolitanism, and global ethics, have been going on in feminist philosophy for at least twenty years, largely unobserved by canonical philosophers.

In feminist theoretical debates concerning postmodernism, deconstruction, identity, and difference, the very notion that "woman" may slither away has emerged, making it impossible to develop a feminist politics. This tendency is particularly pronounced in the work of Judith Butler (1987) and Luce Irigaray (1984). Irigaray's view resembles Butler's insofar as both present a self in interior conflict, a disunited subjectivity; both rely on the insights of psychoanalytic theory, particularly Freud and Lacan, in putting unresolved and unsymbolized desires to the fore. The identity of the subject has, of course, been a matter of concern in mainstream philosophy since Locke's time, at least; but there is no parallel in mainstream philosophy to the manner in which feminist *deconstructionism* has conflicted with more essentialist feminisms, concerned with preserving the notion of "woman" to retain the necessary political and conceptual apparatus to fight the oppression of women. Feminisms such as the genealogical models proposed by Butler and Irigaray doubt whether such a category as the subject exists at all, as distinguished from interpretation feminisms that enhance women's status as subjects by stressing their unique experience and voice (Ferguson 1983, 14). Without a unified category of "woman," there can be no political impetus toward the ending of women's oppression. A feminist deconstructionist therefore seems to be trying to make herself disappear.

The positive aspect of feminist deconstructionism, however, has been the manner in which it has drawn attention to the possibility of a subjectivity that women can actually own, rather than one borrowed from male psychological development. While Irigaray, for example, is often seen as one in a chain of postmodernist and poststructuralist attempts to deconstruct the subject, she is more concerned about creating a subjectivity that women can call their own. Since women have been deprived of an appropriate symbolic by psychiatric theory rooted in male experience, "they have never had a subject to lose" (Whitford 1991, 83).

In other words, a modified feminist deconstructionism, and feminism more generally, suggests the following for global ethics: ethical systems and ethical universals can still exist, but they must be truly universals. They cannot be particularist theories masquerading as ethical universalism. Much of modern feminist theory, particularly such powerful critiques of liberal democracy as Carole Pateman's *The Sexual Contract* (1988), demonstrated in its early days with great perspicacity exactly how shaky were the claims to universalism of the liberal concepts of political selfhood: citizenship, contract, property, and rights. Later feminist work has reconstructed those concepts to make them genuinely universal, incorporating women's experience as well: for example, feminist theories of the state (MacKinnon 1989), political obligation (Hirschmann 1992), property (Dickenson 1997b), democracy (Phillips 1991), justice (Young 1990), and authority (Jones 1993).

These theoretical developments matter a great deal to feminism for the same practical reason that they should matter to global ethics. If feminists had abandoned the notion of women as a universally identifiable and frequently oppressed group, they would have lost the political possibility of trying to do something about women's rights. If global ethics abandons the notion of universal human rights, it loses the political possibility of trying to do something about autocratic regimes or oppression by the economic forces behind globalization. This is the point I made earlier about why a communitarian, particularist analysis, which says there are only the moral norms of community X and community Y rather than any absolute global ethics, is intrinsically status quo. The same problem applies if feminists concede that there are only women in class X or society Y; we lose any chance of appealing to women's rights as universal human rights to criticize practices that oppress women. Yet without a unified, universal category of "woman," in both North and South, there can be no political impetus toward the ending of women's oppression. But on the other hand, Western feminists have also had to contend with charges from communitarians that they are imposing the values of their own liberal cultures on non-Western women. This is something that feminists from both North and South have also begun to overcome.

Particularly instructive for global ethics has been the way in which feminist theory increasingly combines universalism and difference. Denying that so-called impartialist theories of justice are truly universal, Iris Marion Young, for example, offers a paradigm that can also be applied to the question of whether there can be global theories of justice.

> Universality in the sense of the participation and inclusion of everyone in moral and social life does not imply universality in the sense of the adoption of a general point of view that leaves behind particular affiliations, feelings, commitments and desires. Indeed . . . universality as generality has often operated precisely to inhibit universal inclusion and participation. (Young 1990, 105)

The parallel in global ethics will be a concern with inclusion and participation at the expense of the unifying attempt to create a singular global ethic or set of principles such as the famous or infamous "four principles" of bioethics. Young might well dismiss such attempts to transcend difference as imbued with "the logic of identity," as she does with Rawls's account of justice. Whereas "the logic of identity . . . constructs totalizing systems in which the unifying categories are themselves unified under principles, where the ideal is to reduce everything to one first principle" (Young 1990, 98), the politics of difference does not seek so relentlessly to reduce all differences to unity. On one level, Young offers a rather thin account of global justice, one more concerned with procedure than with substance. On the other, however, her account is deeper, if not necessarily thicker, than *principlist* accounts seeking to unify disparate global experience into a single framework. Difference is foregrounded in Young's account of justice, but the proselytizing power of injustice is not relativized out of existence. Indeed, she would argue that opponents of oppression are in a better, more realistic position if they employ a transformational rather than an assimilationist model, if they take difference into account rather than impose a single model of justice with no respect for group identities.

What Feminism Can Teach Global Ethics II: Practice and the Global South

So far, I have concentrated on global ethics in the first sense, that is, the question of ethical universals.[1] I have argued that feminism's response to essentialism and difference, and its growing awareness that too much emphasis on diversity can obscure inequality (Phillips 1991), can teach global ethics possible ways to transcend the two extremes of full-fledged multiculturalism and inflexible human rights. Now I examine the impact of specific feminist responses to more particular issues in global public policy, particularly in the wake of economic globalization (Adam 2002): the second sense of global ethics. This is the second thing that feminism can teach global ethics: its legal and political solutions are more concrete, and its discourse further advanced, because it has been dealing with the problems for longer, having perceived much earlier that there could be problems.

The impact of feminism's response to the multiculturalism question at the global public policy level was strongly felt at the 1995 Beijing conference. Whereas previous world women's conferences had been far more willing to subordinate women's rights as universal human rights to indigenous cultural and religious demands in particular countries, women from both South and North rejected that escape route at the fourth world women's conference (Dickenson 1997a; Okin 2000). The final policy document noted firmly that "while the significance of national and regional particularities and various historical, cultural and religious backgrounds must be borne in mind, it is the duty of states, regardless of their political, economic and cultural systems, to promote and protect all human rights and fundamental freedoms" (Covenant 1995, para. 9–10, cited in Okin 2000, 39). In Beijing, as well as before and afterward, feminist activists also joined forces with more academic or theoretical feminists in a manner that may well be instructive for global ethics (Jaggar 2000; Dickenson 1997a).

Similarly, concepts of women's rights have been incorporated into development ethics and development policy, but tailored in such a fashion as to enable some sort of accommodation with important aspects of traditional cultures. Practical examples include the Indian antirape campaign (Gangoli 1998), the establishment of women's NGOs and the mainstreaming of gender- by non-gender-based ones (Stubbs 2001), the applicability of Western rights frameworks to the political activity of the female Indian village organizers known as *sathins* (Madhok 2002), and campaigns for women's land rights in Southeast Asia (Agarwal 1994). More specifically, in bioethics, this accommodation has been explored in relation to a wide range of subjects: for example, research ethics in the global South (Khan 2000), genetic justice (Mahowald 2000), female genital mutilation and reproductive rights more generally (Hellsten 2002), and the impact on women in the global South of the commodification of gametes and other forms of human tissue (Dickenson 2001, 2002).

The charge that Western feminists are imposing a liberal model on women in the South has been emphatically rejected by such non-Western feminists as Uma Narayan, who has condemned the dereliction of duties to help on a global scale, caused by an overconcern for cultural tolerance. Narayan offers cogent practical illustrations of the latter phenomenon in her book *Dislocating Cultures: Identities, Traditions and Third-World Feminisms* (1997). Well-intending Western feminists, Narayan argues, are too ready to concede toleration of non-Western practices that oppress women; they are crippled by their own guilt, as members of the Western elite that benefited from imperialism, colonialism, and neocolonialism and that continues to benefit from economic globalization. They are too quick to abandon the possibility of a global ethics that genuinely works for women and are too prone to dismiss non-Western feminists who actually agree with them on its foundational principles of equal gender justice. When Narayan mentions her opposition to *sati*, female genital mutilation, or sex-selective abortion, for example, she is usually met—even by feminists—with the accusation that she is too Westernized to be an authentic voice of Indian women. The only acceptable role for Indian women, she feels, is as oppressed victims. Mired in their own discouragement and stereotypes, Narayan accuses, together with their doubts about the very category of woman, Western feminists too readily ignore what is really a very simple matter of justice—and a call for help. Efforts to avoid gender essentialism and the imposition of a universal human rights framework, she claims, fall instead into the trap of cultural essentialism. "While gender essentialism often equates the problems, interests and locations of some socially dominant groups of men and women with those of 'all men' and 'all women', cultural essentialism often equates the values, worldviews, and practices of some socially dominant groups with those of 'all members of the culture'" (Narayan 1997, 82).

Western feminists concerned with avoiding gender essentialism at all costs wrongly assume that neocolonialism proceeds by privileged subjects, such as colonial powers constructing the "Other"[2] in their own image, taking their situation to be typical of that of all women. Actually, Narayan argues, neocolonialism and imperialism work by enshrining *difference* between the colonizer and the "Other." Thus, Western feminists are not as vulnerable as they may fear to charges of neo-colonialism if they attempt to work for women's rights as human rights (Narayan 1997, 83). In fact, one might argue, Western feminists such as Chilla Bulbeck (1998), desperate to avoid Orientalism (Said 1995), actually fall prey to it—by taking a favorable view of any non-Western practice to which women in the global South have accommodated themselves, no matter how oppressive. This, too, is a form of treating the South or Orient as "other" and, to my mind, is both patronizing and politically naive.

This argument could be reinforced with practical examples of colonial powers deliberately undermining indigenous traditions in which women's rights were upheld far more effectively than under colonial rule. For example, before the British Raj, widows in Haryana (then in the Punjab) could legally inherit their husbands' property, but male elders sometimes informally circumvented this legal entitlement by forcing widows to remarry within their husbands' families, a practice known as *karewa*. Rather than intervening to protect women's statutory rights, British colonial administrators actually strengthened *karewa* with legal sanctions against widows who resisted remarriage, all in the name of preserving customary law—even when the practice was challenged in British courts by the women of Haryana (Dickenson 1997b, 40). In other jurisdictions of the global South, Spanish feminist philosopher Celia Amoros, who has had a particularly great influence in Mexico and Argentina, has argued that feminisms of difference have played an important part in demonstrating that women are differently positioned before the law. A feminism of rights and equality can use that concrete knowledge to overturn that disadvantage (Amoros 1986, 1994).

Conclusion

By using a bottom-up, inductive approach rather than a top-down, principlist one, feminists have become adept at seeking agreement on concrete reforms and practical issues rooted in women's experience: what Alison Jaggar terms "feminist practical dialogue" (Jaggar 1995, 115). Similarly, whereas "typically, philosophical theories of justice have operated with a social ontology that has no room for a concept of social groups," Iris Marion Young argues that only a concept of justice that begins with the concepts of group domination and group oppression, attending sensitively to real social differences, can succeed in social reform (Young 1990, 3).

Particularly in relation to health and biomedicine, attending to gender difference is not incompatible with women's rights as human rights, but crucial to implementing those rights. Although women are affected everywhere by globalization of both the causes of disease and the liberal packages of health care "reforms," globalization does not affect them in the same way, and the issues for gender equity vary. For example, while the dominant issues in the Americas and Europe concern decentralization of service delivery, powerful women's advocacy groups in these nations are better placed to protest and influence policy at the local level than in Africa, where distances are great and civil society often weak (Sen, George, and Ostlin 2002). As Rosemarie Tong puts it,

> we all experience pain, suffering and death; and since we are all equal in this way, it is the task of health care to serve each of us as if we were the paradigm case of treatment for everyone. Feminist bioethicists are among the leaders in the movement to make health care attentive to peoples' *differences* so that it can help people become the *same*—that is, equally autonomous and equally the recipients of beneficent clinical practices and just health care policies. (Tong 2000, 24)

We do not have to indulge in any claims about the global feminist "community" as being either unified or powerful to think that feminism has something to teach global ethics. To do so would be to fall into the same trap for which I criticized MacIntyre, at the very beginning of this chapter. The notion of "imagined community," which originates in Benedict Anderson's 1983 book of that title on nationalism, has been used by some feminist writers such as Ann Ferguson to enable us to imagine a global feminism, but others such as Margaret Urban Walker are skeptical: "Imagined communities are seductive because they yield real psychic comforts, powerful feelings of belonging and mattering; imagined communities are irrelevant or dangerous because they distract our attention from actual communities" (Walker 1994, 54)—and power inequalities within them. Nevertheless, Alison Jaggar, from whom this summary is taken, thinks the global feminist community is already becoming something of a reality, in terms of practical efforts around the world against women's subordination. The notion is still useful, provided we think not in terms of global feminism but of global feminisms (Jaggar 2000, 21): a precise parallel to my own preference for "global ethics" in the plural.

Notes

1. I use the term *global South* in conformity with much work in development studies, as an economic and political rather than geographical term. By global South I mean those states characterized by relative poverty, significant international debt, vulnerability to structural adjustment programs, and concomitant scaling back of governmental provision. In common with many analysts from these countries, I reject the term *developing countries* as a euphemism.

2. The concept of the "Other" refers to the idea prominent in the work of Simone de Beauvoir (1952) and elsewhere of a generalized and fictionalized foil to the dominant gender's characteristics. In this case, the "Other" is the colonized people.

References

Adam, Barbara. 2002. "The Gendered Time Politics of Globalization: Of Shadowlands and Elusive Justice." *Feminist Review* 70: 3–29.

Agarwal, Bina. 1994. *A Field of One's Own: Gender and Land Rights in South Asia.* Cambridge, UK: Cambridge University Press.

Amoros, Celia. 1986. *Hacia una Critica de la Razon Patriarcal.* Madrid: Anthropos.

———. 1994. *Feminismo: Igualdad y Diferencia.* Mexico City: UNAM PUEG.

Barry, Brian. 2001. *Culture and Equality.* Cambridge, Mass.: Harvard University Press.

Bulbeck, Chilla. 1998. *Re-Orienting Western Feminisms: Women's Diversity in a Postcolonial World.* Cambridge, UK: Cambridge University Press.

Butler, Judith. 1987. *Subjects of Desire: Hegelian Reflections in Twentieth-Century France.* New York: Columbia University Press.

de Beauvoir, Simone. 1952. *The Second Sex,* translated and edited by H. M. Parshley. New York: Knopf.

Dickenson, Donna. 1997a. "Counting Women In: Redefining Democratic Politics." In *The Transformation of Democracy? Globalization and Territorial Democracy,* edited by Anthony Mc-Grew, 97–119. Cambridge, UK: Polity Press.

———. 1997b. *Property, Women and Politics: Subjects or Objects?* Cambridge, UK: Polity Press.

———. 2001. "Property and Women's Alienation from Their Own Reproductive Labour." *Bioethics* 15, no. 3: 205–17.

———. 2002. "Commodification of Human Tissue: Implications for Feminist and Development Ethics." *Developing World Bioethics* 2: 55–63.

Dworkin, Ronald. 1978. "Liberalism." In *Public and Private Morality,* edited by Stuart Hampshire, 113–43. Cambridge, UK: Cambridge University Press.

———. 2000. *Sovereign Virtue: The Theory and Practice of Equality.* Cambridge, Mass.: Harvard University Press.

Ferguson, Kathy E. 1983. *The Man Question: Visions of Subjectivity in Feminist Theory.* Berkeley: University of California Press.

Gangoli, Geetanjali. 1998. "The Right to Protection from Sexual Assault: The Indian Anti-Rape Campaign." In *Development and Rights,* edited by Deborah Eade, 128–37. Oxford: Oxfam UK.

Held, David, and Anthony McGrew, eds. 2001. *The Global Transformations Reader.* Cambridge, UK: Polity Press.

Hellsten, Sirkku K. 2002. "Multicultural Issues in Maternal-Fetal Medicine." In *Ethical Issues in Maternal-Fetal Medicine,* edited by Donna L. Dickenson, 39–90. Cambridge, UK: Cambridge University Press.

Hirschmann, Nancy J. 1992. *Rethinking Obligation: A Feminist Method for Political Theory.* Ithaca, N.Y.: Cornell University Press.

Irigaray, Luce. 1984. *Ethique de la Difference Sexuelle.* Paris: Editions de Minuit.

Jaggar, Alison. 1995. "Toward a Feminist Conception of Moral Reasoning." In *Morality and Social Justice,* edited by James Sterba, 115–46. Lanham, Md.: Rowman & Littlefield.

————. 2000. "Globalizing Feminist Ethics." In *Decentering the Center: Philosophy for a Multicultural, Postcolonial and Feminist World*, edited by Uma Narayan and Sandra Harding, 1–25. Bloomington: Indiana University Press.

Jones, Kathleen B. 1993. *Compassionate Authority: Democracy and Its Representation of Women*. London: Routledge.

Khan, Kausar. 2000. "Justice and Research in Relation to Women: It Is Not a Matter of Theory Alone." Paper delivered at the Fifth International Conference of the International Association of Bioethics, London, September 21.

Kymlicka, Will. 1989. *Liberalism, Community and Culture*. Oxford: Clarendon Press.

————. 1995. *Multicultural Citizenship: A Liberal Theory of Minority Rights*. Oxford, UK: Clarendon Press.

MacIntyre, Alasdair. 1988. *Whose Justice? Which Rationality?* London: Duckworth.

MacKinnon, Catharine A. 1989. *Toward a Feminist Theory of the State*. Cambridge, Mass: Harvard University Press.

Madhok, Sumi. 2002. "Rights, Agency and the *Sathins*: Towards a Transcultural Dialogue on Autonomy." Paper presented at ESRC workshop, University of Warwick, UK, September 19.

Mahowald, Mary. 2000. *Genes, Women, Equality*. Oxford, UK: Oxford University Press.

McGrew, Anthony, ed. 1997. *The Transformation of Democracy: Globalization and Territorial Democracy*. Cambridge, UK: Polity Press.

Narayan, Uma. 1997. *Dislocating Cultures: Identities, Traditions and Third-World Feminisms*. London: Routledge.

Narayan, Uma, and Sandra Harding. 2000. "Introduction." In *Decentering the Center: Philosophy for a Multicultural, Postcolonial and Feminist World*, edited by Uma Narayan and Sandra Harding, vii. Bloomington: Indiana University Press.

Ngwena, Charles, and Michelle Engelbrecht. 2001. "Health Care Professionals and Conscientious Objection to Abortion in South Africa: Some Legal and Ethical Responses." Paper presented at the Second International Conference on Development Ethics, Tampa, Florida, February.

Nussbaum, Martha Craven. 2000. *Women and Human Development: The Capabilities Approach*. Cambridge, UK: Cambridge University Press.

Okin, Susan Moller. 2000. "Feminism, Women's Human Rights and Cultural Difference." In *Decentering the Center: Philosophy for a Multicultural, Postcolonial and Feminist World*, edited by Uma Narayan and Sandra Harding, 26–46. Bloomington: Indiana University Press.

O'Neill, Onora. 1996. *Towards Justice and Virtue: A Constructive Account of Practical Reasoning*. Cambridge, UK: Cambridge University Press.

Parekh, Bhikhu. 2000. *Rethinking Multiculturalism: Cultural Diversity and Political Theory*. Cambridge, Mass.: Harvard University Press.

Pateman, Carole. 1988. *The Sexual Contract*. Cambridge, UK: Polity Press.

Phillips, Anne. 1991. *Engendering Democracy*. Cambridge, UK: Polity Press.

Rawls, John. 1971. *A Theory of Justice*. Cambridge, Mass.: Harvard University Press.

Said, Edward W. 1995. *Orientalism*. Reprinted with new afterward. London: Penguin.

Sen, Gita, Asha George, and Piroska Ostlin, eds. 2002. *Engendering International Health: The Challenge of Equity.* Cambridge, Mass.: MIT Press.

Shachar, Ayelet. 2001. *Multicultural Jurisdictions: Cultural Differences and Women's Rights.* Cambridge, UK: Cambridge University Press.

Stubbs, Josephine. 2001. "Gender in Development: A Long Haul, but We're Getting There!" In *Debating Development,* edited by Deborah Eade and Ernst Ligteringen, 348–58. Oxford: Oxfam UK.

Tong, Rosemarie. 2000. "Is a Global Bioethics Both Desirable and Possible?" Paper delivered at the Fifth International Conference of the International Association of Bioethics, London, September 21.

Walker, Margaret Urban. 1994. "Global Feminism: What's the Question?" *American Philosophical Association Newsletter on Feminism and Philosophy* 94: 53–55.

Whitford, Margaret. 1991. *Luce Irigaray: Philosophy in the Feminine.* London: Routledge.

Young, Iris Marion. 1990. *Justice and the Politics of Difference.* Princeton, N.J.: Princeton University Press.

Integrating Bioethics and Human Rights
Toward a Global Feminist Approach

2

ANNE DONCHIN

L IKE FEMINIST SCHOLARSHIP generally, feminist bioethics has been continually remaking itself as conceptual flaws surface and new issues unfold. This
dimension of our work is dramatically illustrated by several recent events
that prodded me to consider how human rights fit into our conceptual framework.
Following the 1998 Feminist Approaches to Bioethics (FAB) conference in Japan,
a newcomer to FAB mentioned her surprise that so few speakers had even mentioned the human rights movement. Initially puzzled, I rethought our mission and
realized that her remark had been provoked not by any limitation in *her* own experience but by an insularity within feminist bioethics that I'd not noticed before.

South African physician Wendy Orr's address at the International Association
of Bioethics (IAB) Congress in London in 2000 profoundly affected all who
heard her relate her experience as a vulnerable young surgeon during the apartheid
regime. Assigned to care for detainees who had been assaulted, abused, and tortured by the police, she was forced to choose between remaining silent, while delivering the best medical care possible under the circumstances, or taking the risk
of speaking out. Because she took the latter course and initiated legal action to
protect those in her care, she was victimized by the controlling political regime.[1]
Her account shows how deeply embedded the medical profession was in the South
African political machinery and how little support doctors who were harassed or
detained by security police received from their colleagues.[2] Her experience challenges physicians to examine ongoing abuses and collusion with violations of human rights and ethical norms, not only in her own country but wherever human
rights are vulnerable.

Then I learned of the handbook recently published by the British Medical Association that explores the extensive overlap and interconnections between the

conceptual frameworks of bioethics and human rights (British Medical Association 2001). Suddenly, I realized how seldom North American bioethicists have recognized linkages between the two frameworks, even though the development of the global human rights movement has paralleled the development of bioethics. And then the horrific act of terrorism on September 11, 2001, sparked a long dormant impetus to reunite feminist theory and activism: Afghan women in exile had been seeking for years to capture the attention of world feminism, but only after this catastrophe were their voices able to ignite a sustained response. An increased engagement with human rights discourse at the 2002 FAB conference in Brasília catalyzed my aspirations for FAB's future course. I am now convinced that the ongoing health of feminist bioethics depends on working toward a more inclusive conceptual framework that forges strong links between bioethics and human rights discourse, cuts through dominant norms that reflect the priorities of wealthy societies, and turns attention to global concerns about the health and well-being of the least well-off.

To develop a more coherent, inclusive, and integrated global framework for feminist bioethics, we first need a better understanding of the currents in feminist thinking that have led us to constrict our range of scholarship. I believe multiple factors impeded the awareness of feminist bioethicists. First, we yielded too uncritically to the feminist trend to turn away from global thinking to emphasize local and contextual knowledges (Benhabib 1995).[3] In attempting to globalize feminist bioethics and advance health and well-being across diverse cultures and traditions, we have added a miscellany of diverse voices without giving adequate attention to major structural injustices that tend to override local boundaries. We have also been hampered by compartmentalization and bifurcations among feminists that discourage collaboration among those who share a common commitment to global change. There has been too little crossfertilization between feminists working in bioethics and those whose primary areas of research overlap our own, such as international human rights law and development studies. Though my attention in this chapter is directed primarily to extending the feminist bioethics agenda, converging connections will, hopefully, encourage partnerships among feminists in all fields who share a common commitment to enhancing women's health and well-being across cultural and national boundaries.

For all these groups already share relevant commonalities. They recognize that health does not depend on behavioral choices alone but is the result of interlocking status determinants that affect people's capacities to realize tenable life goals. They also understand the need to shift the attention of providers and policy makers from overemphasis on the delivery of health care services to greater investment in preventive programs. And they are acutely aware of conditions that impair women's health and diminish their agency, particularly the health care needs of marginalized groups and those subject to abuse and neglect. They also recognize the impact of local, national, and international power hierarchies on the distribution of health care resources. Rather than merely deploring existing injustices, some have called for programs of social change to rectify inequities, empower marginalized people to define their own health care needs, and configure local programs to meet them (Cook 1999; Holmes 1999; Nicholas 1999).

Yet despite these commonalities, barriers to collaboration among these groups persist. I consider these barriers in some detail, particularly critiques of rights-based theories. Then I take up leading responses to them and recent initiatives within the international bioethics community to incorporate human rights perspectives. Next, I shift to efforts within the human rights movement to advance global health and consider impediments generated by the dominant economic development paradigm. I then take up an alternative paradigm that seeks to forge a global ethic conjoining development and human rights theories. I evaluate an influential version of this approach and indicate respects in which it is flawed, noting particularly its failure to make adequate provision for group associations and power relations that frame the context of individual human lives. Finally, I propose an alternative framework for a global feminist bioethic that sees human rights as flowing from human material embodiment and social relations and also prioritizes rights to fundamental goods that sustain human life over, say, the property rights of major corporations. My ultimate aim is to lay the groundwork for a theory that is fully responsive to practices that would strengthen all people's capacities to enjoy healthy, productive lives.

Rights Speech: Reservations, Rebuttals, and Revisions

Feminist resistance to a conceptual apparatus that stresses rights language has sprung from sources external to feminism as well as tendencies within it. Prominent among the first group is the negative/positive rights polarity rooted in the liberal tradition. Feminist theorists often point out that a claim to a negative right obligating others to abstain from interference has little value without resources to facilitate its exercise. The right to noninterference, for example, is vacuous without authoritative implementation (say, to access abortion facilities or to be protected against rape). Even the right to self-determination requires considerable social cooperation, for it cannot be exercised even minimally without mutual recognition of people's interdependence. Optimally, it requires mastery of appropriate cognitive and emotional skills, opportunities to shape one's identity in nonoppressive ways, and social support to achieve personal agency.

An overlapping concern is the tendency of rights-based theories to lapse into a rigid individualism that disregards the basic human needs of socially excluded groups. Developing this thread, feminists from a variety of traditions have cautioned against overemphasizing individual rights that constrict personal and social values and dismiss moral aims not expressible as matters of individual preference, including relational ties, sexual equality, and a nurturing, stable child-rearing environment. Some stress affinities between the appeal to rights and masculinist ideologies of personal control and domination; they chide those who emphasize rights discourse for neglecting relational values tied to care and interpersonal connection. In a related vein, others fault the conception of personal autonomy associated with rights discourse for its mentalistic assumptions that valorize a distinctively masculine ideal of autonomy, an ideal that diminishes the importance of embodied particulars and relegates women to a natural sphere severed from human reason (Lovibond 1989, 10).

Appeals to rights, Diana Meyers notes, are often made when a breakdown occurs in loving and caring relationships—when people's interests are neglected. She takes the morality of rights to be primarily a morality of self-defense used to protect people from assaults on their personal integrity. Invoking a right introduces a generalized perspective that captures one dimension of morality but does not tell us how to respect people individually (Meyers 1994, 155).

A further factor in feminist distrust of rights-based theory stems from the early history of the international human rights movement when women's concerns were relegated to the periphery. Despite the 1948 UN charter's inclusion of a right to the highest attainable standard of health, linkages between health and human rights did not become a focal concern until the 1980s. The initial formulation addressed only civil and political rights. In response to pressures to formulate more concrete and potentially enforceable rights, in 1966 the UN General Assembly adopted a covenant incorporating social, cultural, and economic rights (known as second-generation rights). But even this extension did not expressly address equal protections for women and other marginalized groups. Not until ratification of third-generation rights (discussed later in the chapter) could women and other marginalized groups anticipate protected access to resources needed to exercise first- and second-generation rights.

Other sources of resistance to rights discourse stem from tendencies within feminist theory. Over the past two decades feminists have turned away from global thinking to emphasize local and contextual knowledges. Under Carol Gilligan's influence, many have stressed patterns of reasoning allegedly characteristic of women—caring, relationships, and responsibilities—and contrasted them with masculine modes of reasoning that privilege justice and rights (Gilligan 1982). Though Gilligan did not regard either as superior, some of her followers did, most notably Nel Noddings. Noddings (1984) believed feminists could dispense with moral principles, including those that use the (masculine) language of justice and rights. Adequate moral guidance could be gleaned from individual cases where people exercise caring duties.

Despite feminist theoretical resistance to the use of rights language, rights talk has been integral to both academic bioethics and feminist activism for decades. Within feminist bioethics, particularly, there has been broad support for women's right to reproductive services and the rights of patients to take control of their own medical decisions. However, little notice has been taken of the compartmentalization of the women's movement into discrete segments. Reproductive rights is but one example of this fragmentation; others include violence, sexuality, adolescent health care, and development. Some have noted that even the most fundamental reproductive rights cannot be assured without access to such enabling conditions as means of transportation to reach a clinic, resources to pay their fees, ability to read package inserts, and so on. Yet even feminist bioethicists have been reluctant to extend rights language to a broader set of practices. Why so? The influence of mainstream North American bioethics may play a part here. U.S. bioethicists, in particular, have been subject to severe criticism by their counterparts in other countries for their supposed obsession with rights language. What critics seldom understood, however, is that appeals to rights are often rooted in specific features of American experience that arose at a time of major change in the expression of ethical principles and marked a significant power shift from physician paternalism to patient autonomy. The articulation of these principles is historically linked to other rights-based initiatives in the United States, particularly the civil rights movement and the struggles for women's rights in the 1960s and 1970s. Both movements awakened public awareness of submerged voices and injustices inflicted on those lacking access to power. Unfortunately, the influence of these movements on bioethics was short-lived. As mainstream bioethics became professionalized, its agenda shifted. Little remains of the initial legacy except a stress on patient autonomy.

Turning now to rebuttals to these critiques of rights talk, I consider grounds for more extensive inclusion of the human rights framework within feminist bioethics. One approach focuses on deficiencies in the theoretical turn exemplified by Noddings, especially on its virtually exclusive emphasis on interpersonal relationships and its neglect of the political dimensions of social connection. Martha Minow addresses the difficulty of holding together a vision encompassing both the personal and political. Responding to injustices suffered by marginalized groups, she has framed what she calls "the dilemma of difference": ignoring group differences undermines efforts to mobilize opposition to group discrimination, but emphasizing differences risks entrenching the dominant group's stereotypes about the discriminated (Minow 1990, 20).[4] She attributes the dilemma to social institutions that establish only one norm, thereby ignoring the perspectives of those who do not fit within that norm (Minow 1990, 94–95). An exclusively case-oriented perspective, such as Noddings advocates, would obscure these effects of social institutions.

Others have pointed out that rights talk cannot be expunged from a language that preserves concepts bound up with duty and obligation.[5] While resisting propensities to totalize rights language, they emphasize its central functions. "For the historically disempowered," Patricia Williams remarks, "the conferring of rights is symbolic of all the denied aspects of their humanity" (Williams 1991, 152). Williams stresses the need to assess the value of rights, not only from the privileged position of those who have always had them but also from the position of those to whom they have been denied. For African Americans particularly, "the attainment of rights signifies the respectful behavior, the collective responsibility, properly owed by a society to one of its own" (Williams 1991, 163). Rights talk, when uttered by people with the protected standing of bearers of rights, is a so-cially empowered form of speech. Lacking access to rights language, Margaret Walker notes, people may voice preferences or complaints but cannot articulate demands that others are required to meet (Walker 2003, 175).

Concurrently, the human rights movement has extended its scope beyond the two categories of rights formerly identified and has turned to explicit recognition of women's rights, the rights of peoples (as distinct from states), and the right to development. The Convention on the Elimination of All Forms of Discrimina-tion against Women (CEDAW) stresses basic education, career, vocational, health, and family planning information. It also incorporates mechanisms for monitoring injustices, including inequitable access to health care services (British Medical As-sociation 2001, 333). Signatory governments, if found deficient, are obligated to respond. Walker notes that many provisions of CEDAW grew out of the women's movements and come much closer than any prior document to reflecting the lives of women who have been systematically silenced and to addressing oppressions that are based on group membership (Walker 2003, 170–72). Michael Ignatieff, reviewing the last five decades of the human rights movement, acclaims its trans-formed agenda that emphasizes social protections against threats to human well-being, the empowerment of victims, and the validation of their entitlements to freedom (Ignatieff 2001c, 169).

Feminist bioethicists could considerably advance the project of globalizing bioethics by reassessing reservations about adoption of a more inclusive rights dis-course and giving greater heed to the aims of CEDAW. Available evidence shows a high correlation between gender oppression and preventable illnesses, particu-larly in countries with a strong preference for boy children (Drèze and Sen 1989). However, to address these issues adequately we need a conceptual apparatus that transcends dichotomies between developed and less-developed countries, incorporates a compatible development ethic, and integrates relevant features of the global human rights movement into feminist discourse. Medical groups in a few countries outside North America have already broken ground at a practical level.

As I mentioned at the outset, some medical organizations have begun to realize that physicians play a significant role in both concealment and exposure of human rights violations. Since physicians are often the first beyond law enforcement officers to see evidence of the systematic violation of human rights, they have a heightened responsibility to protect the rights of those in their charge, and they deserve protection for reporting abuses. The handbook published by the British Medical Association (British Medical Association 2001) facilitates understanding of how bioethics and human rights provide complementary approaches to improving the health of vulnerable populations, particularly within poorer countries, advancing their well-being, pressing for equitable access to treatment, protecting women's health and reproductive rights, developing nondiscriminatory HIV/AIDS policies, and encouraging practitioners to act as agents and advocates for social justice.

Issues intersecting bioethics and human rights include the health care of vulnerable groups, how to respect cultural diversity without jeopardizing the rights of individuals and groups, securing meaningful informed consent to research (particularly where drug companies from advanced industrialized countries exploit people in less-developed ones to test drugs for market), discrimination in the delivery of health care services, and connections between such underlying determinants of health as nutrition and sanitation.[6] Poor nutrition associated with poverty aggravates the health problems of pregnant and lactating women and increases their vulnerability to poverty-related diseases.[7] Rebecca Cook observes that "promotion of women's health depends on the interaction of most, if not all, human rights" (Cook 1999, 260). She specifically mentions protection of women's employment, equal pay for work of equal value, education, information, political participation, influence, and democratic power within legislatures.

To summarize, though feminist reservations about rights language are often directed more toward misleading theoretical expositions of rights than toward activist strategies, they have practical consequences too. Theories that make inadequate provision for rights risk obstructing the advancement of subordinated groups. But moral theories that give primacy to individual rights can provide only a partial moral vision. Rights-based moral thought alone can tell us nothing about what should be done in the absence of claimant procedures. To develop a more adequate global bioethic, we need a moral framework that encompasses rights claims within a broad range of moral norms, a framework that is fully responsive to conditions that shape human health and well-being across the globe. However, efforts to shape such a framework must be responsive to resistances to a global bioethic that incorporates human rights. I turn now to principal sites of resistance.

Global Health and the
Dominant Development Paradigm

Of course, critiques of rights language extend well beyond feminist contexts to moral thought in general, as well as to central claims of the human rights movement. Despite successive reformulations of human rights, some bioethicists still think human rights language is too closely tied to Euro-American bioethics to contribute meaningfully to a global bioethic. According to Ruth Macklin, opposition to human rights is widespread among Chinese scholars (Macklin 1999, 228–33). Though some Asian scholars support the human rights movement, others advocate a very particularized global approach that counters claims to universal human rights. Defenders of this view assert two related claims. First, in many countries in East and Southeast Asia, people have no theoretical background for the concept of human rights. Second, these people seek primarily to overcome starvation and poverty by increasing national wealth and mutual aid (Sakamoto 1999). Arleen Salles and her collaborators report similar arguments against human rights claims among some Latin American scholars (Salles 2002).

Several considerations need to be taken into account to evaluate these responses. Regarding the second objection, it is often not commodity scarcity that causes famine, injustice, and other factors that contribute to ill health but socially produced deprivations such as lack of legal and other entitlements to food and income (Sen 1990).[8] Among these missing entitlements is appropriate maternal education to enable mothers to avoid food contamination, infant dehydration, and other life-threatening conditions that are responsible for so many infant and child deaths (Freedman 1999; Mata 1988). I will turn to a more detailed discussion of this issue in the next section, where I consider the mutual compatibility of economic assistance to poorer countries and human rights advocacy. The denial of a human rights tradition in Asia is also highly questionable. Amartya Sen has unearthed evidence dating human rights advocacy within the Indian tradition to the twelfth century (Sen 2000). And Salles points out that the independence movements of several Latin American countries based their demands on claims to natural rights, the antecedent of human rights (Salles 2002).

Though the modern formulation is undoubtedly Western in origin, as Sen's evidence illustrates, moral discourse that emphasizes rights is a descendant of older concerns about obligation and justice, virtue and happiness, concerns that have been ubiquitous in ethical discussion since antiquity. However, not until the seventeenth century were the legal dimensions of this discourse extended to women and other disenfranchised groups. The agendas of the social movements that culminated in the French and American revolutions provided the context for a conceptual shift to human rights discourse, as well as a family of interrelated concepts that have been central to moral discourse ever since. Though these movements fell far short of their ideals, their stress on the universality of rights laid the groundwork for contemporary rights claims. The struggles for voting rights, for full participation in the workforce, and for equal opportunity for minority populations are all descendants of these movements and are grounded in a conception of a common humanity based on shared human needs.

Seen in this light, the unqualified rejection of human rights discourse that marks some non-Western approaches to bioethics seems directed more to those who already have control over the basic conditions of their lives than those living on the margins who lack the economic security and reliable social support that the more privileged take for granted. However, as I noted previously, the value of rights needs to be assessed not only from the privileged position of those who already have them but also from the position of those to whom they have been denied. Once human rights are understood as the moral rights of all people in all situations, the central issue is transformed from whether human rights claims should be included within moral discourse to how to identify and characterize them.[9]

The application of this criterion provides a yardstick for evaluating models of economic development that aim to improve living conditions in developing economies. In the next section, I examine in detail the human capabilities model advanced by Amartya Sen and Martha Nussbaum, but first I take up the model that has dominated international assistance programs in developing economies. Based on a quasi-utilitarian construction of preferences that prioritizes economic values, it takes a country's gross domestic product as the measure of its inhabitants' quality of life and assumes that people's expressed preferences represent their actual needs and wants. Institutions that direct globalization support this paradigm. Control of these institutions intensifies the West's economic dominance through programs of national and multilateral "security" that exacerbate the marginalization of populations that cannot contribute significantly to wealth expansion.

Alison Jaggar documents how economic globalization contributes to growing disparities in health outcomes for women worldwide (Jaggar 2003). She, among others, has taken the International Monetary Fund to task for championing market supremacy and insisting on repayment of wealthy creditors even when reimbursement impoverishes the domestic economy of the debtor nations and intensifies their poverty, because forcing debtor countries to repay loans regardless of the conditions of their economy severely diminishes the resources available to support the health and well-being of their people. For example, the intellectual property rules that require poor nations to honor drug patents will result in a transfer of $40 billion a year from poor countries to corporations in the developed world (Rosenberg 2002).[10] Other stratagems employed by Western economic interests include co-optation of rights language to distort and threaten alliances between Western women and those in developing economies, thereby intensifying the fragmentation of human rights initiatives referred to earlier. Some feminists fault these interests for using the cloak of reproductive rights to hijack the agenda of population control programs by manipulating women's reproductive capacity to achieve the demographic goals set by dominant elites (Freedman 1999, 234).

However, feminist groups have begun to seize the initiative, restoring the vitality of rights discourse and opposing the treatment of women as "targets" of contraceptive programs. Women from Asia, Africa, and Latin America have played leading roles in defining the terms and setting the direction of women's human rights movements (as well as reproductive health and rights movements) both in their own countries and at the international level. Several groups are now seeking to counteract programs that would narrow the human rights agenda to the advantage of the West. In a recent address to the World Bank, Mary Robinson, then United Nations high commissioner for human rights, summarized recent efforts within the UN system to channel economic growth resulting from globalization to eradicate poverty, inequality, and deprivation. She called for "ethical globalization" that would make the full complement of rights articulated in the international human rights standards available to all (Robinson 2001).

Human Rights and Capabilities
Models of Human Development

Economist Amartya Sen, joined by a number of development scholars, has questioned the dominant economic development model on two interrelated grounds. First, as I mentioned earlier, famine, injustice, and other factors that contribute to ill health are often due not primarily to commodity scarcity but to socially produced deprivations including lack of entitlements to food and income. Second, the desires and preferences expressed by people who live under oppressive conditions may not provide an adequate guide to their actual needs for either survival or flourishing. Sen cites health surveys in India that document disparities between women's self-reports about their health and their actual health status (Sen 1985). The weight of patriarchal social structures and the ancestral history of women's subjection may distort their consciousness so they internalize prevailing social norms and fail to recognize their own actual needs. In such instances, Sen insists, their preferences are deformed.

Based on these criticisms, Sen has developed a comprehensive economic strategy for encompassing development goals within a more inclusive theoretical framework that takes into account aspects of all three generations of human rights ratified by UN member states: civil and political rights; social, cultural, and economic rights; and rights that protect marginalized social groups. The approach to human development that he pioneered is known as the capabilities approach because, instead of taking gross domestic product as the measure of wealth, it weighs people's capability to lead lives of their own choosing.

In 1986, Nussbaum and others joined Sen in a collaborative UN-sponsored project to incorporate interdisciplinary perspectives into development projects.[11] In a succession of works, Nussbaum has sought to provide philosophical grounding for a specific version of the capabilities approach (Nussbaum 1992, 1998, 1999, 2000). She distinguishes her model from Sen's by its explicit disavowal of relativism, its conception of human functioning derived from Marx and Aristotle, and its enumeration of specific central capabilities.[12] Following John Rawls's thought experiment (Rawls 1971), she imagines a hypothetical group of people deprived of all knowledge about their social position, natural assets, and specific conception of the good life. They assemble to specify fair terms of cooperation for regulating the basic structures of society. She reasons that they would aim at equality of capability rather than equality of resources, since the latter would more likely lead to unequal outcomes that could affect them adversely. For example, disabled people or those who need more food because they perform hard physical labor might need more resources than others to achieve a comparable quality of life (Nussbaum 1992). In several successive works she has developed and refined an enumeration of ten functional capabilities that people require to freely choose lives they personally value (Nussbaum 2000, 78–80).[13] Among them are bodily health, adequate nourishment, and shelter. Understood in this way, the capabilities approach has profound implications for development strategies aimed at implementing health-related rights.

Nussbaum, like an increasing number of other scholars and development organizations (such as the World Bank 2001), has recently turned her attention to the broad economic and social implications of gender discrimination in developing and transitional countries. Her concern, however, also extends to the influence of patriarchal religious communities on women's ability to enjoy healthy, satisfying lives. A recent remark by Ignatieff, reputedly an ardent supporter of human rights, aptly illustrates the kind of insensitivity to gender hierarchies that creeps into the attempts of Western scholars to avoid criticism of other cultures' religious practices. In the course of a discussion urging equal political representation of the interests of the powerless, he asserts: "If, for example, religious groups determine that women should occupy a subordinate place within the rituals of the group, and this place is accepted by the women in question, there is no warrant to intervene on the grounds that human rights considerations of equality have been violated" (Ignatieff 2001b, 19).

Unlike Ignatieff, Nussbaum is not averse to taking on the naturalizing hierarchies of power and privilege that persist in many religious communities and that contribute to the continuing impoverishment of women. She also recognizes connections between these hierarchies and privatized family structures that exploit women's labor only as a means to collective family well-being. Her sensitivity to these issues leads her to focus on the embodied individual as the basic unit for political thought. She develops a rationale for distributing resources in ways that attend to the well-being of all individuals, whatever their capabilities and wherever they fall in the lifespan. This approach has the advantage of addressing specific development goals within a more encompassing global context than do other leading development paradigms. In this respect, her model, like Sen's, is compatible with features of third-generation human rights that attempt to specify human rights more concretely than earlier conceptualizations.

Nussbaum recognizes the dominance of rights language in the international development world and acknowledges a very close relationship between capabilities and rights, but she prefers to take capabilities as her starting point (Nussbaum 2000, 97–101). She believes that rights language often obscures difficult questions and can create the illusion of agreement where there is actually deep philosophical disagreement. Examples she cites include differences about the basis of rights claims, relationships between rights and duties, whether rights are held by individuals or groups, and the specific entitlements of rights holders. She regards both first-generation (liberty) rights and second-generation (welfare) rights as combined capabilities that provide a benchmark for thinking about what it means to secure someone's right. However, she does not wish to do away with rights language altogether. She enumerates several important roles it plays in public discourse: reminding those in power that people have certain justified claims whether or not anyone has done anything about them, emphasizing people's choice and autonomy where rights are guaranteed by the state, and preserving a sense of a terrain of agreement. Her comments suggest the possibility of interweaving both the capabilities model of development ethics and rights discourse within a common pluralistic framework. But before addressing this point, I consider some limitations in her theoretical framework that cry out for more comprehensive strategies. I focus first on the most serious: disregard of individuals' connection to a nexus of group relationships that shape their identities, regulate their social and political positioning, and provide the material conditions to sustain human life. Then I briefly mention several others.

Integrating Group Identifications
into a Development Paradigm

Nussbaum's account of capabilities recognizes only two levels of identification: the universal and the individual. Within her scheme, the individual is the basic unit for political thought. She understands the central capabilities I have enumerated as universal norms of human functioning. To protect the universality of her account and save it from charges of relativism, she deliberately excludes social groups from her structural framework. Feminist accounts, she is convinced, have a tendency to slide into relativism by employing "collectivist means to individual ends" (Nussbaum 1999, 67). She apparently believes that the only way to avoid this snare is to base moral claims on universal human capabilities rather than social endowments or relations (Nussbaum 1999, 72). To her conviction that individuals have an essential core of moral personhood, she recognizes only one alternative, "communitarian anti-essentialism."[14]

But feminists who call her formulation into question are not, by and large, either Marxist "collectivists" or liberals (in the classical sense defined in Jaggar [1983]). They tend to resist commitment to essentialist doctrines of human nature because such beliefs have historically been used to obscure gender-specific differences, shield oppressive political practices from scrutiny, and justify patterns of discrimination that exclude women from educational and social opportunities. Feminists seeking to circumvent cultural relativism commonly employ other strategies that bypass essentialist commitments. Though Nussbaum's version of essentialism may be comparatively benign, the case for a capabilities approach might be articulated in other ways that avoid appeals to both human essences and individual and collective dichotomies.[15] The case for universal human rights is often launched on grounds that presuppose no comprehensive theory of human capacities. Ignatieff builds such a case on human history, taking into account memory of the horrors unleashed by the Nazis (Ignatieff 2001a, 80–81). In an extended response to ethical relativism, Macklin distinguishes between values specific to cultural groups and a class of actions falling under the umbrella of human rights that pertain to health, well-being, and survival universally (Macklin 1999). She declines to delve into deep theoretical questions about the sources of the latter group, preferring to rely on agreement within the international community. Feminist scholars have utilized several overlapping strategies to counter moral relativism. Susan Sherwin (1992) mounts a persuasive case for universal condemnation of all forms of oppression, and Benhabib (1999) defends a modified version of Kantian autonomy that emphasizes the universalizable ability to adopt the standpoint of the other. Hence, the advantages that Nussbaum associates with individualism (freedom from domination by oppressive families or political regimes) might be achieved without foregoing either a universal perspective or the affirmative values of group affiliation.

Even liberal scholars such as Rawls view human rights within the context of associations that are necessary if individuals are to enter into schemes of social cooperation (Rawls 1999). The World Health Organization (WHO) definition of health and subsequent documents based on it all extend the conception of health promotion to groups as well as individuals (Mann et al. 1999, 8). Moreover, many rights proclaimed by the United Nations, including the right to development, entitle people to goods that are accessible only through participation in a particular community or group. Other rights specific to groups include nationality, civil association, political participation, union affiliation, and cultural life as a group member. David Ingram points out that freedom of religion, freedom to work, and freedom from insecurity and ignorance are also rights that individuals are unlikely to exercise apart from group participation (Ingram 2000, 242–43). He holds that all rights are inherently relational since they presuppose social guarantees and other positive enabling conditions (Ingram 2000, 247). In sum, a development theory could accommodate groups as collectivities without jeopardizing the basic rights of individuals or privileging protections afforded to one group over those of others.[16]

Recent feminist accounts depart conspicuously from the individualism of Nussbaum's perspective in their recognition that individuality is inevitably situated within particular configurations of power relations and social connections that provide nurture, care, and identity (Donchin 2000). They recognize that groups are often agents of oppression but realize that group life is necessary for human development, sustenance, and individuality. People depend on their social milieu not only to satisfy their basic physical needs but also to guarantee their self-affirmation and dignity (Freedman 1999, 237). Without the collaboration provided by cohesive groups, marginalized and impoverished individuals are unlikely to gain the widespread social support and resources needed to develop their individual capabilities and act on their autonomous preferences. Failure to take systematic account of the social, political, and relational matrices on which identity is produced and maintained seriously weakens any program aimed at implementing a conception of justice that dislodges traditional gender and class hierarchies. Moreover, when claims to conditions needed to ensure human dignity and well-being are couched in rights language, it is especially vital that rights be viewed as flowing from human material embodiment and social relations. Not all rights carry the same weight. Recognition of distinctively *human* rights establishes priorities among rights claims. Access to those goods that all people require to sustain embodied life have a far weightier claim than, say, the intellectual property rights of multinational corporations (Farmer 2003).

Many feminists also now recognize that local group collaboration is indispensable for personal and social change. Struggles to alter conditions under which women live on any part of the globe are bound to misfire if they disregard local group arrangements. Local people are uniquely situated to anticipate dislocations arising from social change, draw on indigenous networks to resist dominant norms, and tailor responses to local conditions. The problems that arise when local perspectives are disregarded were exemplified in the controversy that erupted over the film *Warrior Marks*, produced by Alice Walker, and the related novel, *Possessing the Secret of Joy* (Walker 1993). This debate aptly illustrates problems that arise when Western activists bypass indigenous local groups. Walker's campaign to rally support condemning the practices of African communities that participate in ritual cutting of young girls' genitals was much criticized by African women as still another manifestation of Western imperialism. Critics charged that her film portrays the African continent as a monolith and uses female genital mutilation as a gauge by which to measure moral distance between the West and the rest of humanity.

These critics insisted that the struggle to transform such traditional practices is better left to those who are sensitive to the social conditions that perpetuate them and who can foster change in ways less likely to intensify the oppression of these women. A *New York Times* op-ed piece by Seble Dawit and Salem Mekuria put it this way: "Genital mutilation does not exist in a vacuum but as part of a social fabric, stemming from the power imbalances in relations between the sexes, from the levels of education and the low economic and social status of most women. All eradication efforts must begin and proceed from these basic premises" (1993, A27). They urge the formation of partnerships with African women; such partnerships would use the power and resources of the West to create space for these women to speak out and to speak with us.

Through such cooperative effort, policies might be developed to change the way such women are socially perceived, both by themselves and by others (Valdés 1995, 428). Crucial to such an undertaking would be encouragement of their capacity to reflect critically on the patriarchal status quo (Li 1995, 409). Uma Narayan points out that without collaborative reflection among similarly situated women, individuals are unlikely to recognize that their own deprivations are part of a pattern of cultural norms that reflect their position within the social structure (Narayan 1997, 11). Narayan speaks of her own mother in India who frequently complained about the oppressive conditions that bound her but was unable to see that her oppression did not stem primarily from the behavior of particular individuals, such as the mother-in-law who maltreated her, but from the social structure that assigned mothers-in-law to positions of such authority. Of course, advances in critical reflection skills cannot bring about constructive change without the power to implement new insights.[17] From this vantage point, an even stronger case can be made for indigenous programs to advance gender equality by expanding opportunities at both individual and group levels and fostering local alliances to diversify individual options and create alternative group practices within communities.[18]

Despite resistance from entrenched bureaucrats, indigenous groups have been effective in building local partnerships for change. They are uniquely suited to mobilize traditional relationships and identify cultural dislocations that foster human potential. In many areas of the globe, the traditional work done by women—and the power these responsibilities confer on them—serve as powerful catalysts for social change and empowerment. Narayan, like many feminists who study the changing position of women in developing areas, recognizes that cultures are seldom monolithic but incorporate within them a diversity of norms and values that may not be mutually compatible (Narayan 1997). Salles, generalizing from her own Latin American experience, points out that "the cultural identity of a community is always in a state of evolution or transformation" (Salles 2002, 18). Martha Chen stresses the evolving character of rural South Asian cultures as they respond to internal (often local) tensions and instabilities that compel women to end their traditional seclusion and seek employment outside the home (Chen 1995, 55).

Margarita Valdés makes an analogous point from the perspective of Mexican culture (Valdés 1995). She extends to developing economies Susan Moller Okin's observation about developed countries: employment makes women less dependent on men and improves their status within the family, thereby strengthening their bargaining position in relation to men (Okin 1995). Moreover, having a job breaks the social isolation of women who had been bound to the domestic sphere, thereby enabling them to function in different social spheres and take action to improve their living conditions. Valdés notes that in the large Mexican cities, many poor women workers have organized themselves to demand urban reforms and contest the division of work according to gender (Valdés 1995, 430). Such examples suggest ways that indigenous women's groups can intervene at the intersection of local tradition and social instability to direct social change along paths they are uniquely qualified to identify as most likely to improve their living conditions.

Nkiru Nzegwu's work (1995) illustrates the numerous practices of cooperative reform and resistance practiced by African women, particularly among grassroots networks of affiliated women's groups that constitute the backbone of local development. Nzegwu chronicles the economic and social power women held in Igbo culture prior to colonial rule (Nzegwu 1995). Indigenous cultural traditions valued female assertiveness and collectivity. Women utilized their networking skills to mobilize across cultural, religious, and economic boundaries, effectively resisting male encroachment on their independence. But after colonial powers imposed their own scheme of gender-specific values on Igbo society, women were reclassified as dependents, a status that precipitated the 1929 Women's War disclaiming their invisibility. Nzegwu's account vividly portrays the effects of the sexist system imported by the British colonizers and shows how co-optation of African men into Western gender stereotyping damaged Nigerian political culture. Today, development projects are still targeted at men, and wide disparities in the incomes of men and women persist. It is not only developers, though, who have hindered Nigerian development. A wealthy multinational oil company has drained their country's natural resources and contributed nothing to local development. Granddaughters of the women who fought the Women's War are now demanding that this company employ more local people, invest in infrastructure projects, and assist villagers to supply food to the company's employees. Their strategies draw on the tradition of market trading by women and modes of protest deeply rooted in their indigenous culture (Peel 2002).

By such means, African women have been challenging both multinational companies and technically oriented development projects for irresponsibly imposing changes that deprive local economies of resources needed to meet subsistence needs. They insist that companies that drain local resources share their profits with the local economy. Their strategy draws on an established tradition of group cohesiveness concentrated in the intermediary political and cultural spaces of established networks and historical relationships stretching between the family and the state.[19]

Nussbaum's interpretation of the capabilities model is largely silent about the tendency of multinational corporations to exploit the resources of developing economies. Sensitivity to varying cultural contexts and crosscultural influences would greatly enhance the case for the universality of the capabilities approach to human development. Recognition of universal human capabilities has major implications for the responsibilities of wealthier countries, both to transitional countries and to pockets of poverty, health care disparities, and gender inequalities in their own economies. Okin notes that when comparisons are made between the living conditions of poor women in developed and developing countries, disparities between economies diminish considerably. She points out that though the severity of their poverty may be greater in poorer countries, patterns of discrimination in developed countries are very similar, particularly within family units (Okin 1995, 284). Moreover, though imbalances in access to health care among economic groups and disparities in maternal and infant morbidity and mortality may not be as severe in richer countries, their injustice is all the more striking since the resources needed to rectify such imbalances are readily available. An analogous point can be made about violence against women. Cass Sunstein cites data showing that women are the victims of both public and private violence in similar proportions in both developed and developing countries (Sunstein 1995, 357).

One final point about Nussbaum's version of development theory: her insistence on locating human rights within liberal political theory risks undermining pragmatic aspects of the human rights movement and getting in the way of efforts by international bodies to forge consensus around practical goals. Within the bioethics community, it has already been shown that it is far easier to reach common ground at the level of practice (on the basis of what Sunstein calls "incompletely theorized agreements") than at the level of moral principle (Sunstein 1995). Anthony Appiah points out that the international human rights framework has an important advantage over the U.S. Constitution in that it does not proceed by deriving human rights from metaphysical first principles (Appiah 2001, 104). This was deliberate strategy on the part of the framers, for they were aiming to achieve universal assent. Even among so-called liberal countries, widespread disagreement exists about how to prioritize theoretical principles. Some question even the desirability of formulating principle-based frameworks for medical decision making. The Scandinavian countries, for instance, tend to emphasize social welfare and patient entitlements, while several others (most notably the United States) emphasize individual rights (Dickenson 1999). The consensus achieved in such agreements as the Council of Europe's Convention on Human Rights and Biomedicine (1997), the Bioethics Declaration approved by the World Conference on Bioethics in Gijón (2000), and the UNESCO document on the human genome (2000) was possible only by focusing on concrete goals and bypassing any single overarching grand theory.

Conclusion

Considering the range of disagreement, a multipronged pluralistic approach seems far more likely to contribute to alleviating injustices than would a unified theoretical design. To be effective in countering global economic and political interests that flout human rights, we must move beyond even the empathetic identification with the situation of the deprived that feminist theorists have endorsed. Feminists need to forge links with like-minded groups to thwart the power elite's intent on bypassing the rights of oppressed people. Narayan's mother failed to understand the forces that victimized her, so she misidentified the source of her oppression. Similarly, many women who submit to traditional patriarchal practices see themselves as having no effective options within the social context that frames their lives. As people are awakened to their deprivations, it is vital that they be empowered to reshape their institutions and practices to expand the range of meaningful choices open to them both individually and collectively.

To implement such a program, we need to be attentive to the work of feminist development theorists who are uncovering the diverse strategies indigenous women's groups devise that draw on their traditional strengths to reconfigure local power relations. As has been shown with HIV/AIDS medical therapy and prevention work in the Asia Pacific region and parts of Africa, individual empowerment is inextricably interwoven with the well-being of communities. In some cultural contexts, such as African communities where a tradition of local women's groups persists, local knowledges and affiliations need to be reinvigorated. In others (such as Mexico) where traditional male privileges have blocked formation of women's alliances, new relational networks need to be encouraged to enhance women's agency and well-being both individually and collectively. Only if human rights are protected at the local level can individuals be empowered to make the fully informed choices that create a climate for dealing effectively with disease prevention and intertwined conditions that perpetuate discrimination and block reconstruction of the cultural fabric of once marginalized communities (Bagasao 1998).

Vital too is support for the expanded definition of health advocated by human rights supporters and the formation of alliances among feminist groups that share overlapping agendas. Promotion of women's health depends on the interaction of many human rights—including rights to employment, education, information, political participation, influence, and democratic legislative processes (Shinn 1999). With a few notable exceptions, infrastructure development has a far greater impact on health than specific medical interventions.[20] And the net must be cast still farther if feminists are to overcome the fragmentation that has eviscerated their global initiatives. As Rosalind Petchesky points out: "compartmentalization obliterates the most important operational principle of a human rights framework: the principle of *indivisibility*" that integrates all three generations of human rights (Petchesky 2002, 75). To press for implementation of the full complement of human rights, feminist groups need to build coalitions and mobilize across issue-oriented programs.

Feminist bioethicists can contribute to this program by rethinking health issues through broader gender and development lenses. We have already made substantial progress in supplanting the individualistic bias dominating much rights discourse, with recognition that the development and maintenance of individuality requires relational bonds. The relational model of autonomy feminist bioethicists have crafted lends itself readily to connection with a conception of human rights that appreciates the importance of interpersonal group networks for implementation of all three generations of human rights.[21] Further reconceptualization of bioethical thought would supplement this work and link it with the recent developments in human rights theory that I have discussed here. Particularly urgent is integration into feminist bioethics of a conception of justice that supplants both contractualism and metaphysical claims about atomistic individuals and speaks to major structural injustices that extend over broad areas of the developing world. We need to intensify our critique of the treatment of health as a commodity and the gender-specific consequences of trade embargoes and economic sanctions that contribute to the exacerbation of economic injustices and mounting poverty.[22] To formulate a more comprehensive framework that is responsive to barriers to women's health across a broad diversity of cultures and traditions, we will need to be attentive to impediments at multiple levels.

To this end, I propose adopting and implementing the strategy Susan Sherwin has put forward for future development of bioethics (Sherwin 2001). Instead of aiming at any single grand theory, we reconceive moral theories as multiple perspectives that provide partial and overlapping resources to address difficult moral issues. Within such a reconception, feminist bioethics, gender studies, development ethics, and human rights discourse would offer overlapping and interlocking "lenses" to illumine dimensions of moral problems obscured by accounts that utilize a single overarching theoretical matrix. Adoption of this strategy does not preclude the search for greater theoretical coherence or closer alignment between theory and practice. More work is needed at the theoretical level to advance thinking about intersections and divergences among these lenses.[23] For instance, we might take a closer look at the few areas where progress has already been made in realizing substantive international consensus among bioethicists and policy makers (for example, basic principles governing medical research and the use of stem cells) for clues that might facilitate extension of the range of theoretical agreement.

On a practical plane, we need to participate actively in efforts to overcome the fragmentation that eviscerates women's health programs and impedes struggles to surmount gender-specific deprivations that thwart women's agency and compromise their health. Coordination of the multiple practices of feminist health activists is bound to enhance crossfertilization among scholars too. Together, such efforts promise to bring theory and practice into closer, more reciprocal, alignment.

Such a revamped moral framework offers the best promise of reinvigorating bioethics in ways that can more adequately expose structural injustices masked by prevailing approaches, remove barriers that impede women's full participation in both local and global alliances, and reshape social conditions to empower marginalized people and advance their health and well-being. Hopefully, through such efforts we can forge a truly global feminist bioethic.

Notes

I wish to express my gratitude to colleagues in the Network on Feminist Approaches to Bioethics, to fellow editors of this volume, and to the editors and reviewers of *Signs: Journal of Women in Culture and Society* for their invaluable contributions to this essay. An earlier version appeared in *Signs* 29, no. 2 (2004). My thanks to the editors of *Signs* for permission to use that material here. My thanks, also, to those who have made valuable comments on previous versions of this essay including Diana Meyers, Susan Dodds, and Edmund Byrne.

1. For a fuller account of her experiences, see the (unnumbered) preface to Baldwin-Ragaven, de Gruchy, and London (1999).

2. For more detail, see British Medical Association (2001, 472).

3. Notable exceptions include Luna (2001) and de Gruchy and Baldwin-Ragaven (2001), who have already begun to explore specific interconnections between feminist bioethics and human rights.

4. Others have constructed variants of this dilemma. See, for instance, O'Neill (1993, 307).

5. For more on this point, see Minow (1990) and Tong (this volume).

6. Several of the other authors in this anthology discuss these issues in considerable detail. See, particularly, the chapters by Bertomeu and Sommer (chapter 11) and Salles (chapter 3). Also, note Luna's essay (2001).

7. For a fuller discussion of associations between health and poverty, see Jaggar (2003, 198–203) and the sources she cites there.

8. Some of these deprivations are politically produced too. For example, the Muslim installed government in northern Sudan has for years kept food and other necessities from Christians in southern Sudan, where the oil deposits happen to be located.

9. This is the characterization of human rights preferred by both Williams (1991) and Macklin. Note Macklin's discussion (1999, 225–28).

10. For a fuller discussion of specific aspects of this issue and intertwined problems, see Bertomeu and Sommer, chapter 11 in this volume.

11. Nussbaum and Sen have occasionally written papers together and jointly edited a collection based on their collaborative projects (1993).

12. For a more detailed discussion of her differences with Sen, see Nussbaum (2000, 11–15).

13. Here I summarize only Nussbaum's most recent version (2000).

14. It is noteworthy that in her subsequent book only a year later, Nussbaum disclaims commitment to any particular view of the person or human nature (Nussbaum 2000, 76). It is not easy to reconcile the two claims even if she is taken to mean that though the capabilities she enumerates are derived from human nature, the more comprehensive theory of justice she avows is not.

15. In response to Nussbaum's position on this point, see Jane Flax (2001). Flax takes Nussbaum to task for conflating human capabilities with human nature, thereby relegating power relations to the background. Note also Dickenson's criticism of Nussbaum's version of the capabilities approach in this volume.

16. Iris Marion Young (1990) has built a conception of groups that are not mere aggregates or associations of individuals but represent a distinctive collectivity whose members have a special affinity with one another based on their similar experience or way of life. They need not have a complete identity of interests but may hold only certain interests in

common around which their group identity is constituted and maintained. Groups that meet these criteria include the traditional groups recognized in the third generation of human rights enumerated by the United Nations, as well as resistance groups such as the Madres de Plaza de Mayo in Argentina and the women's networks in Nigeria that I discuss here.

17. This position has been developed particularly forcefully by Benhabib (1999).

18. On this point, see Sherwin's cogent discussion (1992, 61–62).

19. For the views of other scholars seeking to counter the dominant development paradigm, see contributors to Munck and O'Hearn (1999).

20. The most obvious exceptions are HIV/AIDS and inoculations. The importance of infrastructure development is vividly illustrated by research on women and reproductive tract infections. Studies have shown evidence of heightened vulnerability in areas of the world where women lack access to sanitary toilet facilities. Because of gender-specific norms of modesty and shame, they wait to urinate and defecate only under cover of darkness. Lack of sanitary pads and private places to use them further undermines their reproductive health (Petchesky 2002, 80).

21. For further examples of feminist writing on relational autonomy, see the anthology edited by Mackenzie and Stoljar (2000).

22. Examples of the latter practices include the U.S. embargo on Cuba that blocks imports including contraceptives and X-ray film for performing mammograms.

23. We might benefit, for instance, by thinking of relationships between "lenses" after the model that guides feminist discussion of relationships between the ethics of care and justice. For possible parallels see Held (1995), particularly the article by Alison Jaggar in that volume (179–202).

References

Appiah, K. Anthony. 2001. "Grounding Human Rights." In *Human Rights as Politics and Idolatry*, edited by Amy Gutmann, 101–16. Princeton, N.J.: Princeton University Press.

Bagasao, Teresita Marie P. 1998. "Moving Forward through Community Response: Lessons Learned from HIV Prevention in Asia and the Pacific." *Health and Human Rights* 3, no. 1: 8–18.

Baldwin-Ragaven, Laurel, Jeanelle de Gruchy, and Leslie London, eds. 1999. *An Ambulance of the Wrong Color: Health Professionals, Human Rights and Ethics in South Africa*. Rondebosch, Africa: University of Cape Town Press.

Benhabib, Seyla. 1995. "Cultural Complexity, Moral Interdependence, and the Global Dialogical Community." In *Women, Culture and Development: A Study of Human Capabilities*, edited by Martha Nussbaum and Jonathan Glover, 235–55. New York: Oxford University Press.

———. 1999. "Sexual Difference and Collective Identities: The New Global Constellation." *Signs: Journal of Women in Culture and Society* 24, no. 2: 335–61.

British Medical Association (BMA). 2001. *The Medical Profession and Human Rights: Handbook for a Changing Agenda*. New York: Zed Books.

Chen, Martha. 1995. "A Matter of Survival: Women's Right to Employment in India and Bangladesh." In *Women, Culture and Development: A Study of Human Capabilities*, edited by Martha Nussbaum and Jonathan Glover, 37–57. New York: Oxford University Press.

Cook, Rebecca. 1999. "Gender, Health and Human Rights." In *Health and Human Rights: A Reader*, edited by Jonathan M. Mann, Sofia Gruskin, Michael A. Grodin, and George J. Annas, 253–64. London: Routledge.

Council of Europe. 1997. Convention on Human Rights and Biomedicine. Oviedo, April 4.

Dawit, Seble, and Salem Mekuria. 1993. "The West Just Doesn't Get It," *New York Times*, December 7, A27.

de Gruchy, Jeanelle, and Laurel Baldwin-Ragaven. 2001. "Serving Nationalist Ideologies: Health Professionals and the Violation of Women's Rights." In *Globalizing Feminist Bioethics: Crosscultural Perspectives*, edited by Rosemarie Tong with Gwen Anderson and Aida Santos, 312–33. Boulder, Colo.: Westview.

Dickenson, Donna L. 1999. "Cross-Cultural Issues in European Bioethics." *Bioethics* 13, no. 3: 249–55.

Donchin, Anne. 2000. "Autonomy and Interdependence: Quandaries in Genetic Decision Making." In *Relational Autonomy: Feminist Perspectives on Autonomy, Agency, and the Social Self*, edited by Catriona Mackenzie and Natalie Stoljar, 236–58. New York: Oxford University Press.

Drèze, Jean, and Amartya Sen. 1989. *Hunger and Public Action*. Oxford, UK: Clarendon Press.

Farmer, Paul. 2003. *Pathologies of Power: Health, Human Rights, and the New War on the Poor*. Berkeley: University of California Press.

Flax, Jane. 2001. "A Constructionist Despite Herself? On Capacities and Their Discontents." In *Controversies in Feminism*, edited by James P. Sterba, 25–46. Lanham, Md.: Rowman & Littlefield.

Freedman, Lynn P. 1999. "Reflections on Emerging Frameworks of Health and Human Rights." In *Health and Human Rights: A Reader*, edited by Jonathan M. Mann, Sofia Gruskin, Michael A. Grodin, and George J. Annas, 227–52. London: Routledge.

Gilligan, Carol. 1982. *In a Different Voice: Psychological Theory and Women's Development*. Cambridge, Mass.: Harvard University Press.

Held, Virginia, ed. 1995. *Justice and Care: Essential Readings in Feminist Ethics*. Boulder, Colo.: Westview.

Holmes, Helen Bequaert. 1999. "Closing the Gaps: An Imperative for Feminist Bioethics." In *Embodying Bioethics: Recent Feminist Advances*, edited by Anne Donchin and Laura M. Purdy, 45–63. Lanham, Md.: Rowman & Littlefield.

Ignatieff, Michael. 2001a. "Human Rights as Ideology." In *Human Rights as Politics and Idolatry*, edited by Amy Gutmann, 53–98. Princeton, N.J.: Princeton University Press.

———. 2001b. "Human Rights as Politics." In *Human Rights as Politics and Idolatry*, edited by Amy Gutmann, 3–52. Princeton, N.J.: Princeton University Press.

———. 2001c. "Response to Commentators." In *Human Rights as Politics and Idolatry*, edited by Amy Gutmann, 161–73. Princeton, N.J.: Princeton University Press.

Ingram, David. 2000. *Group Rights: Reconciling Equality and Difference*. Lawrence: University of Kansas Press.

Jaggar, Alison. 1983. *Feminist Politics and Human Nature.* Totowa, N.J.: Rowman & Allanheld.
———. 1995. "Caring as a Feminist Practice of Moral Reason." In *Justice and Care: Essential Readings in Feminist Ethics,* edited by Virginia Held, 179–202. Boulder, Colo.: Westview.
———. 2003. "Vulnerable Women and Neoliberal Globalization." In *Recognition, Responsibility, and Rights: Feminist Ethics and Social Theory,* edited by Robin N. Fiore and Hilde Lindemann Nelson, 195–209. Lanham, Md.: Rowman & Littlefield.
Li, Xiaorong. 1995. "Gender Inequality in China and Cultural Relativism." In *Women, Culture and Development: A Study of Human Capabilities,* edited by Martha Nussbaum and Jonathan Glover, 407–25. New York: Oxford University Press.
Lovibond, Sabina. 1989. "Feminism and Postmodernism." *New Left Review* 178, no. 1: 5–28.
Luna, Florencia. 2001. "Globalization, Gender and Research." In *Globalizing Feminist Bioethics: Crosscultural Perspectives,* edited by Rosemarie Tong with Gwen Anderson and Aida Santos, 254–65. Boulder, Colo.: Westview.
Mackenzie, Catriona, and Natalie Stoljar, eds. 2000. *Relational Autonomy: Feminist Perspectives on Autonomy, Agency, and the Social Self.* New York: Oxford University Press.
Macklin, Ruth. 1999. *Against Relativism.* New York: Oxford University Press.
Mann, Jonathan, Lawrence Gostin, Sofia Gruskin, Troyen Brennan, Zita Lazzarini, and Harvey Fineberg. 1999. "Health and Human Rights." In *Health and Human Rights: A Reader,* edited by Jonathan M. Mann, Sofia Gruskin, Michael A. Grodin, and George J. Annas, 7–20. London: Routledge.
Mata, L. 1988. "A Public Health Approach to the Food-Malnutrition-Economic Recession Complex." In *Health, Nutrition, and Economic Crisis: Approaches to Policy in the Third World,* edited by D. Bell and M. Reich. Dover, Mass.: Aubern.
Meyers, Diana Tietjens. 1994. *Subjection and Subjectivity: Psychoanalytic Feminism and Moral Psychology.* New York: Routledge.
Minow, Martha. 1990. *Making All the Difference: Inclusion, Exclusion, and American Law.* Ithaca, N.Y.: Cornell University Press.
Munck, Ronaldo, and Denis O'Hearn, eds. 1999. *Critical Development Theory: Contributions to a New Paradigm.* New York: Zed Books.
Narayan, Uma. 1997. *Dislocating Cultures: Identities, Traditions, and Third World Feminism.* New York: Routledge.
Nicholas, Barbara. 1999. "Strategies for Effective Transformation." In *Embodying Bioethics: Recent Feminist Advances,* edited by Anne Donchin and Laura M. Purdy, 239–52. Lanham, Md.: Rowman & Littlefield.
Noddings, Nel. 1984. *Caring: A Feminist Approach to Ethics and Moral Education.* Berkeley: University of California Press.
Nussbaum, Martha. 1992. "Justice for Women!" *New York Review of Books* (October 8): 43–48.
———. 1998. "Public Philosophy and International Feminism." *Ethics* 108, no. 4: 762–96.
———. 1999. *Sex and Social Justice.* New York: Oxford University Press.
———. 2000. *Women and Human Development: The Capabilities Approach.* Cambridge, UK: Cambridge University Press.

Nussbaum, Martha, and Amartya Sen, eds. 1993. *The Quality of Life*. Oxford, UK: Oxford University Press.

Nzegwu, Nkiru. 1995. "Recovering Igbo Traditions: A Case for Indigenous Women's Organizations in Development." In *Women, Culture and Development: A Study of Human Capabilities*, edited by Martha Nussbaum and Jonathan Glover, 444–65. New York: Oxford University Press.

Okin, Susan Moller. 1995. "Inequalities between the Sexes in Different Cultural Contexts." In *Women, Culture and Development: A Study of Human Capabilities*, edited by Martha Nussbaum and Jonathan Glover, 274–97. New York: Oxford University Press.

O'Neill, Onora. 1993. "Justice, Gender, and International Boundaries." In *The Quality of Life*, edited by Martha Nussbaum and Amartya Sen, 303–23. Oxford, UK: Oxford University Press.

Peel, Michael. 2002. "Peacefully, Nigerian Women Win Changes from Big Oil." *The Christian Science Monitor*, at www.csmonitor.com/2002/0812/p07s02-woaf.htm.

Petchesky, Rosalind P. 2002. "Human Rights, Reproductive Health, and Economic Justice: Why They Are Indivisible." In *The Socialist Feminist Project: A Contemporary Reader in Theory and Politics*, edited by Nancy Holmstrom, 74–82. New York: Monthly Review Press.

Rawls, John. 1971. *A Theory of Justice*. Cambridge, Mass.: Belknap.

———. 1999. *The Law of Peoples*. Cambridge, Mass.: Harvard University Press.

Robinson, Mary. 2001. "Bridging the Gap between Human Rights and Development: From Normative Principles to Operational Relevance." *World Bank Presidential Fellows Lecture*, at www.worldbank.org/wbi/B-SPAN/sub_mary_robinson.htm.

Rosenberg, Tina. 2002. "Globalization: The Free-Trade Fix." *New York Times Magazine*, August 18, 28.

Sakamoto, Hyakudai. 1999. "Towards a New 'Global Bioethic.'" *Bioethics* 13, nos. 3–4: 191–97.

Salles, Arleen L. F. 2002. "Autonomy and Culture: The Case of Latin America." In *Bioethics: Latin American Perspectives*, edited by Arleen L. F. Salles and María Julia Bertomeu, 9–26. New York: Rodopi.

Sen, Amartya. 1985. *Commodities and Capabilities*. Amsterdam: North-Holland.

———. 1990. "Gender and Cooperative Conflicts." In *Persistent Inequalities: Women and World Development*, edited by Irene Tinker, 123–49. New York: Oxford.

———. 2000. "East and West: The Reach of Reason." *New York Review of Books* (July 20): 33–38.

Sherwin, Susan. 1992. *No Longer Patient: Feminist Ethics and Health Care*. Philadelphia: Temple University Press.

———. 2001. "Foundations, Frameworks, Lenses: The Role of Theories in Bioethics." In *Globalizing Feminist Bioethics: Crosscultural Perspectives*, edited by Rosemarie Tong with Gwen Anderson and Aida Santos, 12–26. Boulder, Colo.: Westview.

Shinn, Carolynne. 1999. "The Right to the Highest Attainable Standard of Health: Public Health's Opportunity to Reframe a Human Rights Debate in the United States." *Health and Human Rights* 4, no. 1: 114–33.

Sunstein, Cass. 1995. "Gender, Caste and Law." In *Women, Culture and Development: A Study of Human Capabilities*, edited by Martha Nussbaum and Jonathan Glover, 332–59. New York: Oxford University Press.

UNESCO. 2000. "The Universal Declaration on the Human Genome and Human Rights: From Theory to Practice." UNESCO, at www.unesdoc.unesco.org.

———. 2001. *Dsigning Democracy: What Constitutions Do.* New York: Oxford University Press.

Valdés, Margarita M. 1995. "Inequality in Capabilities between Men and Women in Mexico." In *Women, Culture and Development: A Study of Human Capabilities,* edited by Martha Nussbaum and Jonathan Glover, 426–32. New York: Oxford University Press.

Walker, Alice. 1993. *Possessing the Secret of Joy.* New York: Harcourt Brace.

Walker, Alice, and Pratibha Parmar. 1993. *Warrior Marks.* New York: Women Make Movies.

Walker, Margaret Urban. 2003. "Truth and Voice in Women's Rights." In *Recognition, Responsibility, and Rights,* edited by Robin N. Fiore and Hilde Lindemann Nelson, 169–80. Lanham, Md.: Rowman & Littlefield.

Williams, Patricia J. 1991. *The Alchemy of Race and Rights.* Cambridge, Mass.: Harvard University Press.

World Bank. 2001. *Engendering Development: Through Gender Equality in Rights, Resources, and Voice.* New York: Oxford University Press and World Bank.

World Conference on Bioethics. 2000. "Bioethics Declaration." Gijón, Spain, at sibi.org/ingles/declaracion.htm.

Young, Iris Marion. 1990. *Justice and the Politics of Difference.* Princeton, N.J.: Princeton University Press.

Bioethics, Difference, and Rights   3

ARLEEN L. F. SALLES

IN WHAT WAYS AND TO WHAT EXTENT should cultural and ethnic considerations play a role in the health care environment? As aspirations to universalism become more suspect in bioethics, it has become fashionable to highlight cultural and ethnic issues, examine their impact on the patient-physician relationship, and argue that they should be clinically and ethically salient (Kleinman, Eisenberg, and Good 1978; Kunstadter 1980; Cross and Churchill 1982; Marshall 1992). Two strategies are generally used to defend this view. The first claims that culture and ethnicity deeply influence a patient's experience of illness and pain. Therefore, if health care practitioners are imbued in their training with a sense that competent care requires cultural and ethnic sensitivity, their relationship with patients will improve and care will be enhanced. In contrast, the second strategy is based on the view that attending to cultural and ethnic particularities is necessary to respect and treat members of diverse groups as equals. Respecting patients requires acknowledgment of the importance of their worlds and their fundamental relationships and values.

It would certainly be a mistake to deny the existence of cultural and ethnic differences. However, like other feminists who have concerns about invoking the concept of difference uncritically (Benhabib 1995; Narayan 1997, 1998; Okin 1999), I worry about assuming that an emphasis on ethnic and cultural differences will invariably promote the health, autonomy, and well-being of patients and other vulnerable groups. First, in societies where essentialist notions of culture and ethnicity are operative and where diverse cultures and ethnic groups are described and understood stereotypically, unjustified beliefs about their supposed values and customs are likely to erode patient rights. Hern and colleagues have pointed out that "the use of the culture concept is often remarkably naïve" in medical practice (Hern et al. 1998, 30). Thus, practitioners influenced by cultural expectations may be inattentive to the unique choices of particular individuals. Second, uncritical emphasis on the importance of culture would harm women if it is used to sustain cultural practices that undermine women's power to represent their own interests and make autonomous decisions.

In this chapter, I address these two concerns by focusing on Hispanic patients.[1] In the first section, I describe some empirical research on Hispanic patients and assumptions underlying its conclusions. I also address some of the ethical issues raised by stereotyping and generalizing about minorities. In the second section, I consider the limitations of uncritical essentialist thinking about ethnicity and culture and propose alternative ways of thinking about these concepts. Finally, in the third section I argue that even if stereotyping and essentialist thinking are avoided, respect for cultural and ethnic differences is morally defensible only within a framework that recognizes basic human rights and goals. Many Hispanic societies impose on women a gender-specific ethic that accustoms them to subordinate their own interests to those of others. Thereby women's right to make decisions on their own behalf and flourish as human beings is subtly undermined.[2] In that case, respecting cultural difference that in fact shields sexism and inequality is morally indefensible.

Hispanics and Medical Decision Making

Within health care practice, Hispanic patients have a distinctive reputation. The general view is that Hispanic patients resent full disclosure of poor prognoses, are not particularly interested in making medical decisions, and embrace a more family-oriented and less individualistic approach to medical decision making than Anglos. This view is influenced by the way the label "Hispanic" is used by the media, the government, and the general population. Ignoring actual differences between one Hispanic individual and another, these labels impose a number of clichés and stereotypes on all Hispanics, thereby conveying the false impression that Hispanics constitute a unitary monolith that thinks and acts in uniform ways. For example, it is frequently stated that Hispanics are overly committed to family values and behaviors (Marín and Triandis 1985; Sabogal, Marín, and Otero-Sabogal 1987) and share traits considered to be inimical to autonomy (for example, being more passionate and intense than intelligent and more tradition loving than self-disciplined) (Fairchild and Cozens 1981; Jackson 1995). Here, the implicit assumption is that a Hispanic culture exists that determines many, if not all, of the attitudes and behaviors of Hispanics.

In the medical context, the profile of the "typical" Hispanic patient is found in several empirical studies (based mostly on findings about Mexican Americans, who make up the largest Hispanic group in the United States). According to the authors of one well-known study on the issue of informed consent and medical decision making, "the decision-making style exhibited by most of the Mexican American and Korean American subjects in our study might be best described as family centered. In this family centered model it is the sole responsibility of the family to hear bad news about the patient's diagnosis and prognosis and to make difficult decisions about life support" (Blackhall et al. 1995, 824). The authors conclude that "insisting on the patient autonomy model of medical decision-making when that model runs counter to the deepest values of the patient may ironically be another form of the paternalistic idea that 'doctor knows best'" (Blackhall et al. 1995, 825). In a different study that focuses on Chinese and Hispanic patients, the authors note that "the culturally diverse patients and their relatives did not consider autonomy when making healthcare decisions. The professional imperative of autonomous, informed decision-making came into conflict with the family's moral imperative—filial duty" (Orona, Koenig, and Davis 1994, 339). In still another study centered on patients' attitudes to advance directives and withholding or withdrawing treatment, the authors compare the attitudes of Mexican Americans, Euro-Americans, and African Americans (Perkins et al. 2002, 17). They report that the majority of all the groups studied shared two beliefs: that the patient should have a say in the treatment and that advance directives can help guide treatment. The authors speculate that expressed agreements probably reflect a common American culture, thus acknowledging that cultures are not closed to one another.[3] Yet the authors do not consider the further possibility that some Hispanics qua Hispanics may actually hold those values. They suggest that the beliefs of "autonomy-loving" Hispanics are the consequence of acculturation and, therefore, they end up relying almost exclusively on an assimilationist analytic framework that obscures the complexity of Hispanic social reality.[4]

In all fairness, the authors of these studies concede that empirical studies are never conclusive, and they acknowledge the limited generalizability of their findings. Nevertheless, they indirectly give support to two views. First, they imply that Hispanics are naturally less concerned about their own personal goals and values than the needs, goals, and values of members of the group to which they belong, and Hispanics are quite willing to sacrifice their personal autonomy for the good of the group. Second, they promote the view that Euro-American patients are models of autonomy, ignoring the reality that many Anglo patients are reluctant to make their own decisions and may prefer a more family-oriented approach to medical decision making (Schneider 1998).

To a certain extent, Hispanic commentators themselves perpetuate the idea that Hispanics are not particularly interested in exercising their right to make decisions in the medical setting. Diego Gracia, an influential Spanish bioethicist, states, "Latin people are profoundly uncomfortable with rights and principles. They are used to judging things and acts as good or bad, instead of right or wrong. They prefer benevolence to justice, friendship to mutual respect, excellence to rights" (Gracia 1995, 205). Gracia argues that people from Latin countries embrace a virtue-oriented approach to ethical issues and give priority to community and family relationships over their personal right to make their own choices. By this line of reasoning, he concludes that an approach based on principles can be very useful in Latin countries. The principle of respect for autonomy, for example, might help counterbalance the paternalism prevalent in medical practice in those countries. Yet however well intentioned Gracia's remarks may be, once again they have the effect of obscuring the heterogeneity of the group. Since people from Latin countries differ in terms of language, race, cultural customs, religions, and practices, they are unlikely to rally uniformly around collectivist values.

Consider, for example, Latin American Hispanics. Latin America is constituted by a diverse array of countries, each with distinct populations that vary in their religious traditions, social practices, and political ideologies. In fact, even within the same population, the degree to which standards of behavior and values are shared depends on many factors, including socioeconomic status,[5] background, gender, education, place of birth, and residence. In general, a more autonomist approach to medical decision making is evident in people from richer and highly developed urban centers than in poorer and underdeveloped areas where people tend to cling to indigenous health practices and display a passive attitude toward their own health care. Thus, when we turn from general and abstract ideas about how Hispanics make medical decisions to the particular contexts in which specific Hispanic individuals make those decisions, a different perspective emerges. It becomes evident that the medical beliefs and values of individual Hispanics in Latin America cannot be predicted solely on the basis of their Hispanic identity.

Turning to Hispanics in the United States, the term *Hispanic* refers to people from all the Spanish American nations, as well as Spain. Can their values and beliefs be predicted on the basis of their ethnicity? Certainly not. Philosopher Ofelia Schutte notes that "in some sectors of Hispanic culture one is expected to approve of bullfights and cockfights, to enjoy eating the entrails of animals, or not to use birth control. I deplore bullfights and cockfights, I follow a semi-vegetarian diet, and as a feminist, I believe a woman has a right to the full control of her body in sexual and reproductive matters" (Schutte 2000, 67). Philosopher Jorge Gracia wonders what he, a Cuban of European ancestry, can have in common with a "poor bracero of Meso-American ancestry who crossed the United States border with Mexico illegally in search of manual labor" (Gracia and De Greiff 2000, 22). What these examples show is not that Gracia and

Schutte are not Hispanic but that Hispanics in the United States constitute a heterogenous group. Despite generalizations about the values, behaviors, and beliefs of Hispanics, the same diversity found in Latin America is also present in the Hispanic American community. There is no common Hispanic race, socioeconomic status, religion, or set of values (del Portillo 1988).

Though general categories probably must be used in certain contexts, considering the complex nature of health care issues, generalizations about all patients or all practitioners are likely to be highly problematic. Ingrained stereotypes can easily exaggerate and distort health care providers' thinking about their Hispanic patients and their treatment of them. Assumptions about cultural uniformity do not foster the kind of communication necessary to determine a particular patient's wishes. Finding values and preferences a priori is a poor substitute for personal communication. Furthermore, such assumptions contribute to the construction of a homogeneous category of patients as the collective "Other," thereby intensifying disparities in power and authority between patients and physicians.

Of course, much of the literature that emphasizes the importance of cultural and ethnic differences in the health care context includes warnings against group stereotyping. Health care practitioners, it is argued, should develop sensitivity, knowledge, and the rational and emotional skills required for the kind of interaction that will prevent them from reducing their patients to embodiments of stereotypical traits. However, it is often extremely hard for the typical health care practitioner to develop those traits and skills. First, there is too little opportunity for most health care practitioners to get to know members of other groups well enough to permit more than a stereotypical understanding of them (Blacksher 1998). Second, many practitioners are uncomfortable with interpersonal communication and tend to avoid it. Cultural generalizations then replace effective communication (Blacksher 1998). A discussion of how notions of family, individuality, health, body, and illness are understood by the patient seems crucial. Yet because many physicians find it difficult to discuss some of these issues, they may reason in this way: since Hispanics are unlikely to share such Anglo values as the primacy of individual autonomy, they probably do not want to know much about their condition and prefer that someone else handle distressing and unpleasant situations for them.

Clearly, those who believe that attention to differences can enrich the patient-physician relationship must proceed with caution lest they undermine the best interests (and human rights) of just those minority groups they intend to benefit. As Barbara Koenig and Jan Williams aptly note, "culture is only meaningful when interpreted in the context of the patient's unique history, family constellation, and socioeconomic status" (Koenig and Williams 1995). For example, Hispanic beliefs about disclosure and truth telling vary within the community (Caralis et al.

1993).[6] When patients expect to be told the truth, treating them according to a simplistic understanding of their culture and ethnic group is not likely to enrich their relationship with health care practitioners or enhance the care they receive (Orr, Marshall, and Osborn 1995). Thus, what passes for cultural sensitivity may impoverish rather than enrich the care of Hispanic patients and their relationship with practitioners. There may be only a short step from seeing an individual as a member of a group with particular traditions to the obliteration of that person's individuality. The individual thereby becomes a mere representative of his or her group, and the underlying basis of his or her ethical choices remains unexamined.

Ethnicity and Culture

Recognition that a focus on culture and ethnicity may be based on stereotypes has led some commentators to highlight the importance of focusing on patients individually (Lock 1993; Orr, Marshall, and Osborn 1995; Hern et al. 1998; Blacksher 1998).[7] Pointing to the pitfalls of generalization and ambiguity about the extent to which cultural norms control the preferences of patients, they recommend that health care practitioners listen to each patient (Lock 1993, 153; Blacksher 1998, 15); put questions to the patient, family, and friends; and negotiate treatment goals and alternatives (Orr, Marshall, and Osborn 1995).[8] Culturally sensitive care, they insist, requires that patients speak out of their personal experience and that practitioners listen with an open mind. However, even more is needed. Before practitioners can hear patients and negotiate with them to use cultural differences in a positive way, they must have a clear conception of what culture and ethnicity represent. Surprisingly, bioethicists have left these important concepts largely unexamined (Wolf 1999). I do not mean to suggest that cultural and ethnic considerations are avoided in bioethical discourse. On the contrary, "culture talk" has become pervasive in the field. But within bioethics there has not been a genuine *philosophical* engagement with the concepts of culture and ethnicity. This would not be a problem if general consensus existed about the meaning of these concepts, but the notions of culture and ethnicity are more problematic than bioethicists assume. Anthropologists and sociologists have had protracted debates about the meanings of these concepts and distinctions between them. Culture has been conceived as social heritage or tradition, as shared and learned human behavior, and as the accumulated symbols and meanings relative to a society or group of persons in a society. As I have argued previously, careful examination of the concept of culture shows that beliefs about the influence of a culture are often overgeneralized.

Uma Narayan cautions against uncritical essentialist conceptions of culture that "depict as homogeneous groups of heterogeneous people whose values, interests, ways of life, and moral and political commitments are internally plural and divergent" (Narayan 1998, 88). Essentialist constructions emphasize the distinctiveness and boundedness of cultures and define cultural identity in opposition to external influences. Cultural essences are assumed to dictate people's fates. Related to this tendency is the belief that cultures are solid, stable, ahistorical, "unchanging givens" (Narayan 1998, 94). This belief is at odds with the tendency of anthropologists to emphasize the changing nature of human societies. Unreflective essentialist understandings of culture obscure internal debates within specific cultures, hide the diversity of normative options available to members, and discourage creative interpretations of cultural identity that would advance autonomous ends (Benhabib 1995).

Essentialist conceptions of ethnicity are comparably problematic. Essentialists define an ethnic group by a set of necessary and sufficient conditions and assign people to that group insofar as they meet those requisites.[9] Group members are identified by common properties such as shared culture or language. Such conceptions raise difficult problems. As Iris Marion Young points out, "oppression has been perpetrated by a conceptualization of group difference in terms of unalterable essential natures that determines what group members deserve or are capable of, and that exclude groups so entirely from one another that they have no similarities or overlapping attributes" (Young 1990, 47). Young uses the term *oppression* to refer to the disadvantages and social inequality suffered by some groups as a result of others' assumptions in everyday life (Young 1990, 41). My discussion in the previous section illustrated how Hispanic patients can suffer from such oppression at the hands of health care practitioners. Indeed, essentialist conceptions of ethnicity may be at the root of this problem. Despite counsel to listen to people and elicit their preferences, health providers who harbor an essentialist understanding of ethnic groups are likely to expect that all Hispanics qua Hispanics share similar values and behaviors.

In response to this, one could argue that even if an essentialist understanding sometimes leads to harmful homogenizing and stereotyping, this does not necessarily count against all essentialist analysis. Homogenizing and stereotyping, the objector might add, have deep roots in human cognitive architecture, and unethical treatment of others could be avoided if agents conducted themselves in morally and epistemically responsible ways. But the fact is that some groups do share common characteristics. Is this objection well founded? Do group traits really exist? Several theorists have pointed out that it is impossible to name a set of enduring characteristics that all members of a group such as Hispanics share in common. Until such traits are found in the lived experience of Hispanic individuals, essentialist analysis is contestable.[10] The variability and diversity of Hispanics' experiences undermine the case for essentialist explanation.

Young articulates a relational account of group membership and argues that group differences should be conceived as "ambiguous, relational, shifting, without clear borders that keep people straight—as entailing neither amorphous unity nor pure individuality" (Young 1990, 171). She believes that people belong to a group insofar as they stand in certain relations to each other (Young 2000, 153). In the case of Hispanics, rather than appealing to race, language, or a common history, Young finds that "what makes it sensible to say that they are nevertheless a single group [is] the fact that social structures similarly position them largely on the basis of their otherwise divergent cultural backgrounds" (Young 2000, 158). In her view, the fact that Hispanics are treated as foreigners, speak Spanish better than English, and are liable to be discriminated against has specific consequences for their opportunities to flourish. Although not all Hispanics are positioned identically with respect to certain social, economic, linguistic, and cultural barriers, "nearly all of them find their lives conditioned by at least one of them" (Young 2000, 153), and it is this fact that accounts for an individual's membership in the group labeled "Hispanics."

Jorge Gracia also defends a relational conception of ethnicity, according to which "what ties the members of an ethnic group together, and separates them from others, is history and the particular events of that history; a unique web of changing historical relations supply their unity" (Gracia 1999, 34). In the case of Hispanics, it is their common historical reality that sets them apart from non-Hispanics in the sense that "at any particular time and place, there are familial relations that Hispanics share and which both distinguish us from non-Hispanics and are the source of properties which also can be used to distinguish us from non-Hispanics" (Gracia 2000, 56).

It is not my intention here to formulate a conception of ethnic affiliation. However, I believe that attention to recent work on a relational conception of ethnicity may enable bioethicists to employ more particularized conceptions of ethnicity and culture in the medical setting. Relational approaches look promising insofar as they do not seek to identify specific attributes shared by Hispanics qua Hispanics. Being Hispanic indicates that one is connected to others in certain ways, but it predicts nothing about one's identity or values. Also, a relational understanding of ethnicity and group membership accommodates internal differences among members (Gracia 1999, 2000; Young 2000). Since it focuses on relations, it retains a conception of Hispanics as a social collectivity without requiring individual compliance with a particular Hispanic ideal or script. Thus, in the context of the patient-physician interaction, a relational understanding of ethnicity is more likely to promote an attitude that fosters meaningful communication between physician and patient. Insofar as it accommodates Hispanic diversity, a relational conception is likely to reduce stereotyping and promote more open communication.[11]

Cultural Differences and Rights

Rejection of essentialist thinking about culture and ethnicity, however, need not imply rejection of all generalization (Narayan 1998). Narayan points to the difference between generalizations that are not empirically accurate and threaten just treatment and those that are arguably true and politically useful in pointing to violation of rights (Narayan 1998, 103). Anthropological evidence suggests that virtually all societies share two features, both of which shape women's lives in ways that tend to disadvantage them. First, all societies distinguish between the public and the private spheres. Women bear primary responsibility for domestic management and child care, and men are dominant in the public domain. Second, all societies are characterized by some forms of female subordination to males within the contexts of both impersonal social institutions and personal relationships (Rosaldo 1974; Ortner 1974).

Many Latin American countries are explicitly organized along patriarchal and authoritarian principles, and the social disparities between men and women seem more evident than in the United States, where male and female disparities are muted and somewhat eroded. It is not that the basic civil rights and political liberties of Latin American women are restricted or violated by the state; in general, they are not (Valdés 1995). Nevertheless, although Latin American women are men's formal equals, at an informal level women's voices are not often heard during decision-making deliberations.[12] Because women's self-sacrifice and self-abnegation is culturally valued, and because of a long history of subjection, women, especially if illiterate and economically disadvantaged, tend to remain silent and defer to men (Luna 1995).

Similarly, patterns of male dominance are prevalent within the Hispanic community in the United States. Cultural demands impose a deferential role on Hispanic women: they care for others but not themselves. Their self-effacing role may render them unable to recognize their own interests. Moreover, cultural expectations impose a self-doubting role on Hispanic women, in which they are perceived as poor decision makers. The combination of the disadvantages of gender, class, ethnic status, and cultural expectations increases the likelihood that a Hispanic woman's request for accurate medical information or a particular treatment will not be heeded. Her lack of social standing may give others the power to dismiss her request as a display of emotionality or a sign of incompetence and may be used to justify health care practitioners turning to the family or the "man in charge" to make women's treatment decisions. If a person's moral agency includes her capacity to express her own preferences, then the traditional silencing of Hispanic women erodes their moral agency.

Such silencing produces harmful consequences that not only adversely affect women's health but also violate their human rights.[13] Recognition that the complex interplay of ethnic and gender-specific barriers deprives minority women of equal opportunities for well-being and advancement necessitates a more comprehensive feminist strategy that includes respect for human rights. The advantage of the human rights framework is that it affirms the inherent worth and equality of all humans, thereby providing support for universal respect.

Yet appeals to rights have been suspect within feminist thought. Underlying the reluctance to think in terms of rights are a number of concerns.[14] I focus on one directly relevant to my theme: the claim that the notion of human rights cannot transcend national borders and cultures. It has been maintained that to press for rights on behalf of people from cultures that do not overtly use the language of rights is an exercise in "cultural imperialism" that undermines their unique moral voices and forces them to do things the "American way."

This line of thinking stresses the advantages of attending to cultural and ethnic differences. However, it overlooks major problems associated with disregarding rights. The view that it is inappropriate to extend the notion of human rights to cultures that do not explicitly affirm them is unjustified; human rights have the potential to reach beyond national borders and specific cultural beliefs. First, the link between rights and the protection of human dignity emphasizes fundamental behavioral and aspirational goals "for a world in which all humans live in harmony and reach their fullest potential" (Knowles 2001, 256–57). Implementation of protections that safeguard the dignity of every human being would empower and promote everyone's well-being regardless of their cultural background. Second, if the problem with rights is that they are generally narrowly interpreted in an ethnocentric and overly individualistic fashion that lends credence to the view that they are inappropriate to some cultures, then the notion of human rights is not beyond repair. A richer understanding must be articulated that escapes the abstract individualism of traditional interpretations and recognizes cultural differences and social commitments without abandoning focus on the shared humanity of those who embody those differences.

Third, from a practical standpoint, rights discourse has done more to promote the well-being of people from diverse cultures (including cultures where rights are not part of the moral repertoire) than any appeal to differences. Notwithstanding the enthusiasm with which attention to differences has been received, when coupled with an attempt to minimize the importance of human rights, emphasis on difference may leave many vulnerable people unprotected. Finally, in the case of Hispanics, only a partial and biased record of their history would support the view that all Hispanics see the notion of rights as foreign. Latin American countries based their declaration of independence from Spain on their claim to natural human rights, rights that their "mother" country, Spain, had unjustly denied them. The rationalism of Descartes and other Continental philosophers, the empiricism of Locke, the social ideas of Rousseau, and the utilitarian thinking of Bentham all contributed to the development of a liberal intellectual tradition in Latin America that supported the independence movements and utilized their ideas as tools for social change. In the past few decades, precisely because of a history of abuses, torture, and authoritarian governments, appeals to human rights are frequently voiced by Hispanics. With respect to claims about women's rights in particular, as early as the seventeenth century, Mexican nun Sor Juana Inés de la Cruz (Paz 1982) questioned the patriarchal culture's representation of women and compellingly defended women's freedom to function in the public as well as private sphere of life. Later, in the nineteenth century her views were reinforced by Latin American female intellectuals, and in the twentieth century a group of women novelists, journalists, and political activists used rights language to claim equality and challenge the tradition that disadvantaged them.[15]

Recently, some feminists have begun to question the prevalent skepticism regarding rights and have attempted to integrate features of human rights discourse into feminist thought (Okin 1998; Freedman 1999; Walker 2003; Donchin 2004). I am very sympathetic to the aim and spirit of their projects. Despite differences in their accounts, they all try to identify ways in which rights express basic human values and lend themselves to the promotion of the well-being of people in general and vulnerable groups in particular. Lynn Freedman expresses this point compellingly: "[the human rights paradigm] seeks to create a world in which human dignity adheres in the still distant ideal of choice: the notion that human beings, constituted through relations with others, can still make choices about their lives, can still have something to say about how to structure and maintain relations with others, be they family, community, or state" (Freedman 1999, 242).

When a woman's right to make her own decisions, including her medical decisions, is not taken seriously, not only is her health adversely affected, but she also is not respected as a possessor of human dignity. Thus, only a very thin notion of respect for persons would support the view that respecting an unreflective cultural tradition that does not listen to every woman patient represents genuine respect. There are reasonable objections to culturally accepted practices that violate basic rights. Such practices should be rejected.

Conclusion

Cultural diversity should be encouraged and protected. In the medical setting, it is a powerful antidote to dogmatism and ethnocentrism and to the tendency to project dominant group experiences and values onto all patients or to judge others according to the majority's norms. Sometimes, however, recognition of difference can be counterproductive, oppressing rather than empowering people who are the carriers of the difference. As Tong has pointed out, within feminist thought an overemphasis on difference "has resulted in feminists' inability to formulate policies aimed at expanding women's freedom and well being in a just manner" (Tong 2001, 29). In this chapter, I have argued that two things are necessary to use cultural and ethnic differences positively in the medical context. First, it is vital to increase awareness of the heterogeneity of collectivities and to direct attention to conflicting interests among their members. If we are to avoid the tendency to homogenize people who belong to a particular social grouping, we need to examine the concepts of culture and ethnicity and replace essentialist constructions of these concepts with a more relational understanding. Second, I suggest that a human rights paradigm be adopted to set the boundaries of morally legitimate cultural practices. This paradigm requires a more inclusive language of rights (Okin 1998; Donchin 2004) that pays attention not only to the defense of basic political and civil liberties of all people but also to the defense of other rights crucial to women's well-being, including the right to speak and to have one's words count, so that one can exercise one's moral agency (Walker 2003). Although often culturally appropriate and hidden under the good intentions of those who are members of a particular culture, the tendency to make medical decisions on behalf of women is troubling because it silences and discredits them. Consequently, it has a negative impact on their ability to function effectively, and it makes it more difficult for women to achieve real equality. Thus, genuine respect for persons and their rights should have priority over cultural and ethnic considerations.

Notes

An earlier draft of this essay was presented at a panel organized by the Society for Iberian and Latin American Thought at the Eastern Meeting of the American Philosophical Association (Philadelphia, December 28, 2002). My thanks to Anne Donchin, Robert Hall, Richard Hull, Rosemarie Tong, and María Victoria Costa for comments on different versions of that article.

1. Although I focus on Hispanics, some of my comments have application to other ethnic groups as well.

2. For a discussion of women in some Latin American countries, see, for example, Margarita Valdés, "Inequality in Capabilities between Men and Women in Mexico," in *Women, Culture and Development*, ed. Martha Nussbaum and Jonathan Glover (New York: Oxford University Press, 1995), 426–32; Juana Armanda Alegría, "La Sexualidad de la Mexicana," in *Anatomía del Mexicano*, ed. Roger Bartra (Mexico DF: Plaza Janés, 2002), 273–81; and Maria Luisa Femenias, *Perfiles del Feminismo Iberoamericano* (Buenos Aires: Catálogos, 2002).

3. For a criticism of the view that cultures are opaque, see Mark Kuczewski and Patrick McCruden, "Informed Consent: Does It Take a Village? The Problem of Culture and Truth

Telling," *Cambridge Quarterly of Healthcare Ethics* 10 (2001): 34–46; and Arleen L. F. Salles, "Autonomy and Culture: The Case of Latin America," in *Bioethics: Latin American Perspectives*, ed. Arleen L. F. Salles and María Julia Bertomeu (New York: Rodopi, 2002), 9–26.

4. For a discussion of assimilationism, see Donna Dickenson, this anthology, chapter I.

5. For a general discussion of the implications of class in medical decision making, see Betty Levin and Nina Glick Schiller, "Social Class and Medical Decisionmaking: A Neglected Topic in Bioethics," *Cambridge Quarterly of Healthcare Ethics* 7, no. 1 (1998): 41–56.

6. See, for example, P. V. Caralis, Bobbi Davis, Karen Wright, and Eileen Marcial, "The Influence of Ethnicity and Race on Attitudes toward Advance Directives, Life-Prolonging Treatments, and Euthanasia," *Journal of Clinical Ethics* 4, no. 2 (1993): 156–65. The authors examine the issue of truth telling and report that Hispanic families wishing to spare a family member from "bad news" frequently request that physicians not inform the patient. However, the authors of the same study note that the Hispanic patients interviewed on the same issue expressed their desire to be informed concerning serious illnesses and life-prolonging treatment. This shows a crucial disagreement about truth telling in the medical context within the same group.

7. Robert Hall has pointed out to me that based on his research on physician-patient communication, he has been led to conclude that the diversity within Anglo patients is so great as to make any single model of decision making unacceptable. His conclusion about both minority patients and Anglo patients is that the physician must find out from the patient how he or she wants the communication and decision making handled. For a more developed account of this issue, see Greg Clarke, Robert Hall, and Greg Rosencrance, "Physician-Patient Relations: No More Models," *American Journal of Bioethics*. Forthcoming.

8. See Margaret Lock, "Education and Self Reflection: Teaching About Culture, Health and Illness," in *Health and Culture: Exploring the Relationship*, ed. Ralph Masi et al. (Oakville, Ontario: Mosaic Press, 1993), 139–58.

9. There are many types of essentialist views. See, for example, Angelo Corlett's genetic view in Angelo Corlett, "Latino Identity," *Public Affairs Quarterly* 13 (1999): 273–95.

10. For an extensive discussion of the problems raised by essentialist views, see Jorge Gracia, "The Nature of Ethnicity with Special Reference to Hispanic Latinos' Identity," *Public Affairs Quarterly* 13, no. 1 (1999): 25–42.

11. I am not implying that physicians and other health care providers should become experts in the philosophical discussion of culture and identity but that they are unlikely to use cultural and ethnic considerations appropriately if these notions are construed in an essentialist fashion.

12. For a discussion of women and Iberoamerican feminism, see Maria Luisa Femenias, *Perfiles del Feminismo Iberoamericano* (Buenos Aires: Catálogos, 2002).

13. For an examination of the harmful consequences of the different forms of silencing and the importance of the right to truth, see Margaret Urban Walker, "Truth and Voice in Women's Rights," in *Recognition, Responsibility and Rights: Feminist Ethics and Social Theory*, ed. Robin Fiore and Hilde Lindemann Nelson (Lanham, Md.: Rowman & Littlefield, 2003), 169–80.

14. See Lynn Freedman, "Reflections on Emerging Frameworks of Health and Human Rights," in *Health and Human Rights*, ed. Jonathan M. Mann, Sofia Gruskin, Michael A. Grodin, and George J. Annas (New York: Routledge, 1999), 227–53; and Anne Donchin, "Converging Concerns: Feminist Bioethics, Development Theory and Human Rights," *Signs: Journal of Women in Culture and Society* 29, no. 2 (2004): 299–324 for a general discussion of this topic.

15. These considerations are not intended to show that all Hispanics think in terms of rights but that it is mistaken to think that rights are not part of Hispanics' moral vocabulary.

References

Alegría, Juana Armanda. 2002. "La Sexualidad de la Mexicana." In *Anatomía del Mexicano*, edited by Roger Bartra, 273–81. Mexico DF: Plaza Janés.

Benhabib, Seyla. 1995. "Cultural Complexity, Moral Interdependence and the Global Dialogical Community." In *Women, Culture, and Development*, edited by Martha Nussbaum and Jonathan Glover, 235–58. New York: Oxford University Press.

Blackhall, Leslie, Sheila T. Murphy, Gelya Frank, Vicki Michel, and Stanley Azen. 1995. "Ethnicity and Attitudes toward Patient Autonomy." *Journal of the American Medical Association* 10, no. 274: 820–25.

Blacksher, Erika. 1998. "Desperately Seeking Difference." *Cambridge Quarterly of Healthcare Ethics* 7, no. 1: 11–16.

Caralis, P. V., Bobbi Davis, Karen Wright, and Eileen Marcial. 1993. "The Influence of Ethnicity and Race on Attitudes toward Advance Directives, Life-Prolonging Treatments, and Euthanasia." *Journal of Clinical Ethics* 4, no. 2: 155–65.

Clarke, Greg, Robert Hall, and Greg Rosencrance. "Physician-Patient Relations: No More Models." *American Journal of Bioethics*. Forthcoming.

Corlett, Angelo. 1999. "Latino Identity." *Public Affairs Quarterly* 13: 273–95.

Cross, Alan, and Larry Churchill. 1982. "Ethical and Cultural Considerations of Informed Consent." *Annals of Internal Medicine* 96: 110–113.

del Portillo, Carlota Texidor. 1988. "Poverty, Self Concept, and Health: Experience of Latinas." *Women and Health* 12, nos. 2/4: 229–42.

Donchin, Anne. 2004. "Converging Concerns: Feminist Bioethics, Development Theory and Human Rights." *Signs: Journal of Women in Culture and Society* 29, no. 2: 299–324.

Fairchild, Halford, and Joy Asamen Cozens. 1981. "Chicano, Hispanic, or Mexican American: What's in a Name?" *Hispanic Journal of Behavioral Science* 3, no. 3: 191–98.

Femenias, Maria Luisa. 2002. *Perfiles del Feminismo Iberoamericano*. Buenos Aires: Catálogos.

Freedman, Lynn. 1999. "Reflections on Emerging Frameworks of Health and Human Rights." In *Health and Human Rights*, edited by Jonathan M. Mann, Sofia Gruskin, Michael A. Grodin, and George J. Annas, 227–53. New York: Routledge.

Gracia, Diego. 1995. "Hard Times, Hard Choices: Founding Bioethics Today." *Bioethics* 9, nos. 3/4: 192–206.

Gracia, Jorge. 1999. "The Nature of Ethnicity with Special Reference to Hispanic Latinos' Identity." *Public Affairs Quarterly* 13, no. 1: 25–42.

————. 2000. *Hispanic/Latino Identity: A Philosophical Perspective.* Cambridge, UK: Blackwell.

Gracia, Jorge, and Pablo De Greiff, eds. 2000. *Hispanics/Latinos in the United States.* New York: Routledge.

Hern, Eugene, Barbara Koenig, Lisa Jean Moore, and Patricia Marshall. 1998. "The Difference that Culture Can Make in End of Life Decision Making." *Cambridge Quarterly of Healthcare Ethics* 7, no 1: 27–41.

Jackson, Linda. 1995. "Stereotypes, Emotions, Behavior, and Overall Attitudes toward Hispanics by Anglos." Julian Samora Research Institute Working Papers Series, Michigan State University.

Kleinman, Arthur, Leon Eisenberg, and Byron Good. 1978. "Culture, Illness, and Care: Clinical Lessons from Anthropologic and Cross-Cultural Research." *Annals of Internal Medicine* 88: 251–58.

Knowles, Lori P. 2001. "The Lingua Franca of Human Rights and the Rise of a Global Bioethic." *Cambridge Quarterly of Healthcare Ethics* 10: 253–63.

Koenig, Barbara A., and Jan Gates-Williams. 1995. "Understanding Cultural Difference in Caring for Dying Patients." *Western Journal of Medicine* 163, no. 3: 244–49.

Kunstadter, Peter. 1980. "Medical Ethics in Cross-Cultural and Multi-Cultural Perspectives." *Social Science and Medicine* 14B: 289–96.

Kuczewski, Mark, and Patrick McCruden. 2001. "Informed Consent: Does It Take a Village? The Problem of Culture and Truth Telling." *Cambridge Quarterly of Healthcare Ethics* 10: 34–46.

Levin, Betty, and Nina Glick Schiller. 1998. "Social Class and Medical Decisionmaking: A Neglected Topic in Bioethics." *Cambridge Quarterly of Healthcare Ethics* 7, no. 1: 41–56.

Lock, Margaret. 1993. "Education and Self Reflection: Teaching about Culture, Health and Illness." In *Health and Culture: Exploring the Relationship*, edited by Ralph Masi et al., 139–58. Oakville, Ontario: Mosaic Press.

Luna, Florencia. 1995. "Paternalism and the Argument from Illiteracy." *Bioethics* 9, nos. 3/4: 283–90.

Marín, Gerardo, and Harry Triandis. 1985. "Allocentrism as the Important Characteristic of the Behavior of Latin Americans and Hispanics." In *Cross-Cultural and National Studies in Social Psychology*, edited by Rogelio Diaz-Guerrio, 85–104. New York: Elsevier Science Publishers.

Marshall, Patricia. 1992. "Anthropology and Bioethics." *Medical Anthropology Quarterly* 6, no. 1: 49–73.

Narayan, Uma. 1997. *Dislocating Cultures: Identities, Traditions, and Third-World Feminism.* New York: Routledge.

————. 1998. "Essence of Culture and a Sense of History: A Feminist Critique of Cultural Essentialism." *Hypatia* 13, no. 2: 86–106.

Okin, Susan Moller. 1998. "Feminism, Women's Human Rights, and Cultural Differences." *Hypatia* 13, no. 2: 32–52.

————. 1999. *Is Multiculturalism Bad for Women?* Princeton, N.J.: Princeton University Press.

Orona, Celia, Barbara Koenig, and Anne Davis. 1994. "Cultural Aspects of Non-Disclosure." *Cambridge Quarterly of Healthcare Ethics* 3: 338–46.

Orr, Robert D., Patricia Marshall, and Jamie Osborn. 1995. "Cross-Cultural Consideration in Clinical Ethics Consultations." *Archives of Family Medicine* 4: 159–64.

Ortner, Sherry. 1974. "Is Female to Male as Nature Is to Culture?" In *Woman, Culture, and Society*, edited by Michelle Rosaldo and Louise Lamphere, 66–87. Stanford, Calif.: Stanford University Press.

Paz, Octavio. 1982. *Sor Juana Inés de la Cruz; O Las Trampas de la Fe.* Barcelona: Seix Barral.

Perkins, Henry, Cynthia M. A. Geppert, Adelita Gonzalez, Josie Cortez, and Helen Hazuda. 2002. "Cross Cultural Similarities and Differences in Attitudes about Advance Care Planning." *Journal of General Internal Medicine* 17: 1–10.

Rosaldo, Michelle. 1974. "Woman, Culture, and Society: A Theoretical Overview." In *Woman, Culture, and Society*, edited by Michelle Rosaldo and Louise Lamphere, 17–42. Stanford, Calif.: Stanford University Press.

Sabogal, Fabio, Gerardo Marín, and Regina Otero-Sabogal. 1987. "Hispanic Familism and Acculturation: What Changes and What Doesn't?" *Hispanic Journal of Behavioral Sciences* 9, no. 4: 397–412.

Salles, Arleen L. F. 2002. "Autonomy and Culture: The Case of Latin America." In *Bioethics: Latin American Perspectives*, edited by Arleen L. F. Salles and María Julia Bertomeu, 9–26. New York: Rodopi.

Schneider, Carl. 1998. *The Practice of Autonomy.* New York: Oxford University Press.

Schutte, Ofelia. 2000. "Negotiating Latina Identities." In *Hispanics/Latinos in the United States*, edited by Jorge Gracia and Pablo De Greiff, 61–76. London: Routledge.

Tong, Rosemarie. 2001. "Is a Global Bioethics Possible?" In *Globalizing Feminist Bioethics*, edited by Rosemarie Tong, 27–36. Boulder, Colo.: Westview.

Valdés, Margarita. 1995. "Inequality in Capabilities between Men and Women in Mexico." In *Women, Culture and Development*, edited by Martha Nussbaum and Jonathan Glover, 426–32. New York: Oxford University Press.

Walker, Margaret Urban. 2003. "Truth and Voice in Women's Rights." In *Recognition, Responsibility and Rights: Feminist Ethics and Social Theory*, edited by Robin Fiore and Hilde Lindemann Nelson, 169–80. Lanham, Md.: Rowman & Littlefield.

Wolf, Susan. 1999. "Erasing Difference: Race, Ethnicity, and Gender in Bioethics." In *Embodying Bioethics*, edited by Anne Donchin and Laura Purdy, 65–81. Lanham, Md.: Rowman & Littlefield.

Young, Iris Marion. 1990. *Justice and the Politics of Difference.* Princeton, N.J.: Princeton University Press.

———. 2000. "Structure, Difference, and Hispanic/Latino Claims for Justice." In *Hispanics/Latinos in the United States*, edited by Jorge Gracia and Pablo De Greiff, 147–66. London: Routledge.

Feminist Bioethics and the Language of Human Rights in the Chinese Context

4

JING-BAO NIE

FOR MANY CHINESE COMPATRIOTS of mine, including well-educated and professional women, *nüquan zhuyi*, the doctrine of women's power, has negative connotations. Chinese feminists who have invoked this term have been viewed as advocating too aggressively for the improvement of Chinese women's conditions, and as importing Western views about gender justice to China, without recognizing that simply because a certain type of feminism works in the West, it does not mean that it will work equally well in China. For this reason and others, Chinese feminists increasingly use the phrase *nüxing zhuyi*, the doctrine of the female gender, to refer to feminism. This phrase, which deemphasizes the political dimensions of feminism, has the advantage of drawing attention to feminism's potential for reconceiving and introducing new conceptual schemes through which to interpret male-female relationships and other relationships characterized by an inequitable distribution of power, opportunities, and resources.

Feminism has changed sociocultural life as well as everyday interpersonal relations in the West. It has also challenged each discipline in the humanities, the social sciences, and the natural sciences. In bioethics, for example, feminist approaches have altered the ways in which ethical issues in medicine and health care are perceived and handled.[1] Though feminist thought and feminist bioethics are characterized by a great variety of perspectives, considerable unity exists within their diversity. For example, according to Rosemarie Tong, "all feminist approaches to bioethics seem interested in asking the so-called women or gender question, raising women's (and men's) consciousness about the subordinate status of women and eliminating gaps between feminist theory and feminist practice" (Tong 1997, 75). More important, feminist bioethics is not about only *women* "talk[ing] about *women's* issues in bioethics" (Little 1996, I); rather, it is about men and women examining "all sorts of bioethical issues from the perspective of feminist *theory*" (Little 1996, 1). Because the primary contribution of feminist bioethics is "to note how imbalances of power in the sex-gender system play themselves out in medical practice and in the theory surrounding that practice" (Nelson 2000, 493), its essential goal is the "elimination of gender inequality" (Tong 1998, 268). Recently, many feminist bioethicists have been particularly concerned about the way in which the sex-gender system seems to value men's rights more than women's rights, as if women's rights were less fully "human" than men's rights. But this is decidedly not the case. Thus, it is crucial that both feminist theorists and activists use the language of rights to serve women's interests. For all its limitations, the language of rights is one that the contemporary world acknowledges as worthy of its attention.

Although feminist approaches to bioethics largely remain a product of Western thought, they have attracted attention in many nations, including China. But because China and the West are so different from each other in politics, culture, and traditional gender relationships, it is not immediately clear that Western feminism in general and Western feminist bioethics in particular can and ought to be applied and taken seriously in Chinese contexts. Thus, the burden of this chapter is to establish that Western feminism, feminist bioethics, and feminist human rights language are highly relevant and significant for China. Collectively, they provide both Chinese theorists and activists with useful conceptual lenses and powerful political strategies to better address bioethical issues in the Chinese context.

The Condition of Chinese Women: Still Oppressed, Still Not Equal to Men

Feminist perspectives, feminist human rights talk, and feminist activism can help the men and women in China better perceive social reality in general and instances of rights violation in particular. At present, many Chinese fail to see the ways in which Chinese women's status is not equal to men's. The Chinese have been indoctrinated to believe that, thanks to Marxist-Socialist efforts, they are the happiest, most fortunate, and most equal people in the whole world. I once believed this to be true. Specifically, I believed that Chinese men and women were equally free and well-off. As a result of being exposed to Western feminist thought, as well as studying and working abroad in several countries, however, I changed my belief. I now think that although Chinese women in the twentieth century are far less oppressed than they were, say, in Imperial China, they are still not men's full equals.

Gender inequality and injustice in China, as in other parts of the world, exist in both blatant and subtle forms, on both the macro and micro level, in both public and private life. When people live under certain conditions long enough, they often get used to them and even try to justify them, no matter how wrong they are. As the ancient Chinese saying goes, "One will not notice how bad smelling it is, if one stays long in a market full of rotten fish; likewise, one will not notice how nice smelling it is, if one stays long in a room full of fragrant flowers."[2] Thus, it is crucial to raise consciousness in men as well as women about all forms of sexual inequality and injustice, especially subtle and unnamed ones. The feminist lens can help Chinese men and women ask themselves why most abandoned babies are girls, why most abortions subsequent to prenatal sex diagnosis result in the elimination of *female* fetuses, and why the suicide rates of Chinese women, especially young rural women, are highest in the world.[3] In other words, the feminist lens of gender can help us Chinese acknowledge the degree to which our relationships smell of "rotten fish" (gender inequity) in China.

Ge Youli, a feminist activist in Beijing, has vividly expressed how Western feminist thoughts helped her see her reality better. Although she always recognized that her parents treated her brother better than they treated her, for a long time she could not identify and articulate what was wrong about this situation. Western feminist thought gave Ge Youli the words and expressions needed to express her dissatisfaction with being treated less well than her brother simply because she was a girl and he a boy (Milwertz 2003, 58):

> I came to acquire words and concepts such as gender discrimination, gender stereotype, gender role and gendered structure. I began to put things in perspective, a gendered perspective. I was amazed at *the effectiveness and forcefulness of these English words in describing and deconstructing [Chinese] women's secondary position in families and societies.* (Milwertz 2003, 58)

Significance of Human Rights and Women's Rights for China

To eliminate gender inequities in China, I contend that feminist human rights language is useful, indeed essential. Admittedly, many arguments or theories reject the relevance and applicability of the idea of human rights, including women's reproductive rights, in the Chinese context. One popular objection builds on Chinese-Western cultural differences. In its typical form, the cultural difference argument runs as follows:

> First premise: The notion of human rights in general and women's rights in particular arose in and is a part of Western culture.
>
> Second premise: The cultural tradition of China is fundamentally different from that of the West.
>
> Conclusion: Therefore, the notion of human rights in general and women's rights in particular is neither relevant nor applicable to China.

A variation of the typical cultural difference argument runs as follows:

First premise: The conception of human rights and women's rights is based on Western individualism.

Second premise: Traditionally, Chinese culture is community oriented.

Conclusion: The notion of human rights and women's rights is neither relevant nor applicable to China.

Although the cultural difference argument contains a grain of truth, it has several problems (Nie 2002). As I see it, it relies on exaggerated assessments of the differences that exist between Western and Chinese cultures, wrong assumptions about the existence of a unified communitarian Chinese culture, and essentialist presuppositions that claim Chinese culture and norms are unchangeable. The cultural difference argument assumes that all those who engage in a given moral practice (such as informed consent) must justify that practice with the same arguments or theories. But, as Carol Gilligan has pointed out, one can use either the language of rights or the language of responsibilities to express the same moral reality (Gilligan 1982). Moreover, one can learn how to translate concepts from these two languages into each other's terms and to speak one or the other as the situation demands. Thus, just because the language of rights has not been spoken as frequently as the language of responsibilities, relationships, and duties in China, it does not mean that the Chinese people lack a concept of rights or that Chinese women do not feel violated and wronged when, for example, their fetuses are coercively taken from their wombs.

The argument against engaging in rights talk in China on the grounds that the idea of human rights is a strictly Western ideal with no place in the Chinese mind or social reality is intellectually flawed. Just because relationships, duties, and responsibilities are the preferred vocabulary for the Chinese does not mean the Chinese are somehow hardwired to reject individual rights and to banish them from their conceptual scheme. As Immanuel Kant's (as well as Gilligan's) ethics show, it is a mistake to assume that a moral tradition emphasizing duty and responsibility will necessarily ignore individual rights and dignity (Kant 1991; Gilligan 1982). It is perfectly possible that a moral tradition, which stresses individuals' relationships to each other and to the community, can treasure and promote individual autonomy at the same time.

Significantly, more and more evidence indicates that the notion of individual rights is compatible with many streams of Chinese thought (see, for example, de Bary and Tu 1998; Hansen 1996, 1997, 2000). According to sinologist and philosopher Chad Hansen, the failure of traditional Chinese thought to find "the inherent dignity and worth of the rational individual to be a natural first principle of morality . . . would not block any Chinese thinkers, ancient and modern, from adopting various kinds of posterior arguments for greater individual freedom" (Hansen 2000, 91). Rights-related concepts such as freedom, self-expression, and choice are quite easy to distill from ancient Daoist thought. Significantly, the works of Zhuang Zi (Chuang Tzu) (for a very readable English translation, see Watson 1968), a founder of Daoist philosophy, stress respecting individual dignity and difference; rebelling against paternalism, authoritarianism, and the constraints of conventional morality; and permitting individuals to "freely and easily wander" in this world, constructing their lives as they wish.

Moreover, even closer approximations of rights talk are present in some modern Chinese works. In her groundbreaking work on the human rights debate in China from 1898 to 1949, Swedish scholar Marina Svensson discovered that in the late nineteenth and early twentieth centuries, many Chinese publications advocated that women and men were equal and should enjoy equal civil and political rights such as freedom of thought and speech. These rights were declared natural or heavenly (*tianfu zhi quanli*). The authoritarian and patriarchal elements in traditional Confucianism were seen as enemies of science, democracy, human rights, and the emancipation of all individuals, but particularly women, whose subjection was epitomized in the harmful practice of foot binding (see Svensson 1996, 112–13, 188). A noteworthy historical fact is that Chinese delegates were directly involved in writing the Universal Declaration of Human Rights, particularly Article I, which is heavily influenced by Confucian moral-political ideals. Were it not for late-twentieth-century developments such as the emergence of the Maoist cult in which (understandably) human rights were totally rejected as part of "capitalist" and "antirevolutionary" theory, the Chinese may have learned to speak the language of rights as fluently as most Westerners do.

In discussing human rights and culture, it is crucial to notice to whom the language of human rights appeals. As Svensson has observed, rights "are called for by those who feel that they are being deprived of them, and those to whom they are directing their calls seldom regard them as legitimate or valid" (Svensson 1996, 14). It is usually those whose power has been undemocratically secured who reject the universality of human rights or redefine the notion of human rights in a way that is favorable and convenient to themselves. And, also not surprising, it is usually those who have been deprived of their freedom who know they have rights and want to assert them in order to empower themselves. In the words of Ruth Macklin, former president of the International Association of Bioethics,

> There is a disconnect between the statements of traditional leaders and the views of activists for social reform, academics and professionals and community leaders who know and care about individual rights, participatory institutions, and other so-called "Western" values. There is a disconnect between the statements of those who defend a status quo perpetuating an oppressive and hierarchical social system,

and people from the same cultures who advocate social change based on ethical principles very much like the principles of humanity and humaneness. Can the beliefs and values of this latter group be explained only under the hypothesis that they are dupes of Western cultural imperialism? This supposition demeans advocates of reform by implying that they are not or cannot be independent thinkers, but are slavish adherents of the Western moral concepts with which they come into contact and seek to emulate. (Macklin 1999, 273)

A common criticism about importing so-called Western values into non-Western societies is that to do so fosters cultural imperialism. This criticism should be taken seriously when Western cultures *impose* values on non-Western cultures regardless of the wills and wishes of people in these societies. But it is an entirely different matter if people in non-Western societies *want* to use Western values in their own struggles against injustice and inequality. For example, Ren-Zong Qiu, a prominent Chinese bioethicist, claims that the Chinese people are now *voluntarily* in the midst of "an awakening of the rights sense" (Qiu 1993, 172).

Although Qiu has reservations about rights-oriented individualism as a theory, like many Chinese he welcomes the practical consequences of rights talk. He views affirmatively that "students and intellectuals are striving for civil rights, girls in villages are claiming the right to freely choose marriage (as opposed to accepting arranged marriages), and patients are asserting the right to self-determination" (Qiu 1993, 172). Moreover, the Chinese government's signing of the United Nations International Covenant on Civil and Political Rights was not only the result of *external* pressure from the international community but also the consequence of *internal* demands from the Chinese citizenry. The 1989 Chinese democratic movement proved to the world that Chinese men and women are willing to die for personal freedom and social democracy. Clearly, within the spirit of the Chinese people there is present a deep sense of their individual worth and value as human persons. In view of the Chinese who died fighting for their rights and individual dignity, how can anyone claim that the Chinese do not treasure their human rights?

Chinese Women's Reproductive Rights as Human Rights

Western academics and political leaders decry the lack of human rights, particularly reproductive rights, in China. Yet as a result of interviewing many Chinese women who have had abortions and many Chinese female physicians who have performed them, I am convinced that simply because Chinese women do not ordinarily use the language of rights to express or defend their reproductive choices, it does not mean that Chinese women are not concerned about controlling their reproductive destiny. On the contrary, Chinese women want more of a say in Chinese family planning policies than they have previously had.

Although most Chinese obstetricians and gynecologists (OB-GYNs) realize that China's population must be controlled if China is to prosper, a growing number of them have serious reservations about the *means* government authorities have used and still use to achieve this goal. For example, in my fieldwork on Chinese views and experiences of abortion conducted in China in 1997, Dr. Zhang, a middle-aged OB-GYN physician, admitted to me that she has had second thoughts about some of the "family planning" operations she performed in the past. Like most Chinese, she does not question the necessity of controlling China's population or the legitimacy of the state family planning program. In fact, she considers limitations on people's procreative choices the business of the state and not, in her own terms, that of an "ordinary OB-GYN doctor." Nevertheless, she is not entirely comfortable with the methods the state employs to achieve its goals. In particular, she is uncomfortable with the role she has played and is asked to play in controlling other women's bodies. For example, she related the following situation to me:

> Some time ago, women in the countryside were compelled to be sent group by group by automobile to the hospital at the city for IUD insertion, abortion, and sterilization. The family planning cadres surrounded them. They guarded the gate out of the ward. They even watched them when they went to the restroom because they were afraid [the] women would run away. Then, I performed many "family planning" operations [that is, abortions and sterilizations]. (Nie forthcoming)

In retrospect, what bothered Dr. Zhang the most about the sterilizations and abortions she performed was that no attempt was made to secure the women's informed consent to them. She was particularly troubled by her participation in a coercive late abortion in which the pregnant woman had no say:

> The reality is that the pregnant woman had no right if the family planning official required her to have [the] late abortion. The woman cannot say whether she wants to or not. She cannot demand or do anything but accept. However, I felt, . . . I do not know how to say it. In present and new-fashioned terms, you should at least get consent from the woman herself (*zhengde benren tongyi*), let her know beforehand (*geita dage zhaohu*). Yet, in that situation in which the pregnant woman was required by the family planning official to have the abortion, no one got consent from her. (Nie forthcoming)

Fortunately, for Dr. Zhang in particular and Chinese women in general, local and state authorities have begun to give Chinese women more say in the kind of birth control methods they use. Since the 1990s, some social experiments have been carried out giving rural women more freedom to choose the method of birth control most congenial to them, a phenomenon called *zhiqing xuanze cun* (the village of informed choice). Dr. Zhang has applauded these experiments, hoping to see them expand:

> Now there have been some experiments regarding informed choice in some villages where people choose their methods of birth control. After bearing a [first] child, people are allowed to choose for themselves what they think is the best method. Even after the second child, sterilization is not forced on people. This practice gives people some degree of freedom of choice (*yiding de xuanze ziyou*). While some experiments have been conducted in some villages, unfortunately, this practice [of informed choice] is not fully under way yet. (Nie forthcoming)

Although Chinese women do not have much choice about participating in the effort to control China's population, it is encouraging to know that local and state authorities are beginning to recognize people's need to have as much freedom as the constraints of necessity permit. Even if the urgent need to control China's population demands that all Chinese exhibit reproductive restraint, that does not mean that women should have no choice about how they exercise reproductive restraint. Sex control, long-term or short-term contraception, sterilization, and early abortion are all reasonable birth control options, provided that women get to choose which method they prefer.

In her important study on how Chinese urban women with only one child view China's family planning program, Danish sociologist Cecilia N. Milwertz discovered that most of these women accept the program despite their wish to have more than one child (Milwertz 1997).[4] Their compliance was a result not so much of fear or coercion as of a "conscientious acceptance" (*zijue jieshou*) of China's need to control its population size. Still, many Chinese urban women with only one child sense that their conscientious acceptance is not entirely free. In particular, they "experience a violation of their reproductive self-determination, but they do not have a concept with which to label the experience" (Milwertz 1997, 198).

The Western feminist language of human rights can help these and other Chinese women label their as yet nameless problem, to express their sense of reproductive loss and possibility. Consider the practice of forced abortion in China, including forced partial-birth abortion, as an example. Examined through the perspective of Chinese state authorities, coerced abortion, for whatever reason, is not a serious problem. Indeed, Chinese state authorities often regard Westerners who oppose such abortions as *dajing xiaoguai* (being surprised or alarmed by the normal things) or *bieyou yongxin* (having ulterior motives, that is, hostile to China and Chinese people). Through the lenses of human rights theorists and activists, however, forced abortions become abnormal—indeed, immoral.[5] They become something to protest as violations of women's human rights to personal privacy and bodily integrity.

Toward a Chinese Feminist Bioethics:
Importance of Native Concerns and Language

Even as Chinese and Western academics continue to debate whether or not the language of human rights and the concepts of Western feminist thought are helpful for China, feminist bioethics has started to take root in practice in China. Among others, Ren-Zong Qiu has organized a series of activities to promote feminist perspectives on bioethics.[6] From its inception, Chinese feminist bioethics has been a part of the international bioethics community. Qiu's projects, including two international conferences on feminism and bioethics in Beijing in 1996 and 2001, were attended by scholars from such countries as the United Kingdom, the United States, India, Australia, and New Zealand. At the same time, Chinese scholars have been eager to participate in international discussions elsewhere (Wang 2001; Nie 2000a, 2001).

Whether feminist bioethics will continue to survive and thrive on Chinese soil is hard to predict. I have so far argued that, in spite of the great sociocultural differences between China and the West, Western feminism, feminist bioethics, and feminist human rights language are relevant to China. They provide the Chinese people with useful lenses to understand the Chinese experience. Thus, it is vital that Chinese thinkers and activists learn from Western feminism and feminist bioethics and that they import to China not only Anglo-American bioethics but all kinds of foreign bioethics.

Yet no matter how important it is for Chinese bioethicists to learn from the bioethicists of other countries, it is even more important for them to focus on native problems and concerns and to create a Chinese feminist language rooted in indigenous Chinese moral and political traditions. It is imperative for Chinese feminist bioethics to integrate academic bioethics with the grassroots activities of Chinese women struggling to make the health care system sensitive to their interests, respectful of their rights and dignity, and appreciative of their labors and bodies. A Chinese feminist bioethics must above all be a bioethics for Chinese women. It must be attentive to, and grounded in, the personal experiences and voices of individual women. Western feminism can help expose the oppressive and unjust nature of Chinese women's individual experiences and collective conditions. Equally as important, Chinese women's experiences and conditions can enrich Western feminism by challenging strictly Western interpretations of them.

The narratives of Chinese OB-GYNs (almost all are female) who perform abortions, and of women who have had abortions, offer good examples of the ways in which individuals' lived experiences can be an effective antidote against the simplifying and overgeneralizing tendency in current understandings of this topic. According to the official Chinese standpoint, Chinese women support the national birth control program because it is beneficial to both the country as a whole and to individual women in particular. In contrast, according to the dominant Western feminist view, the Chinese national population policy is a serious violation of women's reproductive rights, and Chinese women are opposed to it. But the reality of the situation is somewhere between these two extreme perspectives. Most Chinese women, as well as Chinese men, support the policy, but not without some reservations and, in particular cases, resistance.

Clearly, Chinese feminist bioethics must resist the impulse to identify as normative for all Chinese women the perspectives and experiences of urban, well educated, professional Chinese women. Instead, it should closely attend to the lived experiences, concerns, and voices of all types of Chinese women: urban and rural, Han and minority nationalities, educated and uneducated, rich and poor, university professors and *sanpeinu* (female sex workers), white-collar professionals and *dagongmei* (countryside women working in the cities). Most important, Chinese feminist bioethics should be centered on and oriented to underprivileged and marginalized groups such as the millions of increasingly illiterate or half-illiterate women in rural China. The concerns and problems of underprivileged groups and individuals—the exploited, the oppressed, the silenced, and the deprived—should always be the focus of the medical social sciences, humanities, and bioethics, be they Chinese or non-Chinese (Nie 2000b).

In the West, the lenses of gender, no matter how powerful, are not sufficient to analyze issues; one must always look at reality through the lenses of race and class at the same time. In the Chinese context, the rural-urban residency as a category of analysis is essential. There exists a caste-like, institutional social stratification in China in which people are divided into two birth-ascribed civil status groups: rural as the lower and urban as the higher. In spite of some recent improvements, social, economic, and cultural inequality between these two groups is so enormous that depriving an urban person of his or her urban residence status constitutes one of the most serious civil punishments inflicted in China.

Rural-urban injustice in China is a form of discrimination that is more serious but much less acknowledged and addressed than, say, racism. Although discussion of rural discrimination in China is beyond the scope of this chapter, I feel compelled to stress that 0.8 billion rural Chinese—the great majority of the total Chinese population—lack adequate primary health care. While the cause-of-death patterns in urban China are similar to those in developed countries, cause-of-death patterns in rural areas are much more typical of those in developing countries. Death rates due to infectious diseases, respiratory diseases, pregnancy and childbirth, injuries and poisoning, and even suicide are much higher in rural areas than in urban areas. The life expectancy of rural residents is several years shorter than that of urban residents. As the county-township-village three-tier health care system collapses, and as the "barefoot doctors" (the primary health care givers who provided basic free services in the countryside in the 1960s and 1970s) are transformed into physician entrepreneurs, urban-rural inequalities are worsening. Rural girls and women suffer the most. In the same way that it is regarded a misfortune to be born a woman in China—*tuocuo le tai* (being conceived in the wrong womb)—it is regarded a misfortune to be born in the countryside. But the double misfortune of being born a rural woman need not be a misfortune at all—not if the Chinese people as a whole decide to improve the situation of women in the rural outposts.

At present, Chinese feminist bioethics remains overly dependent on Western feminist bioethics. In addition to focusing on and addressing specifically Chinese problems, Chinese bioethics also needs to explore indigenous moral and ethical traditions for new insights to stimulate the development of Chinese feminist bioethics in particular and bioethics in general. Chinese feminist bioethicists must overcome the radical antitraditionalism that grounded the New Culture Movement of the 1920s, the Cultural Revolution of the 1960s and 1970s, and the New Era of the 1980s. The twentieth century in China is a century of revolutions that have destroyed not only millions of lives and a great amount of material civilization but also traditional institutions and values, including those important or even essential for a good society.

All of these losses are sad, but as an intellectual, it disturbs me in particular that often Confucianism, Daoism, and Buddhism are dismissed as entirely retrograde and repressive systems of thought that oppress women in particular. But this is not an accurate evaluation of traditional Chinese thought. Within it are several revolutionary perspectives for Chinese feminists to use. The concept of yin-yang is a good example here. Admittedly, since the Han Dynasty (205 B.C.E.–221 C.E.), the yin-yang concept has been used by Confucians to justify men's power and dominance over women and women's inferior status in sociocultural life. However, according to the original yin-yang concept, yin and yang (symbolizing the female and the male) are not only fundamentally different but also completely equal. They originate in each other, depend on each other, nourish each other, and struggle with each other. One cannot exist without the other. One is neither superior nor inferior to the other. In Daoist theories and practice, yin, being often associated with water, plays an even more critical role than yang in the everlasting metamorphoses of nature. Early Daoist ethical theories, as articulated by Lao Zi and Zhuang Zi, use yin to explain yang, implying that one begins explanations of difference from a female perspective rather than a male perspective (see Watson 1968; for an English translation of Lao Zi, see Chan 1963). Certainly, properly interpreted, the yin-yang concept and ancient Daoism can help Chinese feminist bioethicists articulate ways in which the two sexes, though different, are nonetheless equal. Old Chinese wisdom can serve today's Chinese women well, provided that it is continually reinterpreted in the context within which it finds itself situated.

Exploring the development of a Chinese feminist bioethics by revisiting Chinese traditions is not the subject of this chapter. My point is this: it is not only desperately needed but definitely possible to create a Chinese feminist language rooted in indigenous Chinese moral-political traditions and to develop not only a Daoist feminist bioethics but also a Confucian feminist bioethics. A new China cannot and should not be built from scratch and free from its ancient traditions, and Chinese feminist bioethics should not fall into the black hole of a totally antitraditionalist and abstract way of thinking.

Conclusion

Western feminism has great intellectual and moral charm for me academically and personally. Because I am a Chinese male, I cannot experience the injustices Chinese women experience as women. However, growing up at the bottom of Chinese society, I witnessed and experienced many instances of social injustice, political discrimination, economic inequality, and cultural prejudice, most notably the uniquely Chinese rural-urban split. Because feminism is deeply and passionately concerned about gender-based discrimination, prejudice, and inequality, it has been a powerful intellectual tool for me to make better sense of my experiences, concerns, and pains of living with a wide range of social injustice in China, especially the reality of urban-rural injustice. In this sense, feminist theory is *my theory* or *a theory for me*. It helped me understand the ways in which all forms of discrimination are interrelated.[7]

A global feminist bioethics without Chinese voices is not truly international. In this chapter, I argued that Western feminism and feminist bioethics provide Chinese women and men with useful perspectives to identify and highlight gender inequality issues and to face squarely the "rotten fish" in everyday Chinese life. Specifically, they give the Chinese people the hope and inspiration, vocabulary and language, and practical strategies and political means to overcome patterns of subordination and domination that block the growth of gender freedom and justice in China. I also pointed out the importance of the Chinese context—focusing on native concerns of Chinese women and developing a feminist language rooted in indigenous Chinese culture. China is ready to incorporate feminist bioethics into its bioethics development. I urge its theorists and practitioners to grow Chinese feminist bioethics from the grassroots.

May a Chinese feminist bioethics grow well in China—my motherland! May Chinese feminist bioethics play a positive role in reforming China into a society with less gender inequality and other forms of social injustice! May all men and women in China and other parts of the world live together fully equally and with mutual respect and dignity, as the ancient Chinese wisdom has dreamed of, yin and yang in a true harmony!

Notes

The earlier version of this essay was first presented in Chinese at the Beijing Symposium on Feminist Approaches to Bioethics in China, November 1–2, 2001, and then published in English in *Ethics and Society* (Newsletter of the Centre for Applied Ethics at Hong Kong Baptist University) 9, nos. 1/2 (2002): 2–15.

1. The year 1992 is of special significance for feminist bioethics in the West. In that year, two influential books that address bioethical issues from feminist perspectives were published: Susan Sherwin, *No Longer Patient: Feminist Ethics and Health Care* (Philadelphia, Pa.: Temple University Press, 1992); and Helen Holmes and Laura M. Purdy, *Feminist Perspectives in Medical Ethics* (Bloomington: Indiana University Press, 1992). Feminist bioethics was international from its inception. In 1992, the International Network on Feminist Approaches to Bioethics (usually abbreviated as FAB), organized by Anne Donchin and Becky Holmes, was launched at the Inaugural Congress of the International Association of Bioethics in Amsterdam, Netherlands.

2. This saying originated from *Kongzi Jiayu* (Confucius's Home Sayings). The original text read: "If one lives together with good people, one's character will become good without noticing it." This is like saying one will not notice how nice a room full of *zhilan* (irises and orchids) smells if he or she remains in that room for an extended period of time. Similarly, if one lives with bad people, one's character will become bad without noticing it. This is like saying one will not notice how foul a market full of rotten fish smells if he or she stays in that market too long. These two metaphors illustrate how people's environments assimilate them. In classic Chinese, *zhilan* (irises and orchids) often symbolize good and noble characters, true friendship, and beautiful surroundings.

3. In the early 1990s, China accounted for 44 percent of all reported suicides and for 56 percent of all female suicides in the world, although its population constituted only 21 percent of the world's population. See Sing Lee and Arthur Kleinman, "Suicide as Resistance in Chinese Society," in *Chinese Society: Change, Conflict and Resistance*, ed. Elizabeth J. Perry and Mark Selden (London: Routledge, 2000), 221. From 1995 to 1999, rural suicide rates were three times higher than urban suicide rates. The rate in women was 25 percent higher than in men, mainly due to the extraordinarily high number of suicides among young rural women. See Michael Phillips, Xianyun Li, and Yanping Zhang, "Suicide Rates in China, 1995–99," *Lancet* 359, no. 9309 (2002): 835–40. In the Chinese context, suicide is a strong indicator of many sociopolitical problems such as rural and gender discrimination. For women in China, especially rural China, suicide has been taken as a desperate act of revenge and rebellion in a moral and spiritual sense. See Liu Meng, "Rebellion and Revenge: The Meaning of Suicide of Women in Rural China," *International Journal of Social Welfare* 11, no. 4

(2002): 300–309. Suicide is a "strategy of resistance" used "by women who feel powerless in situations of political and social domination" (Lee and Kleinman 2000, 221).

4. The results of my survey of twelve different population groups throughout China, conducted in 1997, also show that a great majority of Chinese men and women in urban and rural areas genuinely support the national birth planning policies. See Jing-Bao Nie, *Voices Behind the Silence: Chinese Views and Experiences of Abortion* (Lanham, Md.: Rowman & Littlefield, forthcoming).

5. For a discussion of the ethical issues related to coerced abortion in China, see Jing-Bao Nie, "The Problem of Coerced Abortion in China and Some Ethical Issues," *Cambridge Quarterly of Healthcare Ethics* 8, no. 4 (1999): 463–79.

6. As part of a research project on reproductive health and ethics chaired by Ren-Zong Qiu, a symposium titled "Reproduction, Sexuality, Ethics and Women's Rights: Feminist Perspectives" was held in Beijing from February 25 to March 1, 1994. Sixty-six physicians, sexologists, sociologists, demographers, philosophers, bioethicists, lawyers, experts in women's work and women's studies, and administrators of birth control attended the conference. They discussed a variety of issues related to women's sexual and reproductive rights. The symposium papers, together with papers presented at two other conferences held in China, were published in 1996. See Ren-Zong Qiu, ed., *Shenyu Jiankang Yu Lunlixue* (Reproductive Health and Ethics) (Beijing: United Press of Beijing Medical University and Beijing Union Medical University, 1996). From November 1 to 3, 2001, yet another international conference on feminist bioethics was held in Beijing. More than fifty scholars from a wide variety of disciplines attended the meeting. The activities organized by Qiu can be regarded as the birth of feminist bioethics in China.

7. Through challenging a number of "common sense" beliefs, feminism has helped me become aware of some of my own biases against and misconceptions about women. For example, until knowing feminism, I assumed that women were biologically or naturally ill-suited for higher learning. I thoughtlessly accepted the view that while girls may do better in elementary school or junior high school than boys do, due to "biological" reasons they could not, as a group, compete with boys in and beyond the university level. This belief is to some extent based on the historical fact that great writers, thinkers, and scientists in China as elsewhere have been mostly men. But, as feminism has firmly established, the fact that there have been relatively few great female philosophers is not the result of women's inability to reason and create but instead the result of gender discrimination, that is, women have not had the same intellectual opportunities and resources that men have had until relatively recently. Increasingly provided with the same education as men, women are proving to have as much natural talent to excel intellectually, including in abstract thinking, as men have.

References

Chan, Wing-Tsit. 1963. *A Source Book in Chinese Philosophy*. Princeton, N.J.: Princeton University Press.

de Bary, William Theodore, and Tu Weiming, eds. 1998. *Confucianism and Human Rights*. New York: Columbia University Press.

Gilligan, Carol. 1982. *In a Different Voice: Psychological Theory and Women's Development*. Cambridge, Mass.: Harvard University Press.

Hansen, Chad. 1996. "Chinese Philosophy and Human Rights: An Application of Comparative Ethics." In *Ethics in Business and Society: Chinese and Western Perspectives*, edited by Gerhold K. Becker, 99–126. Berlin: Springer-Verlag.

———. 1997. "Do Human Rights Apply to China? A Normative Analysis of Cultural Difference." In *Constructing China: The Interaction of Culture and Economics*, edited by Kenneth G. Lieberthal, Shuen-fu Lin, and Ernest P. Young, 83–100. Ann Arbor: University of Michigan.

———. 2000. "Why Chinese Thought Is Not Individualistic: Answer I of N." In *The Moral Status of Persons: Perspectives on Bioethics*, edited by Gerhold K. Becker, 79–93. Amsterdam: Rodopi.

Holmes, Helen, and Laura M. Purdy. 1992. *Feminist Perspectives in Medical Ethics*. Bloomington: Indiana University Press.

Kant, Immanuel. 1991. *The Metaphysics of Morals*, translated by Mary Gregor. Cambridge, UK: Cambridge University Press.

Lee, Sing, and Arthur Kleinman. 2000. "Suicide as Resistance in Chinese Society." In *Chinese Society: Change, Conflict and Resistance*, edited by Elizabeth J. Perry and Mark Selden, 221–40. London: Routledge.

Little, Margaret. 1996. "Why a Feminist Approach to Bioethics?" *Kennedy Institute of Ethics Journal* 6, no. 1: 1–18.

Macklin, Ruth. 1999. *Against Relativism: Cultural Diversity and the Search for Ethical Universals in Medicine*. New York: Oxford University Press.

Meng, Liu. 2002. "Rebellion and Revenge: The Meaning of Suicide of Women in Rural China." *International Journal of Social Welfare* 11, no. 4: 300–9.

Milwertz, Cecilia N. 1997. *Accepting Population Control: Urban Chinese Women and the One-Child Family Policy*. Surrey, UK: Curzor.

———. 2003. "Organizing for Gender Equality in China: A Process of Cultural and Political Change." Paper presented at the Ecole des Hautes Etudes en Sciences Sociales, Paris, June.

Nelson, Hilde Lindemann. 2000. "Feminist Bioethics: Where We've Been, Where We're Going." *Metaphilosophy* 31, no. 5: 492–508.

Nie, Jing-Bao. 1999. "The Problem of Coerced Abortion in China and Some Ethical Issues." *Cambridge Quarterly of Healthcare Ethics* 8, no. 4: 463–79.

———. 2000a. "Are Privacy and Informed Consent Culturally Specific? A Reflection on Studying Chinese Women's Experiences of Abortion." Paper presented by a Zambian physician, Laurel Baldwin, on behalf of the author at a panel organized by Mexican bioethics Juan-Guillermo Figueroa-Perea, in the Third International Conference of Feminist Approaches to Bioethics, affiliated with the Fifth World Congress of International Association of Bioethics, London, September.

———. 2000b. "Toward the Medical Humanities Centered with Individual Patients and the Underprivileged Groups." *Yixue Yu Zhexue* (Medicine and Philosophy) 21, no. 10: 8–9.

———. 2001. "'So Bitter that No Words Can Describe It': Mainland Chinese Women's Moral Experiences and Narratives of Induced Abortion." In *Globalizing Feminist Bioethics: Crosscultural Perspectives*, edited by Rosemarie Tong, Gwen Anderson, and Aida Santos, 151–64. Boulder, Colo.: Westview.

———. 2002. "Is Informed Consent Not Applicable to China? Intellectual Flaws of the Cultural Difference Argument." *Yixue Yu Zhexue* (Medicine and Philosophy) 23, no. 6: 18–22. For an English version of this paper, see *Formosa Journal of Medical Humanities* 2, nos. 1–2 (2001): 67–74, at www.csmu.edu.tw/genedu/public_html/vol2/Nie.doc.

———. *Voices Behind the Silence: Chinese Views and Experiences of Abortion.* Lanham, Md.: Rowman & Littlefield, forthcoming.

Phillips, Michael R., Xianyun Li, and Yanping Zhang. 2002. "Suicide Rates in China, 1995–99." *Lancet* 359, no. 9309: 835–40.

Qiu, Ren-Zong. 1993. "Medical Ethics and Chinese Culture." In *Transcultural Dimensions in Medical Ethics*, edited by Edmund Pellegrino, Patricia Mazzarella, and Pietro Corsi, 155–74. Frederick, Md.: University Publishing Group.

———, ed. 1996. *Shenyu Jiankang Yu Lunlixue* (Reproductive Health and Ethics). Beijing: United Press of Beijing Medical University and Beijing Union Medical University.

Sherwin, Susan. 1992. *No Longer Patient: Feminist Ethics and Health Care.* Philadelphia, Pa.: Temple University Press.

Svensson, Marina. 1996. *The Chinese Conception of Human Rights: The Debate on Human Rights in China, 1898–1949.* Lund, Sweden: Lund University Press.

Tong, Rosemarie. 1997. *Feminist Approaches to Bioethics: Theoretical Reflections and Practical Applications.* Boulder, Colo.: Westview.

———. 1998. "Feminist Ethics." In *Encyclopedia of Applied Ethics*, vol. 2, edited by Ruth Chadwick, 267–68. San Diego, Calif.: Academic Press.

Wang, Jin-ling. 2001. "HIV/AIDS and Prostitution in Mainland China: A Feminist Perspective." In *Globalizing Feminist Bioethics: Crossscultural Perspectives*, edited by Rosemarie Tong, Gwen Anderson, and Aida Santos, 238–47. Boulder, Colo.: Westview.

Watson, Burton, trans. 1968. *The Complete Works of Chuang Tzu.* New York: Columbia University Press.

Feminist Perspectives, Global Bioethics, and the Need for Moral Language Translation Skills 5

ROSEMARIE TONG

G LOBALIZATION IS USUALLY PRESENTED as a new development in the history of humankind, related primarily to advances in information and travel technologies, the creation of world financial markets, and the modernization of traditional cultures. It is an invitation for the nations of the world to understand that, increasingly, their best interests are no longer separate but linked together. Specifically, Lori P. Knowles, a human rights advocate, has written:

> In the wake of the HIV pandemic, growing environmental consciousness, and a series of sensational advances in biotechnology, there is a dawning realization that problems such as improving public health, regulating advances in biotechnology, and achieving sustainable environmental development transcend national borders. (Knowles 2001, 253)

The "dawning realization" to which Knowles alludes is, I believe, the motivation behind many health-related collaborative projects, including bioethicists' recent attempts to globalize bioethics.

Although I am among those bioethicists who believe a global bioethics is desirable, I am not quite confident it is feasible. Can bioethicists really find a conceptual foundation particularist enough to accommodate their diversities and yet universal enough to serve as a common base from which they can launch collaborative moral action? Although I do not have a complete answer to this enormously difficult question, I believe the beginnings of such an answer can be found in several feminist approaches to bioethics, including the ones offered by Donna Dickenson and Anne Donchin in this volume (see chapters 1 and 2). In particular, I endorse those feminist approaches to bioethics that use some combination of the languages of human rights, human responsibilities, human capabilities, and human needs to highlight that our rich diversities—our particular political, social, and cultural identities—need not negate our common human unity.

Feminist Approaches to Bioethics

Although there are many and diverse feminist approaches to bioethics, they share three goals: (1) to provide moral critiques of actions, practices, systems, structures, and ideologies that perpetuate women's subordination; (2) to devise morally justifiable ways to resist the economic, social, and cultural causes of women's subordination; and (3) to envision morally desirable alternatives to the world as we know it: sexist, racist, ableist, heterosexist, ethnocentric, and colonialist (Jaggar 1992, 364–67). Initially, most feminists sought to achieve this threefold goal by stressing women's *sameness* to men, but the weaknesses of this approach soon became apparent. First, by insisting that women can measure up to men, feminists inadvertently conceded that men, men's traditional roles, and men's domain (the public world) are more valuable than women, women's traditional roles, and women's domain (the private world) (Chanter 1998, 267). Second, and more important, in some respects women's needs differ significantly from men's needs, and ignoring or downplaying these differences only harms women (Gilligan 1982). Consider, for example, the harm that was done to women in the United States by virtually excluding women from clinical research studies for fear of causing risk to their possible or actual fetuses. As a result of this protective measure, clinical research was often conducted on men only, and then it was simply assumed that whatever treatment worked best for adult men would also work for adult women, with some minor adjustments for weight differentials. But clearly this is not the case. Women's bodies significantly differ from men's bodies, and sometimes the pharmaceuticals that work well for men work poorly for women.

Acknowledging that it was probably a mistake to encourage women to totally reject their differences from men and to unreflectively embrace those traits and values many cultures label masculine/Western—namely, "independence, autonomy, intellect, will, wariness, hierarchy, domination, culture, transcendence, product, asceticism, war and death" (Jaggar 1992, 364)—an increasing number of feminists began to present as better than masculine/Western traits and values those traits and values many cultures label feminine/non-Western—namely, "interdependence, community, connection, sharing, emotion, body, trust, absence of hierarchy, nature, immanence, process, joy, peace and life" (Jaggar 1992, 364). "Woman's" difference from "Man" was stressed so much, however, that women's differences from each other were obscured. Gradually, the idea of "Woman" was rejected by most feminists as an essentialist abstraction implicitly biased toward a certain kind of woman: white, relatively affluent, highly educated, and from a developed nation (Echols 1983).

At first, it might strike us as ethically counterintuitive to reject ideas such as the idea of "Woman." After all, the concept of sameness has enabled human beings to respect and consider each other as equal persons, to acknowledge each other as responsible agents and rights-bearers. We have reasoned that people cannot be equal if they are not somehow the same. Yet upon careful reflection, it becomes possible to see how the idea of essential human sameness can function arrogantly and even oppressively. For example, hoping to break down the kind of racial barriers that existed fifty years ago in the United States, historian Kenneth Stampp asserted "that innately Negroes are, after all, only white men in black skins, nothing more, nothing else" (Spelman 1988, 12). Rather than affirming Stampp's words as an enlightened plea for universal brotherhood, contemporary feminist philosopher Elizabeth Spelman interprets them as unreflectively racist. Why, she asks, is it that white men are the standard for black men? Why not instead make black men the standard for white men? Could it be, asks Spelman, that white people think their way of being is superior to black people's way of being and, therefore, that all black people want to be white but no white people want to be black?

Many feminists in developed nations embraced the idea of difference enthusiastically in the 1980s and 1990s so as not to be viewed as absolutists or colonialists—insensitive to, and disrespectful of, people's diversity. For fear of denigrating or demeaning the "Other," this group of feminists refused to condemn systems, institutions, or practices in developing nations that they would immediately condemn as morally wrong and oppressive in their own developed nations. But there was a serious problem with this well-intentioned reticence on the part of a socially and economically privileged group of feminists. It threatened not only *feminist* political action but also any type of political action that requires nations to come together to forge just global policies, including ones related to health care. After all, if feminists cannot agree on what is in women's best interests, on what policies promote gender justice, then how can bioethicists from a multitude of nations, proud of their unique identities, politics, and heritages, be expected to develop policies that promote world health in general or women's health in particular? Clearly, taken to its extreme, the idea of difference, like the idea of sameness, can become an ethically counterproductive concept.

Toward Resolving the Sameness-Difference Question: The Relativism-Universalism Debate

Fortunately, the new millennium is witnessing among feminists, including feminist bioethicists, a desire to recalibrate the balance between respecting people's differences on the one hand and recognizing people's samenesses on the other. Feminists in developed nations are increasingly joining feminists in developing nations to search for ways to articulate women's and other vulnerable populations' needs and to facilitate women-focused and women-led collaborative projects. Among these feminists is Uma Narayan, a feminist of Indian background who now lives in the United States. In her book *Dislocating Cultures: Identities, Traditions, and Third-World Feminisms* (1997), Narayan observes that it is indeed right for Westerners (Narayan's term) to acknowledge their role both in creating unfavorable representations of the "Other" as uncivilized, primitive, barbaric, or animalistic and in letting their negative ideas about the "Other" be used as conceptual ammunition to defend unjust colonial policies. However, she adds the important point that Westerners should not seek forgiveness for their past sins by now refusing to engage in moral criticism of cultures other than their own (Narayan 1997, 127). Narayan stresses that she does not want guilt-ridden Westerners to unreflectively respect her birth culture (Indian) as incapable of evil; rather, she wants Westerners to insist with her that what was wrong about such practices and policies as segregation in the United States and apartheid in South Africa is what is wrong about the Indian caste system, for example. In addition, Narayan pleads that when she, Uma Narayan, condemns female genital mutilation, the sale of human organs, or sex-selective abortion, she should not be dismissed by Westerners as, after all, only a "Westernized" Indian woman, unable to speak on behalf of "authentic" Indian women who, as non-Westerners, presumably endorse every feature of their society, no matter how morally dubious or unjust (Narayan 1997, 146).

Narayan's conviction that the peoples in developed (Western/Northern/first world) nations and the peoples in developing (Eastern/Southern/third world) nations need to be less relativistic and more universalistic is not unique to her.[1] For example, in her 1992 book, *No Longer Patient: Feminist Ethics and Health Care* (Sherwin 1992), Susan Sherwin claims that feminists cannot afford to be what she terms "traditional relativists" when women's basic health and even lives are at stake. Sherwin focuses on the widespread practice of female genital mutilation in many African and Middle Eastern countries,[2] though she could have just as easily focused on the self-immolation of Indian widows (Macklin 1999, 6) or, in the United States, the popularity of liposuction, a risky elective surgery performed to remove fat cells from women's bodies to make them lean enough to fit popular idealizations of the female body (Tong and Kirkland 1996, 151–59).

In her analysis of female genital mutilation, Sherwin, like many other feminists, notes that most of the justifications typically provided for this practice—namely, that it meets a religious requirement; preserves group identity; helps maintain cleanliness and health; preserves virginity and prevents promiscuity; and furthers marriage goals, including greater sexual pleasure for men (El Dareer 1982)—are gender biased or even empirically false. For example, the belief that female genital mutilation advances cleanliness and health does not square with reliable scientific data that links the practice to bodily harm such as shock, infertility, infections, incontinence, maternal-fetal complications, protracted labor, and even death. Thus, because of the ways in which it harms women and girls, Sherwin condemns the practice of female genital mutilation as wrong, despite the fact that many of the women who bear its marks continue to defend it (Sherwin 1992, 65).

Realizing that in the act of condemning female genital mutilation, she risks being dismissed as a moral absolutist, Sherwin explains her primary reason for not respecting cultural diversity in this matter (Sherwin 1992, 62). She claims that feminists should not accept a community's practices if they are the result of "coercion, exploitation, ignorance, deception, or even indifference" (Sherwin 1992, 69). Instead, feminists should accept only those cultural traditions, including religiously based ones, that are the products of a long history of conversations and negotiations in which all social groups have reflectively participated with ample opportunities to freely voice their interests and concerns. Thus, *to the degree* that a practice such as female genital mutilation, self-immolation of widows in India, or liposuction in the United States is the product of a community that silences voices of internal dissent, structuring its relations in terms of patterns of domination and subordination, Sherwin maintains that feminists are not obligated to tolerate, let alone respect, its standards.

Sherwin is not alone in her assessment of the limits of relativism. Philosopher Ruth Macklin, who chooses not to label herself as a feminist but who nonetheless works actively on behalf of women's human rights, has argued that cultural sensitivity and respect for people's diversity does not include, for example, accepting the practice of sacrificing newborn infants to prevent famine. Macklin relates a heated exchange she had with a young anthropologist who defended this practice, prevalent among an isolated indigenous group in Chile, as morally permissible "for them." When Macklin told the anthropologist that the indigenous group was doing something morally wrong based on a false empirical belief, the anthropologist retorted, "That is their belief; the belief in modern science is your belief: Both are simply beliefs" (Macklin 1999, 8). Insisting that if people wish to collaborate globally, they must have some way to condemn practices such as infant sacrifice—no matter where they occur. Macklin asserts that although there are universal ethical principles, acknowledging their existence is not "a commitment to moral absolutism" (Macklin 1999, 273). In other words, just because an ethical principle is universal does not mean that its content is invariable, that it must be adhered to without exception, or that its application does not vary from culture to culture (Macklin 1999, 35). On the contrary, says Macklin, "ethical principles always require interpretation when they are applied to particular social institutions, such as a health care system or the practice of medicine. In the particulars, there is ample room to tolerate cultural diversity" (Macklin 1999, 273–74).

Sherwin and Macklin have other allies in their related attempts to find unity in diversity. Feminist thinkers and activists from all over the world have addressed ways in which women are both the same and different at several recent international women's conferences. To be sure, women's conversations at these conferences have not always been congenial, let alone productive. Indeed, at each of the three international women's conferences the United Nations (UN) sponsored during the International Decade for Women (1975–1985)—in Mexico City (1975), Copenhagen (1980), and Nairobi (1985)—as well as at Forum 85, a loosely confederated group of 157 nongovernmental organizations, problems emerged among women who were variously labeled as Western, Northern, or from developed nations on the one hand and women who were variously labeled as third world, Eastern, Southern, or from developing nations on the other (Morgan 1984, 35). Specifically, in Mexico City, women from some developed nations alleged that many of the women who had come from developing nations, particularly from some of the socialist Asian, African, and South American nations, had been instructed by their respective governments to criticize women's human rights talk as a capitalist/colonialist plot to undermine religious traditions and family relationships in developing nations. Similarly, in Copenhagen, women from some developed nations complained that "more heat had been generated about 'Zionism,' 'racism,' and 'Western imperialism' than about the basic rights of women and their legally deprived status in over 75 of the 118 countries attending" (Rhoodie 1989, 19). Finally, in Nairobi at Forum 85, women from some developed nations complained that "once again, political clichés and ideological harangues, associated with East-West and North-South disputes in the General Assembly of the U.N., [had] dominated proceedings" (Rhoodie 1989, 19). Referring in particular to the Nairobi conference and Forum 85, critic Eschel Rhoodie observed:

> Even the subject of the right of women to choose when and how many children to have did not make the grade. Yet this issue is one of the most important ones to be addressed by women's organizations and governments in the Third World. It failed to become a central rallying point in Kenya, the venue of the conference, the capital of a country where men's blind and irresponsible resistance to birth control has produced the highest birthrate in the world, creating catastrophic social and economic problems and condemning women to remain in a centuries-old stereotype. (Rhoodie 1989, 20)

The leader of the U.S. delegation, Maureen Reagan, reportedly summed up the Nairobi conference as "an orgy of [political and ideological] hypocrisy" (Gillian 1991, 218).

The Possibilities of Feminist Human Rights Language

Fortunately, the 1995 Beijing women's conference succeeded where previous international women's conferences had faltered. Because they were able to draw upon and share from their previous experiences, women came to Beijing determined to avoid the "ideological sloganeering" of Mexico, Copenhagen, and Nairobi and to find common ground for productive discussion (Dickenson 1997, 107–13). In particular, women from the developed nations came to Beijing with a better understanding of the needs of women in the developing nations, and, in turn, women from the developing nations came to Beijing better prepared to view women from developed nations as capable of understanding their particular circumstances.

According to feminist political theorist Susan Moller Okin, it was not that difficult for the women assembled in Beijing to find common ground, that is, some experience or set of experiences that affect all women irrespective of their race, class, culture, religion, and education.[3] Because women *everywhere* are still regarded as the "second sex," women throughout the world have relatively less sexual freedom, fewer reproductive rights, and a worse health and socioeconomic status than men (Okin 1995, 294). Given this state of affairs, Okin stresses the importance of women working together, both to secure for women full equity with the men in their respective nations and to secure for their respective nations full equity within the human community. Somewhat more controversially, at least in some circles of feminist theorists, Okin claims that the language of human rights is the language women should use to achieve the two goals just mentioned. She stresses that using the United Nations Universal Declaration of Human Rights (UDHR), the Convention on the Elimination of All Forms of Discrimination against Women (CEDAW), and the United Nations Declaration on the Elimination of Violence against Women, feminist activists have been able to improve women's status and condition worldwide. Okin's view is reiterated by Anne Donchin in chapter 2 of this volume, in which she shows how, over the past five decades, women have used the human rights card to achieve more parity with men and to make their environment a safer one.

The Limits of Women's Human Rights Talk

Given that a significant number of feminist thinkers and activists have used the language of women's human rights so effectively on many occasions, why do other feminist thinkers and activists express concerns about continuing to use—or, in those nations where rights talk has yet to be spoken, starting to use—rights talk? One reason behind some feminists' reservations about rights talk is that there remains a tendency to privilege first-generation civil and political rights over second-generation economic, social, and cultural rights and certainly over third-generation collective/group rights (Peterson and Parisi 1998, 142–53). Typical first-generation rights include freedom *from* oppression and *from* governmental interference with liberty of action. Typical second-generation rights include "food, clothing, shelter, education, the right to work, rest and reasonable payment" (Faison 1997, A8), and, I would add, health care. Typical third-generation rights are harder to express succinctly, mainly because this generation of rights, which "seeks to preserve the integrity of a particular cultural, ethnic or indigenous group through the rights of self-determination" (Peterson and Parisi 1998, 151), remains in the process of articulation. Still, a typical third-generation right may be the general right to resist "the homogenizing and/or genocidal practices of colonization and/or centralization" (Peterson and Parisi 1998, 151), specified in some contexts as the right to resist the "McDonaldization" of one's national cuisine and in others as the right to resist the theft of one's genetic material for the purpose of developing pharmaceutical products meant to serve not one's own people but other people (see Harvey-Blankenship and Hocking, chapter 12 in this volume, and Bertomeu and Sommer, chapter 11 in this volume).

Clearly, if people have only first-generation rights and not second- and third-generation rights, they are at a real disadvantage. Such a state of affairs is, as many feminist thinkers correctly point out, likely to be particularly bad for women. For example, a woman's right to have an abortion does not mean much if it simply prevents others from interfering with her decision to abort her fetus. Unless such a woman has the funds to pay for her abortion and unless there are physicians willing to help her, her negative right to have an abortion will prove hollow. Comments feminist philosopher Alison Jaggar: "A real choice about abortion requires that a woman should be able to opt to have her child, as well as to abort it. This means that the full right to life of the child must be guaranteed, either by community aid to the mother who wishes to raise it herself, or by the provision of alternative arrangements that do not put the child who is not raised by its own mother at any significant disadvantage" (Jaggar 1976, 357). Moreover, a woman's right to have an abortion is also not likely to mean much to her if she belongs to an indigenous group whose people are few in number and whose number is being further reduced by genetic screening technologies that encourage her to abort her fetus because it, like she, is imperfect (see Shanthi, this volume).

In a variation of the argument outlined previously, feminist activists and thinkers suspicious about the benefits yielded for women through rights talk claim that even if first-, second-, and third-generation rights were equally emphasized, women's interests might still not be served that well. They reason that people's rights are generally better protected in the public domain than in the private domain. Specifically, a woman may have the right to free speech, but she may have grown up in a society where she never learned to voice her opinion authoritatively because men do all the talking and women do all the listening (see Salles, chapter 3 in this volume). Or a woman may have the right to work, but the work she does may go uncompensated or undercompensated because it is done at home or not recognized as "real" work (that is, income-generating work performed in the officially recognized marketplace). Or a woman may have the right not to abort her fetus so that the indigenous group to which she belongs may survive, but she may find herself "disciplined" by her group to produce more children than she thinks are necessary (Peterson and Parisi 1998, 152).

Perhaps the strongest objection of some feminists against rights talk is that, to them, it is a morally impoverished kind of talk, either because it is too "male" in tone—that is, too aggressive and assertive, thereby conveying the impression that it is self-absorbed, self-preoccupied, and unnecessarily oppositional—or because it offers principles and rules so abstract, general, and vague that they are unable to provide meaningful and specific action guides for people who live in very concrete and particularized situations. For example, Australian feminist Chilla Bulbeck, author of *Re-Orienting Western Feminisms* (1998), describes her reaction when she attended a 1992 pro-choice rally in Washington, D.C.:

> I was struck by the anger of many of the speakers and participants. A black and white women's vocal group from Manhattan, named Betsy, shouted out the slogan "We are fierce, we are feminist, and we are in your face". Robin Morgan urged us to buy T-shirts proclaiming "Rage plus women equals power". One placard read "Abort Bush Before His Second Term". Angry arguments erupted between the pro-choice women and the pro-life women who had erected a "cemetery of innocents" nearby (representing aborted fetuses and the twenty-three women who had died during legal abortions). I went to the United States believing I knew it intimately from the flood of films, television programs and academic books that pervade Australian popular and intellectual culture. Yet I felt battered and cut adrift by the assertiveness and anger, by the incessant refrain of rights and freedoms. This fashion of feminism was unfamiliar to me. (Bulbeck 1998, 5)

If this fashion of feminism was unfamiliar to Bulbeck, a feminist from Australia, a nation quite like the United States in many ways, it is likely to be much more alien to women from nations that, even more than Australia, value harmonious human relationships and view societies in which people must continually assert their individual rights as societies whose people have failed to fulfill their responsibilities to each other.

The notion that moral concerns might be better addressed in terms of people's responsibilities to each other rather than in terms of peoples' individual rights is present in the work of those feminist thinkers and activists who espouse a so-called ethics of care. Among the most widely known exponents of the ethics of care is Carol Gilligan. In her book *In a Different Voice*, Gilligan notes that in the Western world, men's tendency to stress their selfhood leads them to develop a style of moral thinking and speaking that emphasizes individuals' personal rights and the virtue of justice. In contrast, in that same world, women's tendency to stress their relationships to family and friends causes them to develop a style of moral thinking and speaking that emphasizes individuals' responsibilities to each other and the virtue of care. Additionally, Gilligan observes that, in the United States at least, there is a tendency to privilege the language of rights and justice as morally superior to the language of responsibilities and care and, therefore, to view women as less morally developed than men, a view Gilligan argues is utterly misguided. Simply because women speak in a different moral voice than men does not mean that they are any less moral than men (Gilligan 1982).

Agreeing with Gilligan's observations, Nel Noddings, another exponent of the ethics of care, provides useful explanations for why it may be a mistake for feminists to rely more on the language of rights and justice than on the language of responsibilities and care. Although Noddings believes that women can speak the language of rights and justice as well as men do, she insists that this language is not their native tongue. Women enter the moral realm through a "different door" than men do, and although women can construct hierarchies of principles and argue deductively, they are apt to regard such displays of reasoning as beside the point. When it comes to deciding whether to withhold further medical treatment from her dying child, for example, a woman is not likely to approach this intensely personal decision as she would approach an extremely difficult math problem. As she struggles to discern what is in her child's best interest, she will prefer to consult her "feelings, needs, impressions, and . . . sense of personal ideal" (Noddings 1984, 3) rather than some set of moral axioms and theorems. Her goal will be to identify herself as closely as possible with her dying child so that her decision will in fact be *her child's* decision.

Ethics, insists Noddings, is about particular relations, where *relation* means "a set of ordered pairs generated by some rule that describes the affect—or subjective experience—of the members" (Noddings 1984, 3–4). There are two parties in any relation: the first member is the "one-caring"; the second is the "cared-for." The one-caring is motivationally engrossed or "displaced" in the cared-for. He or she makes it a point to attend to the cared-for in deeds as well as in thoughts (Noddings 1984, 9). Although Noddings concedes that we tend to care about our family members and friends more than about anyone else, she recommends that we move beyond our present circle of intimate connections by means of what she calls "chains." These chains, meant to deliver us from what would be a regrettable moral incestuousness, apparently function in two ways: one personal and the other formal (Noddings 1984, 47). On the *personal* interpretation, we widen our circles of human relationships directly by revealing ourselves to persons linked to individuals for whom we already care: for example, a spouse of a grown child, or a friend of a friend. On the *formal* interpretation, we widen our circle of human relationships by imagining, for example, possible relationships we could have were it not for certain boundaries created by the limits of space and time. Thus, I can care about all the authors of the chapters in this volume, including the ones with whom I do not have (at present) a personal relationship. Similarly, I can care about the people about whom I/they write or for whom I/they speak.

Unlike Gilligan, Noddings claims that an ethics of care is not only *different* from but also ultimately *better* than an ethics of justice. As she sees it, we must reject rules and principles as major guides to ethical behavior and with them the accompanying notion of universalizability. For Noddings, relationships are not about universals but about particulars—what makes each man or woman uniquely different from any other man or woman. Noddings qualifies her rejection of universals and affirmation of particulars, however. Specifically, she insists that she is not espousing relativism, since there is something properly "universal" about the "caring attitude" that underpins her ethics. Comments Noddings: "Indeed, I am claiming that the impulse to act on behalf of the present other is itself innate. It lies latent in each of us, awaiting gradual development in a succession of caring relations" (Noddings 1984, 83).

As someone who believes that virtue can be taught, Noddings insists that an ethics of caring can be communicated just as effectively as an ethics of rules and principles can. Our initial experiences of care come easily, almost unconsciously, and certainly spontaneously. We act from a natural caring that impels us to help others because we *want* to:

> The relation of natural caring will be identified as the human condition that we, consciously or unconsciously, perceive as "good". It is that condition toward which we long and strive, and it is our longing for caring—to be in that special relation—that provides the motivation for us to be moral. We want to be moral in order to remain in the caring relation and to enhance the ideal of ourselves as one-caring. (Noddings 1984, 5)

Noddings does not describe moral development as the process of *replacing* natural (spontaneous) caring with ethical (deliberate) caring. Although ethical caring requires efforts that natural caring does not, Noddings disagrees with Immanuel Kant's view that ethical caring is somehow better than natural caring. For Kant, an action is not a morally worthy one unless an agent does it out of duty and not merely out of inclination. Kant even suggests that to the degree an action goes against our grain, to that same degree we can be certain that we are doing it because we *ought* to and not simply because we *want* to (Kant 1956, 74–75). In contrast to Kant, Noddings believes that our "oughts" build on our "wants": "An ethic built on caring strives to maintain the caring attitude and is thus dependent upon, and not superior to, natural caring" (Noddings 1984, 80). Morality is not about affirming others' needs through the process of denying one's own interests. Rather, morality is about affirming one's own interests through the process of affirming others' needs. When we act morally (engage in ethical caring), we act to fulfill our "fundamental and natural desire to be and to remain related" (Noddings 1984, 83). If we have any duty when our interests conflict with others' needs, it is our duty to ourselves to be moral—that is, to be and to remain related.

The Intersection of Feminist Human Capabilities and Needs Language with Feminist Human Rights Language

Given the importance of "responsibilities talk"—the voice of care, which women speak so effectively and eloquently—the reluctance of some feminists to use rights talk is, in my estimation, understandable. Rights language can be too adversarial, conflictual, and self-focused, and it can be used in ways that suggest relational responsibilities are not as important as individual rights. Nevertheless, I am convinced that, politically, the language of rights is one of the languages feminists need to use if they wish to serve women's best interests *worldwide*. Properly spoken, as it was by most of the women who attended the International Women's Conference in Beijing, rights language can be profoundly feminist talk. Its words can be interpreted not only through the grid of the ethics of care but also through the lens of what have been termed human capacities. According to philosopher Martha Nussbaum, human capabilities are those resources and opportunities for life functioning that are always rational to want, whatever else one wants (Nussbaum 1999, 41). Among these capabilities are several of particular interest to bioethicists, including "being able to live to the end of a human life of normal length" (Nussbaum 1999, 41); "not dying prematurely or before one's life is so reduced as to be not worth living" (Nussbaum 1999, 41); and "being able to have good health, including reproductive health" (Nussbaum 1999, 41).[4]

To be sure, Nussbaum's complete list of human capabilities (Nussbaum 2000) can be faulted as either overinclusive or underinclusive. It can also be contested on the grounds that it is the product of a self-appointed Western/Northern/developed-world expert who has decided what all people, and not simply she, need to lead a human life. But this objection is answerable. Although Nussbaum specifies the ten general categories (life; bodily health; bodily integrity; senses, imagination, and thought; emotions; practical reason; affiliation; other species; play; control over one's environment) on her human capabilities list in terms of the particular experiences she has had (Nussbaum 1999, 41–42), her ten general categories nonetheless transcend the limits of her unique moral imagination. Indeed, her list of human capabilities is virtually indistinguishable from the list of human needs that Maria Mies, a sociologist known for her work on development economics, and Vandana Shiva, a physicist known for her interests in spirituality, have enumerated in their jointly authored book on ecofeminism (Mies and Shiva 1993, 13). Specifically, the fundamental function of morality, according to Mies and Shiva, is to keep "intact and alive enough life-sustaining social and political networks to meet all people's fundamental needs for food, shelter, clothing; for affection, care and love; for dignity and identity, for knowledge and freedom, leisure and joy" (Mies and Shiva 1993, 322).

As I understand all ethics of care, including Nussbaum's capabilities approach and Mies and Shiva's fundamental needs approach, they are attempts to further articulate and develop second-generation economic and social rights and third-generation collective group rights in ways that serve women's and men's interests equally. They use the language of human relationships, responsibilities, capabilities, and needs to clarify that first-generation human rights (that is, political and civil liberties) are but some of the rights required to lead a good human life. Second-generation and third-generation rights are equally required. Thus, I do not see responsibilities, capabilities, and needs approaches to morality so much as rivals to rights approaches to morality as complements and specifications of them.

Conclusion

Feminist bioethicists are in a unique position to teach all bioethicists how to translate between the language of justice and rights on the one hand and the language of care, responsibilities, capabilities, and needs on the other. Although examples of moral translation are present in virtually every one of the chapters in this volume, a particularly good example is in *Negotiating Reproductive Rights*, a collection of essays written by members of the International Reproductive Rights Research Action Group (IRRRAG). In one of the IRRRAG essays, low-income urban women from Brazil, Egypt, Malaysia, Mexico, Nigeria, the Philippines, and the United States all justify their reproductive rights in terms of their maternal responsibilities. Specifically, they reason "that since they (not husbands or partners) suffer the greatest burdens, pains and responsibilities of pregnancy, childbearing and childrearing, they therefore have earned the right to make decisions in this arena" (Petchesky and Judd 1998, 362).

By engaging in ongoing discussions with diverse women about the particular conditions that limit their ability to function as human beings who have enough self-respect to proclaim their human rights, feminist bioethicists will be supplied with the content they need to speak the language of women's human rights more effectively in national and international forums. In the course of discussing women's perceived responsibilities as well as women's common needs and capabilities, particularly those born of human beings' carnality and mortality, feminist bioethicists may actually be motivated to personally *care* enough about women's situations worldwide to collaboratively produce *just* health care policies, practices, and institutions. We need to confront oppression and exploitation with a language of rights filled with the cry of human needs, the promise of human capabilities, and the demand of responsibilities. Only then will we be able to effectively voice women's human rights in ways that those in power can understand and honor.

Notes

I wish to acknowledge Westview Press for permitting me to base some of this chapter on a section from a chapter I wrote titled "Is a Global Bioethics Possible as Well as Desirable? A Millennial Feminist Response," in *Globalizing Feminist Bioethics: Crosscultural Perspectives*, edited by Rosemarie Tong with Gwen Anderson and Aida Santos (Boulder, Colo., 2001).

1. See, for example, Chilla Bulbeck's discussion about fracturing binarisms in her book *Re-Orienting Western Feminisms: Women's Diversity in a Postcolonial World* (Cambridge, N.Y.: Cambridge University Press, 1998), 18–56. Bulbeck shows that no binary opposition, no matter how much it tries to avoid privileging one set of values and circumstances over another, can succeed in its effort. In particular, in view of the fact that so many people have hybrid racial, ethnic, and national identities, language is increasingly failing "us" as "we" look for terms to refer to each other and words to communicate with each other. Frustrated by my own inability to pick my binary "poison," I have decided to use the opposition developed nation/developing nation when I speak in my own voice. When it comes to discussing gaps between the world's "haves" and the world's "have-nots," the North-South divide probably reflects the enormity of these gaps better than the West-East divide.

2. See also Loretta M. Kopelman, "Female Genital Circumcision and Conventionalist Ethical Relativism," in *Globalizing Feminist Bioethics*, ed. Rosemarie Tong with Gwen Anderson and Aida Santos (Boulder, Colo.: Westview, 2001), 219–37.

3. See, for example, the impressive list of names in Susan Moller Okin's "Feminism, Women's Human Rights, and Cultural Differences," *Hypatia* 13, no. 2 (1998): 46.

4. For a detailed explanation of Nussbaum's capabilities opportunities, see Anne Donchin (chapter 2 in this volume) and Donna Dickenson (chapter 1 in this volume). Both Donchin and Dickenson illuminate the strengths and weaknesses of Nussbaum's approach, offering their own more rights-emphatic approaches as better alternatives to Nussbaum's capabilities approach unmodified.

References
Bulbeck, Chilla. 1998. *Re-Orienting Western Feminisms: Women's Diversity in a Postcolonial World*. Cambridge, UK: Cambridge University Press.

Chanter, Tina. 1998. "Postmodern Subjectivity." In *A Companion to Feminist Philosophy*, edited by Alison M. Jaggar and Iris Marion Young, 267. Malden, Mass.: Blackwell.

Dickenson, Donna. 1997. "Counting Women In: Globalization, Democratization, and the Women's Movement." In *The Transformation of Democracy*, edited by Anthony G. McGrew, 107–13. Cambridge, UK: Polity Press.

Echols, Alice. 1983. "The New Feminism of Yin and Yang." In *Powers of Desire: The Politics of Sexuality*, edited by Ann Snitow, Christine Stansell, and Sharon Thompson, 439–59. New York: Monthly Review Press.

El Dareer, Asma. 1982. *Woman, Why Do You Weep? Circumcision and Its Consequences*. London: Zed Books.

Faison, Seth. 1997. "China Turns the Tables, Faulting U.S. on Rights." *New York Times*, March 5, A8.

Gillian, Angela. 1991. "Women's Equality and National Liberation." In *Third World Women and the Politics of Feminism*, edited by Chandra Talpade Mohanty, Ann Russo, and Lourdes Torres, 218. Bloomington: Indiana University Press.

Gilligan, Carol. 1982. *In a Different Voice: Psychological Theory and Women's Development*. Cambridge, Mass.: Harvard University Press.

Jaggar, Alison M. 1976. "Abortion and a Woman's Right to Decide." In *Women and Philosophy: Toward a Theory of Liberation*, edited by Carol C. Gould and Max W. Wartofsky, 357. New York: Putnam.

———. 1992. "Feminist Ethics." In *Encyclopedia of Ethics*, edited by Lawrence Becker with Charlotte Becker, 364–67. New York: Garland.

Kant, Immanuel. 1956. *Groundwork of the Metaphysics of Morals*, translated by H. J. Paton. New York: Harper & Row.

Knowles, Lori P. 2001. "The Lingua Franca of Human Rights and the Rise of a Global Bioethic." *Cambridge Quarterly of Healthcare Ethics* 10, no. 3: 253.

Kopelman, Loretta M. 2001. "Female Genital Circumcision and Conventionalist Ethical Relativism." In *Globalizing Feminist Bioethics*, edited by Rosemarie Tong with Gwen Anderson and Aida Santos, 219–37. Boulder, Colo.: Westview.

Macklin, Ruth. 1999. *Against Relativism*. New York: Oxford University Press.

Mies, Maria, and Vandana Shiva. 1993. *Ecofeminism*. London: Zed Books.

Morgan, Robin. 1984. *Sisterhood Is Global*. Garden City, N.Y.: Anchor.

Narayan, Uma. 1997. *Dislocating Cultures: Identities, Traditions, and Third-World Feminisms*. New York: Routledge.

Noddings, Nel. 1984. *Caring: A Feminine Approach to Ethics and Moral Education*. Berkeley: University of California Press.

Nussbaum, Martha. 1999. *Sex and Social Justice*. New York: Oxford University Press.

———. 2000. *Women and Human Development: The Capabilities Approach*. Cambridge, UK: Cambridge University Press.

Okin, Susan Moller. 1995. "Inequalities between Sexes in Different Cultural Contexts." In *Women, Culture and Development*, edited by Martha Nussbaum and Jonathan Glover, 294. Oxford: Clarendon Press.

———. 1998. "Feminism, Women's Human Rights, and Cultural Differences." *Hypatia* 13, no. 2: 32–52.

Petchesky, Rosalind, and Karen Judd, eds. 1998. *Negotiating Reproductive Rights: Women's Perspectives Across Countries and Cultures.* London: Zed Books.

Peterson, V. Spike, and Laura Parisi. 1998. "Are Women Human? It's Not an Academic Question." In *Human Rights Fifty Years On: A Radical Reappraisal,* edited by Tony Evans, 132–60. Manchester, UKs: Manchester University Press.

Rhoodie, Eschel M. 1989. *Discrimination against Women: A Global Survey of the Economic, Educational, Social, and Political Status of Women.* London: McFarland.

Sherwin, Susan. 1992. *No Longer Patient: Feminist Ethics and Health Care.* Philadelphia: Temple University Press.

Spelman, Elizabeth V. 1988. *Inessential Woman: Problems of Exclusion in Feminist Thought.* Boston: Beacon.

Tong, Rosemarie, and Anna Kirkland. 1996. "Working Within Contradiction: The Possibility of Feminist Cosmetic Surgery." *Journal of Clinical Ethics* 7, no. 2: 151–59.

On Learning How to Care Appropriately   6
A Case for Developing a Model of
Support for Those in Need

CAROL QUINN

IN THIS CHAPTER, I OFFER a support model that is sensitive to the ways in which people in developing nations articulate their own needs. To do so, I first argue that such a model is necessary. Here I work within a needs-based justice structure, drawing on insights from Amartya Sen, Martha Nussbaum, and Martin Hoffman, among others. I explain that a mere description of human needs does not require us to *care* that those needs are met or to develop the means to meet them. This is especially true when caring for people significantly different from oneself. Empathetic identification with those in distress moves us to care, but then we must learn how to care, recognizing the limitations and difficulties of caring across differences in power as well as culture. To generate normative rules for such caring, we need an ethical framework. I argue that this framework should be rights-based. We have a right to have our needs met in virtue of our universally shared right to lead a life of human flourishing and dignity. Here I appeal to the Hebrew concept of *kavod*, which most closely translates as a relational notion of dignity. To have *kavod* requires (1) control in the sense of self-determination, (2) community acknowledgement of value, (3) living a life worthy of pursuit, and (4) acting morally responsibly. Living a flourishing life is living a life of *kavod*, and certain needs must be met to have such a life. Meeting those needs requires (global) community recognition, support, and responsibility. In developing this argument, I also appeal to other authors in this volume—Donna Dickenson (chapter 1), Anne Donchin (chapter 2), Arleen Salles (chapter 3), and Rosemarie Tong (chapter 5).

After arguing for the necessity of a support model, I develop one suited for people in positions of power who want to help people in positions of relative powerlessness. I discuss the problems as well as the potentialities of helping others from one or more positions of power. I speak particularly to Western feminist bioethicists who want to help people in developing countries, especially women whose basic health needs are often either neglected or not met. I claim that, despite certain limitations, a care ethic often has the strength to go further than a justice ethic in public as well as private life. Finally, I apply this support model to the public health care system in Chile. I have chosen to focus on Chile not because I think Chilean women's health care is worse, say, than that of Brazilian or Argentinean women, but because my friend and international colleague, Dr. Nicolas Guiliani, a scientist at the University of Chile in Santiago, has sparked my interest in his country. Through him, I have come to care, concretely, about the Chilean people.

Feminist Grounds for Developing a Support Model

Historically, ethicists have favored a justice-based model of morality, whether it is justice as fairness, egalitarian justice, distributive justice, retributive justice, and so forth. Justice-based morality has traditionally appealed to men's universal rights. It is rule-based, abstract, and impersonal rather than relationship-rooted, concrete, and personal. Supporters of justice-based thinking do not rule out care-based thinking altogether. Indeed, they recognize the importance of care, describing it as a virtue exemplified by a mother caring for her child. However, because care-based morality lacks the formal properties of justice-based morality, they tend to think that care should be subordinated to justice in situations where they conflict (Hoffman 2000). Note, though, that with this assumption comes the presumed moral superiority of abstract "male" reasoning over concrete "female" caring. Care-based morality is personal and affective, looking at the lives of particular persons in particular contexts. Justice-based morality, on the other hand, is impersonal and rational, free from emotions getting in the way.

Many feminists argue against what they rightly consider to be a largely masculine and, in particular, white, educated, Western justice and rights morality and instead favor a care-oriented morality. Nel Noddings, for one, notes the important feminine qualities of care-based morality, which is context-based and particular rather than rule-based and acontextual; therefore, it is better able than justice-based morality to acknowledge and respect people's differences (Noddings 1984). Care-based morality is grounded in empathy toward others and especially in empathic distress when others are in need. It refers to a particular orientation toward others, in which we care not so much about others' abstract rights as about their concrete needs.

Some feminists, including feminist bioethicists, now recognize problems with a morality based on care only. They are specifically concerned that such a morality tends to be too relativistic and too tolerant of various injustices at times, especially where women's health is at stake. Thus, these feminists see the need for a more universalistic, rights-based morality and recognize health as a basic human rights issue. Feminists including Virginia Held (1995), Donna Dickenson, Anne Donchin, Susan Sherwin, and Rosemarie Tong suggest the need for a reconciliation of care-based and justice-based moralities, one that transcends "the two extremes of full-fledged multiculturalism and inflexible human rights" (Dickenson, this volume). Dickenson, Donchin, Salles, and Tong argue in favor of linking feminist bioethics and human rights discourse. They discuss feminist resistance to and distrust of rights language, yet point out that this resistance has been largely theoretical. In practice, rights talk has been integral to feminist activist strategies (Donchin, chapter 2 in this volume), and feminists would do well to adopt rights talk, which is the dominant language of the international and political arenas.

Reconciling justice and care is not altogether unfamiliar work. One can sympathize with, indeed feel empathetic distress for, a hardworking fifteen-year-old female Mexican worker laboring in one of the many maquiladoras (which are little more than sweatshops) along the United States–Mexican border; or for families living in communities that get their drinking water from the Rio Grande, where much of the toxic waste from the maquiladoras is illegally dumped; or for the many anencephalic children—four times the national average—born in the border cities of Brownsville, Texas, and Matamoros, Mexico (Bullard 2001). One can feel empathetic distress for all of these people and yet also believe they are being treated unjustly, that their rights as human beings to food, shelter, a clean environment, education, health care, and a flourishing future are being violated or outright ignored.

One way to frame the compatibility of justice and care is to understand justice as feeling distressed when people's needs are not met. People have a right to a life of human flourishing and dignity. Such a right requires, minimally, that people's basic needs be met, and we should rightly feel distressed when they are not. The International Federation of Red Cross and Red Crescent Societies and the United Nation's 1948 Declaration of Human Rights recognize that the right to have one's basic needs met is universal, absolute, and applicable to all people equally. Such societies and declarations focus on human worth and the oneness of the human condition and also work toward realizing a multicultural, global, peaceful coexistence. Specifically, they identify health as a basic human need and agree with thinkers such as Rebecca Cook, who claims that good health is a precondition to exercising other basic rights, including equal participation in communal and social life (Cook 1999, 263).

Why We Need a Support Model

As Amartya Sen (2000), Martha Nussbaum, and others argue, human beings have a right to live a life of human flourishing and dignity and a right to have those needs met that contribute to that flourishing life (Nussbaum 2000). Nussbaum grounds this idea of human flourishing and dignity in an intuitive idea of what it is to live such a life. But intuitive ideas are shaky foundations for a universal morality, and Dickenson rightly criticizes Nussbaum for appealing to intuition on the grounds that intuitions are culture-driven. A warrior culture, for example, would include violence as part of a dignified life, which is unacceptable. Thus, we must appeal to a less culture-bound notion of human flourishing and dignity than one grounded in intuition. I suggest we turn to the Hebrew concept *kavod*. I discovered this word while presenting a paper on dignity at the University of Haifa. I was told by a Holocaust survivor in the audience that instead of using the word *dignity* throughout my paper, I should have instead used the word *kavod*.

A much richer notion than our common understanding of dignity, *kavod* is essentially relational, based on community recognition, support, and esteem. *Kavod* is connected with one's projects and life pursuits. More important, it has a moral element to it. One attains *kavod* as a side effect of engaging in work. However, it cannot be just any work. Rather, it must be some meritorious accomplishment or worthy project that bears positively on the community. *Kavod* requires self-determination, community acknowledgement of value, living a life worthy of pursuit, and acting morally responsibly; more specifically, it requires that each person's basic needs be met. One cannot lead a life of *kavod* alone. Unless people care for each other—feed each other; minister to each other's physical, psychological, and spiritual needs, especially the need to be esteemed, respected, and loved—*kavod* cannot be achieved. Achieving *kavod* requires community recognition and support of one's basic human needs.

We should feel empathetic distress for those whose needs are not met, and we should feel moved as responsible, caring, global community members to meet those needs. In his insightful work *Empathy and Moral Development*, psychologist Martin Hoffman develops a needs-based justice and care ethic that helps us understand why we need the support model I propose. He argues for a responsibility-oriented morality, where one feels it is one's responsibility to consider others, empathize with others, and work to meet the needs of others. Such an ethic is global in nature, focusing on our interdependence and connectedness to each other—to others close by, but also to those more distant; to those who are alike, but also to those different. A needs-based justice and care model sees crosscultural needs, life goals, preferences, and fears, and it recognizes similar crosscultural emotional responses to being praised, criticized, and treated unfairly, as well as to attachment, separation, and loss (Hoffman 2000, 299). Such an orientation places greater value on global community obligations than on the celebration of individual autonomy, a value much favored in U.S. ethics and politics. On this view, we care that people's needs are met; we feel distressed when they are not. We want all people to lead flourishing lives and not merely to get by. Furthermore, those of us in positions of power have a responsibility—indeed a paramount moral duty—to help relatively powerless people whose basic needs are not being met. It is a moral outrage to be bystanders to the world's injustices. The needs-based justice and care ethic, in which I ground my support model, is especially fragile in large part because human beings—our very moral lives—are so fragile.[1] As Hoffman notes, it is our human nature to feel empathy toward others, but such a caring response can be diminished or destroyed by power-asserting individuals and cultures valuing competition, interethnic rivalry, hostility, and violence over cooperation, help, and kindness (Hoffman 2000).

Although experiencing empathetic identification with those deprived or distressed is necessary, I agree with Donchin that we must move beyond this (Donchin, chapter 2 in this volume). Having an empathetic connection moves us to care, but we must then learn how to care, working cooperatively at both the theoretical and practical levels, challenging moral paradigms that inhibit or even block our attempts to recognize each other's right to live a life of *kavod*.

On Caring Appropriately: Avoiding Colonizing Care—A Lesson for Those in Power

> *We who are strong gather together to tighten the knots and knit a net of safety to catch those who are falling.*
>
> —SHIRLEY VOGLER MEISTER, *THREADS OF HOPE* (1998)

What problems should those of us in positions of power attend to in developing a model of support for developing countries?[2] I speak as a Western feminist bioethicist, an educated white woman with a PhD and a university position. That is, I speak from a position of relative power wanting to help those who suffer various injustices across the globe. The problem can be articulated as follows. When we as feminist bioethicists recognize a problem with a country's practices—for example, its freedom-denying reproductive policies—we incur an obligation to help change or even overturn those practices to the degree they do not meet people's basic needs. But how can we offer to help those largely unfamiliar to us, when our care for them can mistakenly be seen as insulting and invasive? That is, how can we effect change across differences, especially when we might be confronted—indeed, are perhaps likely to be confronted—with the question, aptly put by Lorraine Code in her work *Rhetorical Spaces*: "How can you care about me when you don't know who I am or what matters to me?" (Code 1995). Code's concern, which is expressed quietly between countries that are not hostile to one another or suspicious of each other's motives, is voiced loudly between countries separated by chasms created by longstanding conflict or violence. It is hard to try to help people who have good reason to hate you.

The solution is not simply a matter of providing reassurance or so-called comfort words to possible recipients of care, however. On the contrary, the problem, which is at least twofold, calls for multiple solutions. First, as Code points out, there is the danger of the "arrogant" privileged who claim to know better than the oppressed about what is going on and what needs to be set right, without making any real effort to compare their perception of reality with that of the people they presume to help. Second, there is the problem of the "humble" privileged who worry there may be no way for them ever to genuinely understand the culture and problem of the people they want to help. Their crucial concern is how to find a way to care without colonizing.

Tong specifies this concern for feminist bioethicists as the problem of feminist bioethicists knowing how to build a bioethics that is relativistic enough to accommodate diversities between individuals and societies—that is, we want to avoid being insensitive and insulting—yet universal enough to serve as a common base from which we can launch collaborative moral action. We want to be morally critical of certain actions and ideologies—often justified under such umbrella terms as *tradition* and *religion*—yet we also want to suggest and implement plans of action when we are convinced that fundamental human values are being violated. This is a delicate and difficult task that requires an appropriate balance, which I discuss later in this section. As Tong suggests, tolerance and silence are utterly morally inappropriate, especially when we recognize gross violations of human rights (Tong, chapter 5 in this volume).

We feminist bioethicists must be committed to making changes, yet such action requires careful self-examination, self-criticism, and when necessary, self-correction. Oftentimes the model one government wants to impose on another is not a morally appropriate model for that country. Indeed, as is the case of the health care system in the United States, it can be a harmful model. Many governments, including the U.S. government, tend to think they know what is best for others wherever they happen to live. They take it upon themselves to remake the recipients of their care into their own image. Code calls this bad caring as contrasted with good caring. But although bad, arrogant caring is to be eschewed, sometimes a government, including the U.S. government, or we ourselves really do know what is best for others. We do have a real idea about how to improve the lives of others. But does this knowledge per se ipso facto make us expert change-makers, especially in cultures about which we know little more than simplistic stereotypes? Acting as experts in such cases may alienate those for whom we feel a responsibility to help. Chandra Mohanty writes of the danger of much Western feminist discourse, which constructs *the* third world woman as a singular, monolithic subject that "carries with it the authorizing signature of Western humanist discourse" (Mohanty 1991). Similarly, Arleen Salles argues against the limitations of essentialist thinking about culture and ethnicity (Salles, chapter 3 in this volume).

Noddings explains that caring involves stepping out of one's own personal frame of reference into that of others. She models her ethics of caring on mothering. Noddings seems to ignore the problem of caring across difference, which is quite different from caring for a child that is "flesh of my flesh." However, she does recognize the need to step into the other's shoes, so to speak, to get the other's perspective. One of the main problems with Noddings's account concerns the power imbalance that the mothering model sets up. Mother and child are definitely not equals. In caring for others, we certainly do not want to be so maternalistic that we presume to always know what is best for them. However, Noddings's mothering model does seem to capture at least the initial relationship between the more powerful caretaker and the approached recipient of care. But we do not want this unidirectional relationship to remain this way, for this would be counterproductive to the effort to work for real change. As Sara Ruddick and others point out, one aim of mothering is to free the child of dependency on the mother (Ruddick 1995).

Given this problem or core set of problems, what should those of us committed to human rights and medical humanitarianism do? Can we—let alone the U.S. government—learn to care appropriately? To answer this concern, I first discuss the notion of power—those who have it (in this case, by and large, the caretakers) and those who don't have it (by and large, the recipients of care). Change of a particular health care principle, policy, or practice ought to be initiated whenever possible by the care recipients so as to reaffirm their agency. It is important for all care recipients (but particularly ones who have been marginalized, subordinated, and silenced) to perceive themselves as in charge of their own destinies. For well-intentioned, powerful caretakers to deprive care recipients of the opportunity to effect changes for themselves on the grounds, say, that they are moving too "slowly" or "ineptly" is to further deny the care recipients' own voice, a voice that is necessary for long-term changes not only in health care but also in education, employment opportunities, political participation, property rights, and so on. Caretakers should not prematurely intervene in armylike fashion to oversee care recipients' efforts to effect change in their own way. The more desired result is that, with the background help of caretakers, care recipients can empower themselves. There should be a genuine sharing of power and not the mere illusion of power sharing between the caretakers and the care recipients.

Another problem occurs when caretakers experience difficulties finding powerful allies within the recipient country, typically men, who will likely be listened to and respected and who can apply political pressure to effect significant policy changes. Indeed, without powerful allies from within the recipient country, it would be tremendously difficult, if not impossible, to effect change—especially to enhance the position of women in society. Thus, caretakers should try to form alliances with national and international health and human rights organizations so that they can make *real* differences in people's lives. But even here, traps await caretakers. Regrettably, even the most humanitarian organizations are subject to abuses of power and influence. For example, both Doctors Without Borders and Doctors of the World have tried to remain politically neutral while acting on the moral obligation to alleviate the suffering of people desperately in need of medical care. They have given public testimony to the human rights abuses and the misery they encounter in the field. Yet despite their efforts to act in a caring fashion, they have become increasingly militarized due to the warfare, violence, conflict, and disorder within which they work. Oftentimes, they find themselves caught in the middle of factions, forced to choose one faction over the other (Fox 1999). Because the moral effectiveness of this kind of group depends on their ability to influence structures of power and authority, their contributions suffer to the extent they are forced to turn, for example, to *military* forces for protection and transportation.

Around the globe we find that women suffer most in terms of not having their needs met or having them ignored outright. As a result, many women do not lead flourishing lives of *kavod*. Throughout the world, women are viewed and treated as inferior and subordinate to men. Thus, feminist bioethicists have a pressing need to address the protection and advancement of women's health interests; for unless women's basic health care needs are met, women will never be able to lead flourishing lives, including lives independent of men if they choose. This directly relates to economic concerns, for poverty negatively affects health through the impact of poor nutrition, crowded and unsanitary living conditions, inadequate medical care, and poor access to social resources and supports (Adler et al. 1999, 182–83). As Tong notes, this is not an easy task; it requires not simply medical intervention but further challenging and ultimately overturning core interpersonal and societal values and attitudes. Presently, in areas around the globe, many people in power care little about women's health needs. They outright endanger them, or they pervert them in their need to sexually control women (to make them either less or more sexually desirable). Even worse, they make females utterly dispensable through the practice of sex-selective abortion.

In learning how to care appropriately, we need to learn how to listen to all sorts of needy people with the goal of getting the facts right, for we cannot care appropriately if our desire to help is based on stereotypes, misinformation, or assumptions that others want to be just like us. We need to learn about the practices of diverse cultures, with the goal of understanding how such practices came about and how people view these practices and participate in them. As Sherwin recognizes, feminist bioethicists should accept a community's practices if they are the result of a truly democratic conversation among all segments of society; but they should reject them if they are the result of coercive, deceptive, exploitive, ignorant, or indifferent attitudes and behaviors (Sherwin 1992, 65). Caretakers need to demonstrate understanding and concern by showing interest and trying to find a connection across differences invoking shared activities such as motherhood and mothers' shared hope that their children will lead healthy, happy, flourishing lives.

Many practices that the U.S. government or well-meaning organizations impose on others or encourage others to model—or others model in virtue of the fact that the all-powerful United States does it—are not good, effective practices. In fact, some are actually outright harmful. To see this, let us briefly consider Chile's public health care system.

The Failure of Chilean Health Care Reform

The current health care system in Chile is an example of those in power (namely, the United States) providing a model of health care that does not work and has indeed been outright harmful to people. In 1973 a military coup, backed by then U.S. president Richard Nixon and national security advisor Henry Kissinger, overthrew the democratically elected Chilean government of Salvador Allende. Before the 1973 coup—and especially from 1952, when Chile's national health care system was introduced as part of that country's social security—Chile's medical system was studied around the world as a model example of equal access to health care services for all. However, with the coup came dramatic government cuts affecting all parts of Chile's social security, including health care, which was eventually privatized (Solowey 2002).

Chile modeled its health care system on the United States, a country that glorifies free-market thinking, competition, and free choice over community support and care, hoping that by fostering competition among health care providers in the medical marketplace, quality of care would go up and costs would go down.[3] Keeping health care costs down and improving quality of care are both worthy goals, but turning to the United States—a system that is grossly unjust and outright harmful to many, a system where more than forty million are uninsured and tens of millions more underinsured, where public health care is often underresourced and facing major cutbacks, and where the quality of care varies drastically according to ability to pay—proved harmful.

In an effort to liberalize health care, the Chilean government sharply reduced government and employer contributions to health care services, shifting the costs to users. By the mid-1990s, 7 percent of the gross pay of each employed person was withheld for health care. Chile now offers public and private health care options.

Employees choose where this 7 percent deduction will go. One option is to put money into a private health insurance plan, modeled on U.S. health insurance plans, offered by Instituto de Salud Previsional (ISAPRE), where employees make co-payments. Another option is to put money into the increasingly bankrupt public health care facilities (the remnants of the national health service, Sistema Nacional de Salud). Opening up a private health care market provides a variety of health care options at various prices and has improved the quality of care—but only for those Chileans who can afford the ISAPRE option. Though such an option is available to each person, the determining factor, as it is in the United States, is not choice but ability to pay. As a result, higher income Chileans have fled from the public system. Almost three-fourths of ISAPRE's clients are in the top 30 percent of Chileans by income; the public system consists largely of the Chilean poor. ISAPRE clients earn seven times that of the average public health system user. Chile's grossly underfunded, underresourced public health care system must meet the health care needs of 70 percent of Chileans as well as 100 percent of the country's public health costs, including environmental health, sanitation control, and occupational health safety needs. It is not uncommon for public hospital staff to ask patients' relatives to bring sheets, medicines, and other necessities from home because the hospitals lack the money, equipment, and facilities to meet even the patients' most basic medical and comfort needs. Patients or their relatives often need to sell furniture and other household goods to afford the most basic medicines. Excessive waiting periods at public clinics result in many patients using emergency care—a problem faced in the United States, resulting in the bankrupting of many hospitals, especially inner-city hospitals such as D.C. General.[4]

The current Chilean health care system is a good example of a developing country wanting to modernize, to improve in the image of the more powerful and presumably more successful U.S. model, but the unfortunate result is new problems of great disparity in quality of care between the rich (only 30 percent) and the poor (70 percent). In this example, those in power (namely, the United States) do not know better and do not provide the correct model for change. It is a moral mistake to presume that just because a solution comes from the United States, it is better. The market-driven Chilean health care system is now faced with new problems and challenges; it will be extremely difficult and costly—economically, socially, and politically—to fix these "improvements" modeled on Western experts.

Conclusion

What could the United States have done if my proposed support model had been in place, and what if anything should the United States do now? Whether the United States was morally justified in backing the 1973 military coup is one question; however, I think that the coup need not have resulted in remaking for the worse Chile's model egalitarian health care system into the U.S. image. This was an especially harmful mistake, since the gap between Chilean rich and poor is far greater than in the United States, and there is a far greater percentage of poor Chileans than poor Americans. The U.S. model—unjust in the United States—is even more unjust in a country such as Chile where so many desperately poor people live. But what can we do now to meet the needs of the Chilean people? Are Chile's current health care problems an important global health care concern to which those in power should turn their attention? I believe so, especially since the United States in large part helped create Chile's current situation. To remedy this state of affairs we need collaborative efforts between those in Chile who are committed to reform, such as my friend Guiliani, and Western feminist bioethicists. Furthermore, we must take part in international meetings, such as the conferences of the International Network on Feminist Approaches to Bioethics, committed to global understanding and change in health care, and the World Social Forum, committed to global social change and alternatives to social change other than imperialistic, Western (especially U.S.) domination. Finally, we need to support international medical humanitarian organizations such as Doctors Without Borders and Doctors of the World.

Notes

1. Laurence Thomas argues for the fragility of human moral lives in his work *Vessels of Evil: American Slavery and the Holocaust* (Temple University Press, 1993).

2. This section of the chapter was presented at the Fourth Conference of the International Network on Feminist Approaches to Bioethics, Brasília, Brazil, 2002.

3. The information in this section is drawn largely from Joseph Collins et al., *Chile's Free Market Miracle: A Second Look* (Oakland: Food First Books, 1995).

4. D.C. General was the Capital's only public, full-service hospital and the only hospital in the district that treated the majority of uninsured and underinsured residents (the poor and working classes) for free. Before closing, D.C. General, which served at least 40 percent of the district's population, faced massive cutbacks in budget, staffing, equipment, and services, resulting in six- to ten-hour waiting periods and not enough patient beds. The impact of the closing of D.C. General has been substantial. For example, gunshot victims who are shot a few blocks from D.C. General sometimes die en route to other, more distant hospitals, and there are now longer waiting periods, and poorer service, at these other hospitals.

References

Adler, Nancy E., Thomas Boyce, Margaret A. Chesney, Sheldon Cohen, Susan Folkman, Robert L. Kahn, and S. Leonard Syme. 1999. "Socioeconomic Status and Health: The

Challenge of the Gradient." In *Health and Human Rights*, edited by Jonathan M. Mann, Sofia Gruskin, Michael A. Grodin, and George J. Annas, 182–83. New York: Routledge.

Bullard, Robert. 2001. "Decision Making." In *Faces of Environmental Racism*, 2d ed., edited by Laura Westra, Bill E. Lawson, and Peter S. Wenz, 3–28. New York: Rowman & Littlefield.

Code, Lorraine. 1995. *Rhetorical Spaces: Essays on Gendered Locations*. New York: Routledge.

Cook, Rebecca. 1999. "Gender, Health, and Human Rights." In *Health and Human Rights*, edited by Jonathan M. Mann, Sofia Gruskin, Michael A. Grodin, and George J. Annas, 263. New York: Routledge.

Collins, Joseph, John Lear, Walden Bello, and Stephanie Rosenfeld. 1995. *Chile's Free Market Miracle: A Second Look*. Oakland: Food First Books.

Fox, Renee. 1999. "Medical Humanitarianism and Human Rights: Reflections on Doctors Without Borders and Doctors of the World." In *Health and Human Rights*, edited by Jonathan M. Mann, Sofia Gruskin, Michael A. Grodin, and George J. Annas, 417–35. New York: Routledge.

Held, Virginia. 1995. *Justice and Care*. Boulder, Colo.: Westview.

Hoffman, Martin L. 2000. *Empathy and Moral Development: Implications for Caring and Justice*. Cambridge, UK: Cambridge University Press.

Meister, Shirley Vogler. 1998. "Threads of Hope." In *At Our Core: Women Writing About Power*, edited by Sandra Martz, 160–61. Watsonville, Calif.: Papier Mache Press.

Mohanty, Chandra Talpade. 1991. "Under Western Eyes: Feminist Scholarship and Colonial Discourses." In *Third World Women and the Politics of Feminism*, edited by Chandra Talpade Mohanty, Ann Russo, and Lourdes Torres, 51–81. Bloomington: Indiana University Press.

Noddings, Nel. 1984. *Caring: A Feminist Approach to Ethics and Moral Education*. Berkeley: University of California Press.

Nussbaum, Martha. 2000. *Women and Human Development: The Capabilities Approach*. Cambridge, UK: Cambridge University Press.

Ruddick, Sara. 1995. *Maternal Thinking: Toward a Politics of Peace*. Boston: Beacon.

Sen, Amartya. 2000. *Development as Freedom*. New York: Oxford University Press.

Sherwin, Susan. 1992. *No Longer Patient: Feminist Ethics and Health Care*. Philadelphia: Temple University Press.

Solowey, Fred. 2002. "Chile's Privatized Social Security, Health Care, Is a Failure." *Revolution: The Journal for RNs and Patient Advocacy*, at www.revolutionmag.com.

Thomas, Laurence. 1993. *Vessels of Evil: American Slavery and the Holocaust*. Philadelphia: Temple University Press.

CONTEXTUALIZING REPRODUCTION: II
PARTICULAR PERSPECTIVES

Feminist Bioethics and Reproductive Rights of Women in India
Myth and Reality

7

K. SHANTHI

WOMEN'S ABILITY TO MANAGE their fertility is a crucial factor in women's emancipation. Although contraceptives have helped many women control their reproductive destinies and remain active in the workforce, they have also enabled both the state and health care institutions to intervene in women's private lives to serve public goals. The scope of reproductive and genetic technologies is vast, including both the old reproduction-controlling technologies (contraception, sterilization, and abortion) and the new reproduction-assisting technologies (artificial insemination, in vitro fertilization, and surrogate motherhood), as well as the new genetic technologies that facilitate sex selection and sex preselection. Because it is impossible to discuss all of these technologies in this chapter, I have decided to focus only on those reproductive technologies that prevent conception and those genetic technologies that aid in sex selection and sex preselection. These technologies are neither neutral nor value free. They can be used for good or evil purposes, for benefit or harm, and their dual nature is evident in many developing nations, particularly those without the legal means or will to regulate their use.

Although the new reproductive and genetic technologies tend to work in largely beneficial ways in developed nations, they often work in harmful ways in developing nations, particularly those nations characterized by unequal gender relations and by the subordination of women to men in the family and the workplace. For example, in India—where a social security system is almost absent—children are regarded as a safety net for one's old age, and boys are preferred over girls for cultural reasons; therefore, the societal pressure on women to produce as many children as possible and at least one boy[1] is quite intense. In such a context, the new reproductive and genetic technologies are not likely to benefit women, particularly poor women who aim to please those who have power over them by procreating a large number of the "right" kind of children. Thus, my overall thesis is that to the extent that women are economically disadvantaged, socially marginalized, and politically voiceless in a society, their reproductive rights will be constrained. Unless issues such as poverty, inequality, unemployment, and environmental degradation are addressed first, women's rights and human rights will remain abstract concepts. They will exist only on paper.

The Demographic Transition in India: An Overview

Although India covers only 2.4 percent of the world's land area, it supports 16 percent of the world's population. Numbering 345 million at the time of its independence from England (1947), the population of India grew to 846 million in 1991 and is expected to reach nearly 1.3 billion by 2016 (Government of India 1996). Many factors have contributed to India's steep population growth. The death rate for India as a whole has dropped from twenty-seven persons per 1,000 population in 1947 to nine persons per 1,000 population in 1995, and the infant mortality rate has declined from more than two hundred infants per 1,000 infants in 1947 to seventy-four per 1,000 in 1995. In addition, men's life expectancy has gone up from forty-two years in 1951 to sixty-one years in 1991, and women's life expectancy has risen from forty-one years to sixty-two years in the same period of time (Government of India 2000).

The only hopeful news about India's population size is that its growth rate seems to be slowing down in certain sections of India for reasons related to women's reproductive lives. The average birth rate has declined from forty per 1,000 in 1947 to twenty-eight per 1,000 in 1995. Moreover, as estimated by the Sample Registration System, the total fertility rate—the average number of children born to a woman during her reproductive span—has declined from six in 1947 to three in 1994 (Government of India 1998).

One reason Indian women are tending to have fewer children is that the rate of contraceptive use has risen from about 10 percent of reproductive-age women in 1971 to 40 percent in 1995. Indeed, as a result of the Indian government's family planning program, about 210 million births were prevented between 1947 and 1997 (Government of India 1998). Unfortunately, the average lower birth rate is distributed unequally across India's regions. Specifically, the actual birth rate varies from a low of 14.3 per 1,000 in Goa, 17.3 in Kerala, and 19.0 in Tamil Nadu and Nagaland, to a high of 35.4 in Uttar Pradesh, 33.7 in Rajasthan, 32.8 in Madhya Pradesh, and 32.5 in Bihar. The latter four North Indian states constitute 40 percent of the country's population; unless their population growth in terms of birth rate is controlled, it is unlikely that the annual population growth rate will decline enough to substantially benefit all Indians (United Nations Population Fund 1997).

Reflections on the Family Welfare Program in India

India's family planning program is the oldest government-sponsored fertility reduction program in the world.[2] Since its inception, the program has undergone several quantitative and qualitative changes. Until the late 1960s, the program existed to provide maternal and child care benefits to expectant mothers.[3] Fertility reduction was not among its main goals. But when India's growing population began to threaten its economic development, the thrust of the program changed. A target method was used between 1969 and 1974, with the aim of achieving a contraceptive prevalence rate of 60 percent and a net reproductive rate of one daughter per mother by the end of the fourth five-year plan (Government of India 1991). Under the target method, the job of a health care worker was to motivate, persuade, pressure, or induce a specific number of women to adopt permanent or temporary fertility control methods. Each health care worker was assigned annual, monthly, weekly, and in some cases daily target numbers. The health care workers were paid Rs. 50 (equivalent to one American dollar) for every woman who "chose" sterilization but were paid nothing for women who chose intrauterine devices (IUDs) or oral contraceptives. Because of this economic incentive, the health care workers tended to present sterilization as a better birth control option than IUDs or oral contraceptives. Moreover, the patients who came to family planning clinics were also offered incentives to choose sterilization. Patients who were sterilized received Rs. 160 (about three American dollars), but patients who chose other methods of birth control received no monetary compensation (Guha 1990; Singh 1990).

During the era of "targets," women were sterilized en masse at government-sponsored sterilization camps, makeshift facilities where teams of gynecologists performed one sterilization after another, in assembly-line fashion, all day long. Patient follow-up was not part of the "camp" experience. Women who developed infections and postoperative complications did not know where to seek much-needed follow-up health care (Guha 1990; Singh 1990). News of patient neglect and abuse started to circulate among the Indian population in general. Academics and the educated elite criticized the state's family planning program not only because of its failure to provide Indian women with a wide variety of birth control methods and general reproductive health care but also because of its uneven success (Government of India 2002). Although fertility rates were slowed down in some Indian states, they continued to explode in others. In addition, Indian activists and outsiders criticized the family planning program as unfairly targeting

poor women who were already weak due to malnutrition, overwork, repeated pregnancies, and inadequate rest. So pathetic was the plight of these women in particular that the Indian public took its shock out on Indira Gandhi's regime. In fact,
her regime was voted out of power largely because of the sterilization scandal.

Not wanting to suffer the fate of Indira Gandhi's administration, the Janata
Party decided to rethink the old family planning program, renaming it the family
welfare program and making family planning simply one part of women's (and
men's) health care. However, the old demographically driven goal of reducing the
birth rate and the population growth rate soon slipped back into the new program's agenda. "Achievements" were once again recorded in terms of sterilizations
performed, couple protection rates, and births averted (Government of India
1992). In relatively short order, the focus of the new program became population
reduction rather than holistic family health care.

Fortunately for Indian women, the present coalition government at the Center
(since no single party won the majority to form the government) has begun to replace the Janata Party's disingenuous family welfare program with a bona fide one.
Following the International Conference on Population and Development (ICPD)
held in Cairo in September 1994 (United Nations 1994), the government realized
it really had to change and improve its public reproductive health services. By insisting that "government goals for family planning should be defined in terms of
unmet needs for information and services" (United Nations 1994, 43–44), the
ICPD Program of Action changed the language, concept, and focus of population
policy in India. One of the most frequently made points in Cairo was that reproductive health is a state of complete physical, mental, and social well-being and not
merely the absence of reproductive disease. In order to flourish as full human beings, women need access to safe contraceptives and appropriate health care services
as well as the freedom to determine when to have sex and to procreate. Women need
others' help to protect themselves from sexually transmitted diseases (including
HIV/AIDS), to time and space their children, and to deal with the bodily discomforts that sometimes accompany natural processes such as pregnancy, breastfeeding, menstruation, menopause, and so forth (Ramachandran 1999).

In addition to linking reproductive health to a sense of physical and psychological well-being, the Cairo conference also stressed the importance of women
themselves contributing to the development of family planning policies. As a result of women-focused, grassroots discussions about new and improved ways to
handle family planning in India, the Indian government launched the externally
aided Reproductive and Child Health Project (RCH) in October 1997. At the
policy level, the government asked Indian states to gradually eliminate incentive
payments for sterilizations and to use their limited public resources to bolster existing reproductive health care services, filling in the gaps with private monies and

services. Moreover, at the delivery level, the government asked Indian states to provide the new reproductive and child health services at the local rather than state level and to keep them client-focused (Visaria and Visaria 1999; Government of India 1997).

Regrettably, circumstances have prevented the Indian government from keeping all of its promises about a new era of reproductive and child health care services. Among these circumstances is a predictable lack of financial resources and skilled medical personnel to deliver high-quality services. Particularly worrisome is the fact that some of the local program managers are not only relatively unskilled but also uncommitted to the objectives of the new program. Far from being vested in the cause of women's and children's health, these particular government workers view their jobs as just a job and not a very interesting one at that. To the extent that local program managers are mediocre or unmotivated, women are not likely to receive the information and counseling as well as medications and devices they need to maintain and control their reproductive well-being. Furthermore, men are not likely to use condoms, let alone care about women's reproductive rights, including their right to time their pregnancies so that they are safe (Visaria 1999).

Invasive Contraceptive Technologies

A survey of the contraceptives promoted by the Indian government over the years clearly indicates a gradual shift from simple contraceptive methods such as diaphragms and jellies, which women can insert themselves, to complex contraceptive methods such as intrauterine devices (IUDs), Depo-Provera, and Norplant, each of which requires the assistance of health care professionals. Specifically, IUDs must be inserted and removed properly by a health care professional to avoid significant harm to the woman's uterus. Depo-Provera, a hormonal drug that lasts at least three months, must be given by injection, and Norplant, another hormonal drug that lasts approximately five years, must be implanted under the skin.

Although a small number of Indian women have expressed dissatisfaction about the side effects of IUDs, a far larger number of Indian women have voiced complaints about Depo-Provera's and Norplant's serious side effects, including heavy and irregular menstrual bleeding, headaches, vomiting, dizziness, and nervousness. Furthermore, because Norplant in particular requires personal hygiene of a high order, good sanitation, the availability of clean water, and accessible medical facilities for safe insertion and removal (Mukherjee 1999; Ravindran and Rao 1997), it is likely to pose considerable health risks to women in a country such as India, where only 14.7 percent of rural women and 48.7 percent of urban women have access to medical institutions (Government of India 1991) and where the temptation for self-removal of Norplant is high.

In many Western nations, health care is largely financed through the public or private sectors. The private sector in these nations is tightly regulated not only by government authorities but also by private insurance companies who make third-party payments. In contrast, in India only 25 percent of health care is financed from sources other than individuals' own pockets (World Bank 1996). Given that most Indians must subsidize their own health care, it is not surprising that many Indians, particularly Indian women, are prone to purchase relatively inexpensive contraceptives that have been abandoned by Western nations because of their possibly harmful side effects. Realizing that their patients cannot afford the best contraceptives that money can buy, Indian doctors push cheap, unregulated Western "leftovers" on them. Worse, many Indian doctors fail to inform their patients that by using these contraceptives they put their health at risk.

The Thorny Issue of Abortion

Given the costs and side effects of contraception and the inadequate health services available to most Indian women, access to safe and inexpensive abortion is of great concern to many Indian women. Although the Medical Termination of Pregnancy Act (Abortion Law) was passed in 1971, the Indian government has yet to make the abortion procedure available to all the women who need or want it. The Abortion Law permits abortion within the first twelve weeks of pregnancy, and in exceptional cases, up to sixteen weeks (provided two physicians agree that the abortion is medically necessary). Because government hospitals refuse to terminate pregnancies after twelve weeks, women seeking terminations in their second (or third) trimesters must use private practitioners who generally charge steep prices for their services. In rural areas, private practitioners are few, and hence late abortions are invariably performed by untrained traditional health providers under unhygienic conditions. Abortions performed by untrained quacks under unsafe conditions during late stages of pregnancy are deemed illegal. Since the incidence of anemia is very high among economically poor women, the government has advised women not to seek late abortions, particularly abortions performed by unskilled persons. Yet it is precisely the government's failure to provide safe legal abortions on a mass scale, as well as its failure to meet the demand for contraceptives, that puts poor Indian women in the hands of untrained traditional health providers.

In India, illegal abortions probably outnumber legal abortions by a ratio as high as eleven to one, for a number of reasons. These include the late recognition of some pregnancies, the negative attitude of many health care professionals toward women seeking abortions, the cultural shame associated with illegitimate motherhood, poor or inadequate service in the public hospitals, and the high cost of legal abortions in the private sector. Sadly, unsafe illegal abortions account for about one quarter of the estimated 100,000 maternal deaths that occur in India annually (Ford Foundation 1997). According to a 1993 survey on the leading causes of death among Indian women of reproductive age, 20 percent die due to complications associated with abortion, 40 percent die due to anemia, 20 percent die due to malposition of the fetus, and 20 percent die due to nonclassifiable factors (Directorate of Public Health and Preventive Medicine 1997).

Population and Sexual Health Education in India

Indian girls and women not only have limited access to appropriate contraception and abortion services, but they also have inadequate access to appropriate population education, family-life education, and especially sex education. The gravity of the problem is evident in the increase in rape of girls under ten years of age (84 percent between 1990 and 1994) (*Health for the Millions* 1998). In addition, the failure of parents and social institutions to provide children with adequate information on sexuality and reproduction leaves young girls and boys at high risk of contracting sexually transmitted diseases such as HIV/AIDS. Survey results at the international level indicate that young people in developing as well as developed nations are increasingly likely to be sexually active outside the marriage bond as a result of economic conditions, peer pressure, mass media influences, migration, and other social changes (Hawkins and Meshesha 1994). And yet in India, contraceptives are denied to young unmarried women and, as noted previously, legal abortion services are difficult to obtain. Hence, young unmarried pregnant women often attempt to self-abort or try to secure an illegal abortion, imperiling their lives. In such a context, the need to work with India's youth to avoid human tragedies related to sex and reproduction cannot be overemphasized.

Misuse of Prenatal Reproductive Technologies and Women's Health

Among women in the Indian middle and wealthier classes, ethical concern shifts from control of pregnancy and sex education to the use and misuse of medical technologies to ensure a "wanted" child. Prenatal diagnostic tests such as ultrasonography, amniocentesis, chorionic villus sampling, fetoscopy, maternal serum testing, and so on are intended to detect serious fetal abnormalities and to prevent the birth of children with major disabilities. But in a country such as India where sons are preferred over daughters, these tests are often used for the purpose of sex selection. Indeed, a significant number of Indians actually think these tests were designed solely for the purpose of sex selection. Of one thousand abortions performed subsequent to amniocentesis, 97 percent of the fetuses were female (Network on Reproductive Rights 1998). Other more recent developments include the relatively wide use of infertility clinics that provide sex preselection techniques[4] and even promise to provide couples with the baby of their "choice" (meaning a male infant).

Given these facts, the educated public and women's groups persuaded the Union government to pass the Regulation and Prevention of Misuse of Diagnostic Techniques Act of 1994, which bans sex selection and sex preselection. However, in a country where the rural population is scattered over 600,000 villages, it is relatively easy for people to escape the grip of the law. Contributing to the problem is the fact that health care professionals as well as many patients are motivated, albeit for different reasons, to defy the law or to interpret it in ways that suit their own interests. For example, because the law does not require the registration of medical equipment that can diagnose other conditions in addition to sex selection, many health care professionals are able to use the equipment for sex selection whenever they think they can escape the scrutiny of the government. Moreover, the removal of import duties has facilitated the purchase of "sex-determination machines." Virtually any private or public clinic can afford one, and health care professionals can make a great deal of money performing illegal sex-determination tests. Thus, it is not surprising that after some initial successes (the 2001 sex ratio in India was 933 females per 1,000 males, an improvement over the 1991 sex ratio of 927 females per 1,000 males), the 1994 legislation seems to be weakening.[5] India's sex ratio continues to compare unfavorably with the global sex ratio (excluding South Asia), which is 106 females for every 100 males (Mahbus 2000).

The issues at stake in the misuse of prenatal screening technologies are demographic, social, cultural, political, and above all ethical. The arguments put forth in favor of sex selection are not only ethically flawed but also factually mistaken. They include the following two points: (1) if fewer girls are born, the number of future mothers will be reduced, and the population size will automatically decrease; and (2) as women become scarcer in number, their status and desirability will increase.

Those who favor sex selection fail to realize that if a society seeks to reduce its population size primarily by targeting girl babies for death in the womb, it is not a civil let alone democratic society. Rather, it is a society for which an end justifies some very morally dubious means. Moreover, making women a scarce commodity will not necessarily increase women's status. On the contrary, it may reduce women's status, as men become frenzied in their search for a woman they can call their own. If women become relatively few in number, rape, kidnapping, forced polyandry, and even female slavery may become the order of the day, posing threats to the safety and security of all women, but particularly widows and deserted or unmarried women. The law of supply and demand will operate in the marriage market to find equilibrium, and in the process of achieving this equilibrium many women will be humiliated, threatened, and even killed. Women will become an "endangered species" subject to violence.

Among other reasons to oppose overuse or misuse of prenatal tests for purposes of sex selection include the following:

1. It is not justifiable to terminate a pregnancy simply on the basis of the sex of the fetus.
2. Some prenatal tests and medical technologies may cause fetal deformity or even death.
3. Using prenatal medical technologies simply to satisfy the dictates and preferences of a largely patriarchal society may undermine women's interests and desires.
4. Prenatal medical technologies may be used to serve "genocidal" causes such as the elimination of a particular caste or minority ethnic group. (Balasubramanyam 1986; Mies 1987)

Feminist Concerns Regarding Population Control Policies

The current situation in India concerning population control policies needs to be understood in the context of global feminist action. Throughout the world, women's organizations have been waging an ongoing war against antiwomen population control policies. In general, these groups have insisted that women be given greater control over their own reproductive decisions and that their bodies not be invaded and violated simply to serve their nation's need for a certain population size. They have also asked that women be provided with the means to protect themselves against sexually transmitted diseases and the kind of contraceptives over which they have the greatest control. Finally, women's organizations have lobbied for greater male involvement in family planning (provided that the involvement is supportive of women's goals as well as men's) and, most important, a reduction in the power imbalance between men and women in the home and in the workplace (Bruce et al. 1995).

In India, women's groups have been particularly active in their struggle to change India's family planning policies, which have a tendency to degenerate into mere population control policies irrespective of the women-friendly rhetoric masking their fundamental intent (Ramachandran 1999; Pachauri 1997; Patel 1994). Admittedly, some women have given up in frustration along the way, feeling they cannot effect real change. Nonetheless, most have continued to protest the government's neglect of women's overall health interests and its attempts to deprive women of meaningful reproductive choices. As I have noted throughout this chapter, Indian women's groups have repeatedly urged that women be given access to the widest range of safe and affordable means of birth control available and that they be given a real choice about the means used to control their fertility. In addition, Indian women's groups have continually reminded government authorities that reproductive health is not only about controlling women's fertility but also about contributing to women's health status and their ability to enjoy the positive features of human reproduction and sexuality (Banerji 2000). Undernourished and overworked women cannot be expected to give birth to healthy children; and physically and psychologically abused women cannot be expected to view their bodies as anything more than objects for others to use.

Obstacles Preventing a Full Realization of Reproductive Rights

Like the majority of women in other parts of the world, most especially in developing nations, Indian women sometimes face seemingly insurmountable obstacles in the realization of their reproductive rights. Gender, poverty, and culture interact very closely and create multiple barriers to the well-being of women (Petchesky 2000). For example, because the majority of Indian girls marry at a very young age, about 10 percent of girls become mothers before their skeletal and reproductive systems are fully developed, and 43 percent of all deaths of girls between the ages of fifteen and twenty are due to complications associated with pregnancy. Moreover, because Indian girls are less well fed and taken care of than Indian boys, about 50 to 80 percent of mothers suffer from anemia (Shiva 1991), and women's overall health status leaves much to be desired. Regrettably, this state of affairs is likely to persist unless India can overcome son preference and a tradition that permits parents (particularly fathers) to make marriage decisions for daughters, and husbands and mothers-in-law to make reproductive decisions for wives and daughters-in-law who are often mere children themselves.

Fortunately, as a result of initiatives such as the 1994 United Nations Third International Conference on Population and Development (ICPD) in Cairo, feminists are helping women throughout the world gain the strength to take control over their own lives, beginning with control over their bodies' reproductive capacities. Realizing that there is no way for India to ignore its population problem, many Indian feminists are trying to develop population policies that give Indian women as much reproductive choice as is possible in the context of a nation that must stabilize its population if it is to thrive economically, politically, and socially (Berer 1991). As Indian feminists see it, respecting women's procreative rights and reducing the size of the world's population are values that can be reconciled. Indeed, even if it is difficult to say no to sex and motherhood in a country such as India where women are valued largely because of what their bodies can do for others, it is actually best not only for Indian women but also for India itself that women procreate less. If the majority of Indian women simultaneously decided to bear only one or two children and refused to abort their female fetuses, the power of the "son" would be diminished.

Conclusion

To be sure, it will not be easy for Indian women to gain enough courage to say no to these ancient traditions, some of which are held as fiercely by women as by men largely because they do not require women to compulsorily share the economic burden of the household by working in the public sphere. Nevertheless, the question for Indian women to ask themselves is the question women everywhere must ask themselves: are the sufferings and pains I have experienced throughout my life ones I wish to pass on to my daughter or do I hope, through my efforts, however small, to give my daughter a future better than my present? The fight for human rights—one's children's rights—is a fierce one; but the self-determination, autonomy, integrity, and self-respect it provides are well worth the wounds.

Notes

1. In the Indian cultural context, a boy is desired for two reasons: to perform the last funeral rites for the redemption of the souls of parents and to provide life support during parents' old age. Girls are not desired since they are considered liabilities in view of the huge dowry (bride price) to be paid at the time of their marriage.

2. While fertility regulation includes all factors such as family planning, abortion, delayed marriage, and breastfeeding, family planning is normally defined as prevention of unwanted pregnancy, information about the importance of spacing between births, reduction in total fertility rate, and services for infertile couples. But the last is never taken seriously. The success of a family planning program is often measured by the number of acceptors of contraceptives, the number of sterilizations performed, and the contraceptive prevalence rate. See Simone Appelman and Fenneke Reysoo, "Everything You Always Wanted to Know: Lexicon and Comments on the New Population Concepts from a Gender Perspective," in New Reproductive Technologies, Women's Health and Autonomy, ed. Gupta Jyotsna Agnihotri (New Delhi: Sage Publications, 1994), 143–44.

3. During this period, women were treated as objects of development rather than subjects of development. The government of India's paradigm shifts from women's welfare to women's development and, finally, to women's empowerment is in tune with changing ideological debates on women's development in the international context.

4. The Ericsson method of sex selection involves the separation of X and Y chromosomes in the sperm. Sperm are placed in a glass column filled with a dense liquid protein (albumin)

in which sperm with the Y chromosome (related to the conception of a boy) have greater mo-
bility. Given this advantage, the Y-bearing sperm tend to swim faster to reach the bottom and
can be separated from the X-bearing sperm. The process is repeated several times until there
is a 75 to 80 percent concentration of Y-bearing sperm. These concentrated sperm are introduced into the cervix so that in contrast to the normal probability of 51.5 percent, the probability of male progeny is increased to 70 to 80 percent. See Voluntary Health Association of
India, "Women and Medical Technology," *State of India's Health* 17 (1992).

5. In the zero to six years age group, the 2001 sex ratio was 927 females per 1,000
males, whereas it had been 945 females per 1,000 males in 1991.

References

Appelman, Simone, and Fenneke Reysoo. 1994. "Everything You Always Wanted to
    Know: Lexicon and Comments on the New Population Concepts from a Gender Per-
    spective." In *New Reproductive Technologies, Women's Health and Autonomy: Freedom or Dependency?*
    edited by Jyotsna Agnihotri Gupta, 143–44. New Delhi: Sage Publication.
Balasubramanyam, Vimala. 1986. *The Contraceptive: As if Women Mattered—A Critique of Family
    Planning*. Bombay: Center for Educational Documentation.
Banerji, Debabar. 2000. "Decaying Health Services and Increasing Sufferings of the
    Voiceless." *Health for the Millions, New Delhi* (January/February): 30–34.
Berer, Marge. 1991. "What Would a Feminist Population Policy Be Like?" *Conscience* 12,
    no. 5.
Bruce, Judith, Cynthia B. Lloyd, Ann Leonard, Patrice L. Engle, and Niev Duffy. 1995.
    Families in Focus: New Perspectives on Mothers, Fathers and Children. New York: The Population
    Council.
Directorate of Public Health and Preventive Medicine. 1997. *Gender and Health: A Handbook
    for Health Workers*. Government of Tamil Nadu Chennai.
Ford Foundation. 1997. "Legal but Still Unsafe: The Complexity of Abortion in India."
    Ford Foundation Bulletin (Autumn/Winter): 9–12.
Government of India. 1991. "Family Planning Programs in India." In *Year Book 1989–90*,
    238–40. New Delhi: Ministry of Health and Family Welfare.
———. 1992. "Action Plan for Revamping the Family Welfare Programme in India." New
    Delhi: Ministry of Health and Family Welfare.
———. 1996. "Report of the Technical Group on Population Projections." In *The Indian Econ-
    omy*, edited by Dutt Ruddar and K. P. M. Sundaram, 71. New Delhi: S. Chand and Co.
———. 1997. "The Approach Paper to the Ninth Five-Year Plan (1997–2002)." New
    Delhi: Planning Commission.
———. 1998. *India: National Family Planning Program: Achievements and Challenges*. New Delhi:
    Department of Family Welfare.
———. 2000. "Statement from the Secretary of the Department of Women and Child
    Development, Ministry of Human Resource Development at the Twenty-Second Ses-
    sion of CEDAW." Paper presented on the occasion of hearing Indian women and chil-
    dren's progress under CEDAW, New York, January 24–30.

————. 2002. "Ninth Five-Year Plan 1997–2002." New Delhi: Planning Commission.

Guha, A. 1990. "Population Programs: The National Scene." In *Corporate Sector and Family Welfare Problems in India*, edited by B. Sengupta, A. Guha, and P. P. Talwar, 19–23. Delhi: Council of Indian Employers.

Hawkins, Kirstan, and Bayeligue Meshesha. 1994. "Reaching Young People: Ingredients of Effective Programs." In *Population Policies Reconsidered: Health Empowerment and Rights*, edited by Sen Gita, Adrienne Germain, and Lincoln C. Chen, 141–48. Cambridge, Mass.: International Women's Health Coalition and Harvard Centre for Population and Development Studies.

Health for the Millions, New Delhi. 1998. 24, no. 1 (January/February): 1.

Mahbus, Ul Haq. 2000. *Human Development in South Asia 2000: The Gender Question*. London: Oxford University Press.

Mies, Maria. 1987. "Sexist and Racist Implications of New Reproductive Technologies." *Alternatives* 12: 323–42.

Mukherjee, Vanita Nayak. 1999. "Gender Dimension of Basic Needs: Women's Access to Menstrual Hygiene and Reproductive Tract Infections." Chicago: MacArthur Foundation Fellowship for Population Innovation.

Network on Reproductive Rights. 1998. "Amniocentesis for Sex Determination Banned in Maharashtra." *Women's Global Network for Reproductive Rights* 23: 134–35.

Pachauri, Saroj. 1997. "Need to Promote Women's Sexual and Reproductive Rights." *The Business Age* 16: 14–16.

Patel, Vibhuti. 1994. "Indian Women's Struggle to Survive: Campaign against Femicide." *The Child and the Law* 16: 16–19.

Petchesky, Rosalind P. 2000. "Human Rights, Reproductive Health and Economic Justice: Why They Are Indivisible." *Reproductive Health Matters* 8, no. 15: 12.

Ramachandran, Vimala. 1999. "Shying Away from Sexuality: Government Reproductive Health Program." *Voices* 3, no. 1: 19–21.

Ravindran, Sundari T. K., and Sumathy S. Rao. 1997. "Is the Diaphragm a Suitable Method of Contraception for Low-Income Women: A User Perspectives Study." In *Beyond Acceptability: User's Perspectives on Contraception*, edited by T. K. Sundari Ravindran, Marge Berer, and Jane Cottingham, 78–88. London: Reproductive Health Matters.

Shiva, Mira. 1991. "Of Human Rights and Women's Health." *Health for the Millions, New Delhi* (June): 34–36.

Singh, H. 1990. "India's High Fertility Despite Family Planning: An Appraisal." In *Population Policy: Contemporary Issues*, edited by Godfrey Roberts, 91–98. New York: Praeger.

United Nations. 1994. *Report of the International Conference on Population and Development*. UN Doc A/Con/171/13, 43–44.

United Nations Population Fund. 1997. *India: Towards Population and Development Goals*. UNPFA: Oxford University Press.

Visaria, Leela. 1999. "Delivering Reproductive Health Services: Innovations and Challenges." Paper presented at the Futures Group International Panel, The Hague Forum for the ICPD +5 Review Health Watch, February 8.

Visaria, Leela, and Pravin Visaria. 1999. "India: Case Study." In *Reproductive Health in Policy and Practice: Case Studies from Brazil, India, Morocco,* and *Uganda,* 27–28. New York: Population Reference Bureau.

Voluntary Health Association of India. 1992. "Women and Medical Technology." *State of India's Health* 17.

World Bank. 1996. "Development in Practice: Improving Women's Health in India." May.

Globalizing Reproductive Control   8
Consequences of the "Global Gag Rule"

KAREN L. BAIRD

THE "GLOBAL GAG RULE" disqualifies foreign nongovernmental organizations (NGOs) from receiving U.S. family planning funds if they provide counseling on abortion, offer abortion services, or participate in political abortion debate in their own country. First articulated by former president Ronald Reagan in 1984 at the United Nations International Conference on Population in Mexico City (the Mexico City Policy), the global gag rule remained in effect until 1993, when President Bill Clinton rescinded it. In 2001, newly elected president George W. Bush reincarnated the policy in its current form. Critics contend that Bush's version of the global gag rule is a "cruel, extremist policy" that has resulted in "more unintended pregnancies, more unsafe abortions, and more maternal and child deaths" than before its promulgation (Reproductive Health Matters 2001, 206). In my estimation, the critics are right. If any rule violates established human rights for women, it is the global gag rule, or so I argue in this chapter.

First, I outline the history of the global gag rule, discussing its complex meaning and the politics surrounding its imposition and repeal. In this connection, I highlight U.S. requirements for funding family planning programs. To demonstrate the policy's consequences, I include data about abortion laws, abortion statistics, consequences of unintended pregnancy, and maternal mortality. Next, I analyze how the global gag rule affects the funding, services, and programs of various NGOs and undermines established human rights principles. Finally, I discuss the overall implications of the policy for women's reproductive health, maternal mortality, and the provision of family planning services.

The Global Gag Rule

In 1973, the U.S. Congress passed the Helms Amendment prohibiting the use of U.S. funds to pay directly for abortion services within family planning programs. This law has been in effect continuously since that time. At the 1984 International Conference on Population in Mexico City, then-president Ronald Reagan introduced further restrictions on the use of U.S. funds for abortion services. The so-called Mexico City Policy, a predecessor to the current global gag rule, states that the U.S. Agency for International Development (USAID) will not fund any non-U.S. organizations that provide abortion services or promote abortion as a method of family planning, even if such activities are undertaken with non-U.S. funds.

When President Bill Clinton, a Democrat and supporter of women's rights, came into office in January 1993, he promptly rescinded the Mexico City Policy. After the 1994 Congressional elections when the U.S. Congress returned to Republican control, however, abortion opponents immediately sought to reestablish funding restrictions on abortion services provided outside U.S. boundaries. To reinstate the Mexico City Policy, they tacked on amendments to appropriations bills withholding funds to the United Nations (UN). Clinton vetoed their first attempt in 1998, but in 1999 he was forced to sign another version of the bill so the United States would not lose voting rights in the UN General Assembly. At that point, the U.S. owed almost $1 billion in unpaid UN dues (Cohen 2000) and needed to show some movement in the direction of reducing this debt. Clinton vowed that the restrictive policy would only be in effect for the fiscal year 2000. He kept his promise, but release of the 2001 appropriations for USAID family planning funds was delayed until February 2001, permitting the newly elected president, George W. Bush, to institute new restrictions on abortion services (Center for Reproductive Law and Policy [CRLP] 2001).

On January 22, 2001, Bush issued an executive order announcing the current global gag rule. The order forbids foreign NGOs from receiving funds from USAID if they "perform or actively promote abortion as a method of family planning or provide financial support to any other foreign nongovernmental organization that conducts such activities."[1] Included in the prohibition are bans on counseling that offer information about abortion (except when the woman's life is endangered or she is a victim of rape or incest) and bans on lobbying foreign governments to legalize or to sustain legalization of abortion (U.S. White House Memorandum 2001; CRLP 2001). Not only are NGOs prohibited from using U.S. funds to engage in such activities, but they are also prohibited from using *any* funds to support such enterprises.

NGOs that wish to accept USAID funds must sign a statement agreeing to the restrictions as part of any new grant or cooperative agreement issued after

February 15, 2001. For existing contracts, the restrictions come into force when the contract is up for renewal or when additional funds for family planning are requested. The restrictions apply only to foreign NGOs and not to foreign governments. If a foreign government engages in the prohibited activities, it must keep U.S. funds separate and be able to show that the U.S. funds are not being used for the restricted activities.

However, NGOs may use any and all funds to treat injuries and illnesses caused by legal or illegal abortions. In addition, they may use these funds to engage in anti-abortion activities (U.S. White House Memorandum 2001; Population Action International 2001). If an NGO wants to speak in favor of women not terminating their pregnancies, it may do so loudly. U.S. authorities will not try to muffle its voice.

International Family Planning and Reproductive Health Programs and Policies

Family planning policies and their predecessor "population policies" are guided by international conferences and organizations and are implemented through governments and international organizations such as the UN Population Fund (UNFPA), the World Health Organization (WHO), and the World Bank. The U.S. government provides the largest amount of money for international family planning, primarily through USAID. Fiscal year 2002 appropriations were $425 million. About half of the money goes to foreign governments and agencies such as the UNFPA; the other half, more than $200 million, funds NGOs (Hwang 2002).

The International Conference on Population and Development (ICPD) held in Cairo in 1994 marked a significant departure in world population policies. Prior to this, family planning policies created at the 1974 conference in Bucharest and the 1984 conference in Mexico City focused on targeted population growth decline or fertility reduction. The slow economic development of many countries was attributed primarily to rapid demographic growth. Accordingly, family planning became a focus of many international development programs, and reduction in birth rates became a leading policy goal. Other important factors such as mortality rates, various other health indicators, human rights, women's status, and education were ignored (Mundigo 2000).

In 1994 at the ICPD at Cairo, a program of action was developed and recognized by more than 180 countries (UN 1994). A new emphasis was placed on the advancement of women, social development extending beyond family planning, and the provision of family planning and contraception within a larger context of reproductive health care for women. This expanded framework included safe pregnancy and delivery, abortion where legal, prevention and treatment of sexually transmitted infections (including HIV/AIDS), and counseling on sexuality. In sum, the new population policies emphasized protection and enhancement of women's reproductive rights (Ashford 2001). Human development became the focus of family planning and the means to curb population growth.

Two other related changes helped effect this transformation in family planning philosophy. First, a growing body of data gathered in many countries showed that a reduction in childbirth correlated with an increase in the relative status of women (Barroso and Jacobson 2000). Second, international women's rights activists emphasized the unequal power relations between men and women and the need to apply fundamental human rights specifically to the conditions of women's lives. At the 1993 UN World Conference on Human Rights in Vienna, women argued that it was no longer sufficient to merely extend existing human rights mechanisms to women; rather, so-called women's rights had to be understood as human rights (Peters and Wolper 1995, 3). Activists pushed the need for women to have greater control over their sexuality and reproduction as an important component of women's rights. They argued that the most important human right is the right to control one's body (Peters and Wolper 1995, 8). Such claims were reiterated at several international meetings, such as the fourth World Conference on Women in 1995 in Beijing, and in documents such as the Convention on the Elimination of All Forms of Discrimination against Women of 1979 and the Declaration on the Elimination of Violence against Women of 1993.[2] Thus, it is not surprising that following the 1994 ICPD meeting in Cairo, the global policy discourse regarding women's rights, social development, and family planning was radically altered. Family planning policies are now more fully conceptualized as reproductive health policies, and reproductive health is defined as a human right.

International Abortion Laws

In most African countries, abortion is either illegal or available only under limited circumstances (see table 8.1). The exception is South Africa, which legalized abortion in 1996. In eighteen of the fifty-nine countries listed, abortion is legal under all circumstances or in cases of rape or fetal impairment. In nineteen countries, abortion is legal under very limited circumstances, such as to protect a woman's health or life; in twenty-two countries it is illegal. This information is important because the implications of the global gag rule differ depending on the status of a country's abortion laws. Where abortion is legal, the rule does not allow NGOs to discuss the option of a procedure that is legal within its own national boundaries. In countries where advocates are fighting to have abortion legalized, NGOs cannot participate in legal advocacy efforts. Such restrictions indirectly affect women's

Table 8.1.   Abortion Laws in Countries with NGOs That Receive USAID Funds

Abortion Is Legal	Abortion Is Legal under Limited Circumstances	Abortion Is Illegal[a]
Albania	Bolivia	Bangladesh
Armenia	Botswana	Benin
Azerbaijan	Burkina Faso	Ivory Coast
Cambodia	Cameroon	Dominican Republic
Georgia	Ecuador	Egypt
India	Eritrea	El Salvador
Kazakhstan	Ethiopia	Guatemala
Kyrgyz Republic	Ghana	Haiti
Moldova	Guinea	Honduras
Nepal	Jamaica	Indonesia
Romania	Jordan	Kenya
Russia	Liberia	Madagascar
South Africa	Mali	Malawi
Tajikistan	Morocco	Nicaragua
Turkey	Mozambique	Nigeria
Turkmenistan	Peru	Paraguay
Ukraine	Rwanda	Philippines
Uzbekistan	Zambia	Senegal
	Zimbabwe	Tanzania
		Togo
		Uganda
		Yemen

Source: Center for Reproductive Law and Policy (CRLP) 2002, with updates by author.
[a] Some of these countries may permit abortion when the mother's life is endangered.

health. Many studies show that illegal abortions are a large source of maternal mortality and morbidity. In addition, unintended pregnancies that are carried to term impose heavy burdens and risks on women, which I discuss in the next section.

Abortion, Unintended Pregnancy, and Maternal Mortality

Grave consequences follow for women forced to maintain unintended pregnancies. Pregnancy-related complications are a major source of disability and death among women in developing countries. Women suffer infections, ruptures of the uterus, pelvic inflammatory disease, vaginal tearing, damage to the reproductive tract, and obstetric fistula (a muscular tear that allows urine or feces to seep into the vagina). Many suffer from incontinence and infertility if repairable damages are not corrected (Global Health Council 2002, 19).

More than 500,000 women die from pregnancy-related causes each year, most in less-developed countries. The Global Health Council estimates that from 1995 to 2000, nearly 700,000 women died from unintended pregnancies; this is about 20 percent of all maternal deaths (Global Health Council 2002). A mother's death has profound consequences for her family. In some countries, her death increases the risk of death for her children younger than five by as much as 50 percent (World Bank 1993).

Many women who have unintended pregnancies undergo unsafe abortions. WHO estimates that each year about 13 percent of maternal deaths result from abortion complications (World Health Organization 1998). These complications and deaths generally arise from unsafe abortions, usually where the procedure is illegal or inaccessible. The Global Health Council estimates unsafe abortion accounts for 64 percent of the women who die from unintended pregnancies (Global Health Council 2002). The highest number of abortion deaths occurs in Africa where approximately 70 percent of unintended pregnancies are aborted, despite prohibitions against abortion in most African countries (Global Health Council 2002, 15).

These data show that the global gag rule, because it limits an organization's ability to provide information about abortion, contributes to the impact of unintended pregnancy on women, especially in the developing world. The problem of unsafe abortion is vital to women's health. Even where abortion is illegal, many women who do not obtain adequate information about the procedure will still attempt to end an unwanted pregnancy—at great risk to their health and life.

International Family Planning Organizations and the Effects of the Global Gag Rule

Most of the NGOs I discuss in this chapter rejected U.S. funding because of US-AID limitations on abortion services, though there are exceptions.[3] International Planned Parenthood Federation (IPPF), the world's largest reproductive health organization, works with more than 150 family planning organizations in 180 countries worldwide. They report that the global gag rule has cost them $18 million (Salter 2003). They are also threatened with the loss of more than $75 million in joint partnership funding over the next four to eight years (Salter 2003). Fortunately, the European Union has agreed to help them cope with the consequences of the withdrawal of U.S. funding (International Planned Parenthood 2002a).

The Family Planning Association of Kenya (FPAK) is a volunteer-based NGO that has pioneered the family planning movement in Kenya, operating as many as fourteen health clinics serving low-income women. Founded in 1962, FPAK is committed to gender equality and equal rights. It promotes the empowerment of young people and sexual and reproductive health within the context of reproductive rights (International Planned Parenthood 2003). In 2003, FPAK was granted the United Nations Population Award for making an outstanding contribution to increasing the awareness of population problems and their solutions (International Planned Parenthood 2003). It formerly received more than half a million dollars per year from USAID. As a result of the global gag rule, FPAK lost 20 percent of its funding and was forced to close three clinics and cut staff so radically that about 5,600 clients—mainly women of reproductive age—were denied services.

Marie Stopes International (MSI) is an international organization that "provides sexual and reproductive health information and services to 3.3 million people in thirty-eight countries including Africa, Asia, Australia, Europe, Latin America, and the Middle East" (Marie Stopes International 2003). Since MSI openly advocates legal and safe abortions, it also lost USAID funds. Specifically, U.S. "policy has resulted in the loss of more than three million dollars to the MSI Partners in Africa, leading to the closure of three centers in Kenya, an outreach program servicing poor communities in Ethiopia and further centers in Tanzania" (Marie Stopes International 2003).

Movimiento Manuela Ramos (MMR) is a women's health NGO in Peru that chooses to receive funds from USAID. Peru has the second highest maternal mortality rate in South America, and abortion is illegal within its boundaries. The president of MMR, Susana Galdos Silva, testified before the U.S. Congress in 2001 that an estimated 60 percent of pregnancies in Peru are unwanted and about 30 percent end in abortion. Every year 65,000 Peruvian women are harmed to the point of requiring hospitalization due to complications from unsafe abortions, which account for 22 percent of maternal deaths (U.S. Congress 2001). Silva testified that she has worked on reproductive rights issues for many years, including efforts to decriminalize abortion. MMR would like to contribute to present decriminalization advocacy efforts. As a first step, it would like to see abortion legalized in cases of rape and incest. A recent survey of pregnant patients between the ages of twelve and sixteen at the Lima Maternity Hospital found that 90 percent of the pregnancies were the result of sexual abuse (U.S. Congress 2001). However, due to the threatened loss of USAID funds, MMR does not participate in advocacy efforts.

Movimiento Manuela Ramos is also a partner in community reproductive health projects, such as ReproSalud, that seek "to empower women to exercise their right to family planning and other essential reproductive health services" (U.S. Congress 2001, 32). ReproSalud must choose between providing important reproductive health services for women or engaging in efforts to reduce maternal mortality, injury, and hospitalizations as well as pregnancies resulting from rape and incest. Silva states, "In the face of serious problems such as these—sexual abuse, dangerous abortion practices, and alarming rates of maternal mortality—how can the U.S. tell us that we must be silent? And yet, we must promise to be silent—even with our own, non-U.S. funds—if we are to save the programs that thousands of women depend upon" (U.S. Congress 2001, 32).

Ironically, because of the restrictions of the global gag rule, Silva was able to discuss issues during her U.S. visit that she cannot discuss in her own country. She obtained a ruling assuring her that she could speak freely about abortion in her testimony before Congress without fear of jeopardizing funding for her organization in Peru. At the hearing, Silva expressed her frustration about this contradictory state of affairs. She stressed the absurdity of the fact that upon returning to her country she would again be "silenced" about the abortion issue (U.S. Congress 2001, 32).

The Family Planning Association of Nepal (FPAN) also lost funding as a result of the global gag rule. Nepal has the fourth highest maternal mortality rate, and it is estimated that 50 percent of these women die from unsafe abortion (about six per day), and many more suffer physical injuries (U.S. Congress 2001). According to FPAN's director, Dr. Nirmal K. Bista, the organization has received generous support from the United States for nearly thirty years. Until 2002 Nepal had the strictest abortion law possible—women were imprisoned for seeking and receiving abortions for any reason whatsoever. The Nepalese Ministry of Health concluded that a more liberalized abortion law would reduce maternal mortality and morbidity and called for NGOs to address the issue (U.S. Congress 2001). As a result of NGO efforts, abortion was legalized in 2002 for pregnancies resulting from rape or incest (International Planned Parenthood 2002b). FPAN has made a commitment to continue addressing the high incidence of maternal mortality. It has called on medical professionals, health NGOs, human rights advocates, and women's groups to educate people and change government policy. This network supports qualified legalization of abortion and improved access to safer services. But such advocacy disqualifies FPAN from receiving U.S. funds. Consequently, it will lose almost $250,000, greatly affecting its ability to provide services, particularly in Nepal's three most densely populated areas. The director of FPAN speaks out:

> This is the challenge: do I listen to my own government that has asked FPAN to help save women's lives or do I listen to the U.S. government? Were we to accept the restricted U.S. funds, I would be prevented from speaking in my own country to my own government about a health care crisis I know first hand. But by rejecting U.S. funds, I put our clinics—clinics addressing that same health care crisis—in very real jeopardy. (U.S. Congress 2001, 39)

Many other international reproductive rights groups have also had to withdraw requests for USAID funding, including the Bangladesh Rural Advancement Committee (BRAC), which was previously one of USAID's top recipients. Prerana of India also rejected funding (U.S. Congress 2001; Sepulveda-Olivia 2003). And in 2002, the U.S. withheld $3 million from WHO's Human Reproduction

Program because it was conducting research on mifepristone, a drug that induces medical abortion and is legally marketed in the United States as RU-486.

In 2002, the U.S. government withheld $34 million from the UN Population Fund (UNFPA)—or 12 percent of its annual budget—on the grounds that UNFPA was supposedly supporting forced abortions and coercive practices in China. Three fact-finding missions found no evidence of UNFPA support of such practices, but the United States nonetheless declined to restore funds to UNFPA, choosing instead to redirect them to finance women's health care needs in Afghanistan and Pakistan (International Women's Health Coalition 2003; Maloney 2003). UNFPA claimed that, as a result of the U.S. decision, two million unwanted pregnancies, nearly 800,000 induced abortions, 4,700 maternal deaths, and more than 77,000 infant and child deaths occurred in Nepal (Mercier 2003). In response to these stark statistics, the European Union agreed to help UNFPA cope with the consequences of the U.S. funding withdrawal (International Planned Parenthood 2002a).

The Global Gag Rule as a Violation of Human Rights

The global gag rule violates many international human rights doctrines, including the 1995 Beijing Platform for Action (UN 1995), the Convention on the Elimination of All Forms of Discrimination against Women (CEDAW) and its committee, and the International Covenant on Civil and Political Rights and its human rights committee (Center for Reproductive Law and Policy (CRLP) and University of Toronto 2002).[4]

The essential message of all these doctrines is best summarized in the 1994 ICPD Programme of Action:

> Reproductive rights embrace certain human rights that are already recognized national laws, international laws and international human rights documents and other consensus documents. These rights rest on the recognition of the basic right of all couples and individuals to decide freely and responsibly the number, spacing and timing of their children and to have the information and means to do so, and the right to attain the highest standard of sexual and reproductive health. (UN 1994)

Significantly, the U.S. government honors these rights within U.S. boundaries but chooses to ignore them in any non-U.S. nation that accepts USAID funds.

Specifically, the global gag rule inhibits the provision of comprehensive reproductive health services to women in non-U.S. countries, thereby imperiling women's health. It restrains NGOs' ability to openly discuss the problem of unsafe abortions in nations that forbid abortions and to provide safe abortions in nations that do permit them. Unaware of just how unsafe an abortion can be or having limited access to safe abortion services, many women submit to unsafe abortions. As a result, thousands of women die. Indeed, worldwide about 13 percent of maternal deaths are attributable to unsafe abortions (World Health Organization 1998).

One of the worst effects of the global gag rule is that it causes organizations such as FPAK, MSI, and UNFPA that reject funding to close clinics or reduce services, including not only family planning services but also cervical and breast cancer screening, infant immunizations, and HIV/AIDS counseling (Raghavan 2003). Ironically, such clinic closings and service reductions almost always result in more unintended pregnancies and more abortions than would have occurred otherwise. In addition, organizations that accept funding may fail to engage in permissible activities, such as offering abortion in cases of rape or incest, for fear of even appearing noncompliant with respect to the terms of the global gag rule.[5]

By prohibiting advocacy for abortion rights but not against abortion rights, the global gag rule also violates rights to free speech, rights to free association, and the right to petition the government. Such restrictions on what citizens say would be unconstitutional in the United States, where free speech is an established international human right (CRLP 2001) and where the government may not dictate what private organizations do with their own nongovernment funds as long as the activities they support are legal. Clearly, the global gag rule reveals a distressing double standard. The U.S. government seeks to restrict abortion debate and abortion services in non-U.S. nations that it would not dare to restrict in the United States.[6]

Conclusion

Worldwide, many women suffer from unwanted pregnancies and obtain abortions, no matter what the cost and toll on their lives. People with varying positions on abortion can all agree that the best action is to reduce the number of unwanted pregnancies. An increase in women's reproductive health services is extremely important, but lack of contraception is not the *only* reason women suffer unintended pregnancies. As Gita Sen and Srilatha Batliwala state, "The control of women's and girls' sexuality and reproduction is at the heart of unequal gender relations, and is central to the denial of equality and self-determination to women" (Sen and Batliwala 2000, 24). They continue:

> There is probably little reason to doubt that when women have greater autonomy, decision-making power, control over their own and household resources, access to adequate services, and freedom from violence and coercion, they also exercise greater power in their sexual and reproductive relations. In such a context, they

tend to make decisions which result in delaying marriage, having fewer children, spacing pregnancies, and even remaining unmarried or childless by choice. (Sen and Batliwala 2000, 26)

Clearly, education, employment, wealth, decision-making power, and many other factors affect women's childbearing.

The complexity of the issue was recognized at the 1994 ICDP in Cairo, and complete reproductive health care for women, as well as complete human development and equality of rights for women, is now the stated goal. But these ambitious targets are unlikely to be achieved in the near future. Without them, large numbers of unwanted pregnancies are still likely to occur.

The global gag rule inhibits the provision of safe abortions for women who need them and in some cases reduces the provision of reproductive services to prevent them. This is not *merely* an issue about U.S. funding of abortions for women. It is about allowing international and indigenous organizations to provide the information and services that women want and need. It is about leaving other countries to pursue policy changes that would better serve their own citizens. The wealth of the United States allows it to be very influential in the family planning arena. Many organizations are forced to choose between providing health services for some of the poorest women of the world or abiding by the dictates of the wealthiest nation in the world—dictates that violate established human rights and harm women. Given the power and wealth of the United States, it has great potential to vastly improve women's lives; it is grossly unjust that it instead chooses to put many women's lives at risk.

Notes

I would like to thank my research assistant, Amber Galeo, for her invaluable work on this chapter.

1. President Bush announced the new rule on January 22, 2001; it was issued as a memorandum to the Administrator of USAID on March 28, 2001, and it was codified in the Federal Register on March 29, 2001. See *Federal Register* 66, no. 61: 17301–13. It will be referred to as the U.S. White House Memorandum. See U.S. White House Memorandum, "Memorandum of March 28, 2001: Restoration of the Mexico City Policy," *Federal Register* 66, no. 61 (March 29, 2001): 17301–13.

2. See Center for Reproductive Law and Policy (CRLP) and University of Toronto International Programme on Reproductive and Sexual Health Law, "Bringing Rights to Bear: An Analysis of the Work of UN Treaty Monitoring Bodies on Reproductive and Sexual Rights," (CRLP Publication, 2002) for a detailed explanation and analysis of various human rights treaties and UN treaty monitoring bodies and how they have incorporated reproductive and sexual health and rights of women into their documents and work.

3. I want to thank CRLP and IPPF for sharing their information with me.

4. For a much more detailed analysis of human rights, reproductive health, and international documents, see CRLP and University of Toronto (2002). Also see Rebecca Cook, Bernard M. Dickens, O. Andrew F. Wilson, and Susan E. Scarrow, *Advancing Safe Motherhood through Human Rights* (WHO publication WHO/RHR/01.5, 2001) for an analysis of human rights and safe motherhood.

5. Studies show that this occurred under the Mexico City Policy. See, for example, Richard P. Cincotta and Barbara Crane, "Public Health: The Mexico City Policy and U.S. Family Planning Assistance," *Science* 294 (October 2001): 525–26.

6. See Center for Reproductive Law and Policy (CRLP), "The Bush Global Gag Rule: A Violation of International Human Rights and the U.S. Constitution" (CRLP Publication, Item: B019, July 2001) for a fuller discussion of this issue.

References

Ashford, Lori S. 2001. "New Population Policies: Advancing Women's Health and Rights." *Population Bulletin* 56, no. 1: 3–43.

Barroso, Carmen, and Jodi L. Jacobson. 2000. "Population Policy and Women's Empowerment: Challenges and Opportunities." In *Women's Empowerment and Demographic Processes*, edited by Harriet B. Presser and Gita Sen, 351–76. New York: Oxford.

Center for Reproductive Law and Policy (CRLP). 2001. "The Bush Global Gag Rule: A Violation of International Human Rights and the U.S. Constitution." CRLP publication, Item: B019, July.

———. 2002. "The Global Gag Rule's Effects on NGOs in 59 Countries." CRLP publication, Item: F034, April.

Center for Reproductive Law and Policy and University of Toronto International Programme on Reproductive and Sexual Health Law. 2002. "Bringing Rights to Bear: An Analysis of the Work of UN Treaty Monitoring Bodies on Reproductive and Sexual Rights." CRLP Publication.

Cincotta, Richard P., and Barbara Crane. 2001."Public Health: The Mexico City Policy and U.S. Family Planning Assistance." *Science* 294 (October 19): 525–26.

Cohen, Susan. 2000. "Abortion Politics and U.S. Population Aid: Coping with a Complex New Law." *International Family Planning Perspectives* 26, no. 3 (September): 137–39.

Cook, Rebecca, Bernard M. Dickens, O. Andrew F. Wilson, and Susan E. Scarrow. 2001. *Advancing Safe Motherhood through Human Rights.* WHO publication, WHO/RHR/01.5.

Global Health Council. 2002. "Promises to Keep: The Toll of Unintended Pregnancies on Women's Lives in the Developing World." Washington, D.C.: Global Health Council.

Hwang, Ann. 2002. "Exportable Righteousness, Expendable Women." *World Watch* 15, no. 1 (January/February): 24–31.

International Planned Parenthood (IPPF). 2002a. "IPPF Welcomes 10 Million from the European Community," at www.ippf.org/newsinfo/pressreleases/EU_00_03_2002.htm.

———. 2002b. "Nepal Legalises Abortion to Save the Lives of Thousands of Women Each Year," at ippfnet.ippf.org/pub/IPPF_News/News_Details_s.asp?ID=2321.

———. 2003. "Family Planning Association of Kenya Wins 2003 United Nations Population Award," at ippfnet.ippf.org/pub/IPPF_News/News_Details.asp?ID=2738.

International Women's Health Coalition (IWHC). 2003. "Bush's Other War: The Assault on Women's Reproductive and Sexual Health and Rights," at www.iwhc.org/index.cfm?fuseaction=page&pageID=468.

Maloney, Carolyn. Member, U.S. House of Representatives, D-NY. 2003. "President Bush: Attack on Women around the World," at www.house.gov/maloney/issues/waronwomen/timeline.html.

Marie Stopes International (MSI). 2003. At www.mariestopes.org.uk.

Mercier, Rick. 2003. "Davis Is Out Front on Family Planning 'Gag Rule.'" *Free Lance–Star* (Fredericksburg), at www.fredericksburg.com/News/FLS/2003/032003/03102003/889423.

Mundigo, Axel I. 2000. "Lessons Learned: The Need to Invest in Reproductive Health." In *Promoting Reproductive Health: Investing in Health for Development*, edited by Shepard Forman and Romita Ghosh, 281–97. Boulder, Colo.: Lynne Rienner.

Peters, Julie, and Andrea Wolper, eds. 1995. *Women's Rights, Human Rights*. New York: Routledge.

Population Action International (PAI). 2001. "What You Need to Know About the Global Gag Rule Restrictions: An Unofficial Guide." Washington. D.C.: Population Action International.

Raghavan, Sudarsan. 2003. "Bush Pulls Funds from Kenyan Women's Clinics." *Charlotte Observer*, October 12, 21A.

Reproductive Health Matters. 2001. "Ipas Declines to Sign the Global Gag Rule: Public Statement." *Reproductive Health Matters* 9, no. 17 (May): 206–207.

Salter, Fiona. 2003. IPPF. Personal correspondence.

Sen, Gita, and Srilatha Batliwala. 2000. "Empowering Women for Reproductive Rights." In *Women's Empowerment and Demographic Processes*, edited by Harriet B. Presser and Gita Sen, 15–36. New York: Oxford University Press.

Sepulveda-Olivia, Lillian. 2003. Center for Reproductive Rights. Personal correspondence.

United Nations. 1994. *Programme of Action Adopted at the International Conference on Population and Development*. Cairo, September 5–13. UN doc. ST/ESA/SER.A/149. New York: UN.

———. 1995. *Report of the Fourth World Conference on Women*. Beijing, China, September 4–15. UN Doc. A/CONF.177/20. New York: UN.

U.S. Congress. Senate. 2001. Committee on Foreign Relations. *Mexico City Policy: Effects of Restrictions on International Family Planning Funding*. 107th Congress, 1st Session, July 19. Washington, D.C.: U.S. Government Printing Office.

U.S. White House Memorandum. 2001. "Memorandum of March 28, 2001: Restoration of the Mexico City Policy." *Federal Register* 66, no. 61 (March 29): 17301–13.

World Bank. 1993. *World Bank Development Report: Investing in Health*. New York: Oxford University Press.

World Health Organization (WHO). 1998. "Unsafe Abortion." Geneva, Switzerland: World Health Organization.

A Boy or a Girl: Is Any Choice Moral? 9
The Ethics of Sex Selection and Sex Preselection in Context

JULIE M. ZILBERBERG

T HE SIGNIFICANCE OF SEX SELECTION depends on geographical location and social situation. In this chapter, I compare and contrast sex-selection practices in the United States and India. I consider technologies employed before and after conception. My overall aim is to show that the contexts within which choices are made have a major bearing on the moral dimensions of the practice.

Sex Selection in the United States

In the United States, prenatal diagnosis has been used to enable women at risk of having a child with a sex-linked genetic condition to determine fetal sex. For example, if a pregnant carrier of hemophilia gives birth to a son, there is a 50 percent risk that he will inherit the disease. If the child is female, she will not have hemophilia, but there is a 50 percent chance that she will be a carrier. Wishing to avoid having a child with hemophilia, parents may therefore sex select against a male fetus even though there is a 50 percent chance that the baby will be born healthy.

One could claim that preconception sex selection for disease avoidance is not really sex selection at all but is solely a matter of selecting against disease; the intent is disease avoidance rather than selection of sex per se. However, despite the differing intent, the practice still involves sex selection. Although parents' primary motivation in this case is not related to gender issues, but instead on biological and social preferences relating to disease and well-being, the practice still results in selection of sex.

Setting aside the ethical merits or difficulties specific to different methods of accomplishing sex selection, sex selection for disease avoidance is, in general, morally acceptable in my view. Its justification is twofold. First, it is based on respect for the autonomy of women to control their own bodies and their own reproduction. Second, its justification is based on acceptable intentions of parents who attempt to ensure healthy offspring. Parents generally strive for the health of their offspring by avoiding infection, treating illness, trying to give adequate nutrition and rest, and seeking prenatal care where available while the fetus is in the womb. It is considered appropriate and admirable to foster good health and well-being for one's children. Attempting to give birth to healthy offspring via sex selection for disease avoidance is an extension of striving for the health and well-being of existing offspring. It is similarly based on ethically appropriate desires that one's children, and perhaps people in general, be subject to as little suffering as possible. If it is considered ethically appropriate and admirable to take care of one's embryo in utero so that one's child is born healthy, it may also be ethically permissible to attempt to avoid giving birth to a child who will inherit a genetic disease. Taking steps to give birth to healthy offspring via sex selection for disease avoidance is one of the ways in which a woman can increase the likelihood that she does not give birth to an unhealthy child. Sex selection for disease avoidance reflects the view that if something can be done to avoid illness or health-related difficulties, then it may be morally permissible to do it,[1] although it is not morally required.

Apart from sex selection for purposes of disease avoidance, sex selection is desired by some for purposes of "family balancing," the view that it is good to have children of both sexes in a family. The following case is reflective of actual cases in which a family balancing request is made:

> A 32-year-old woman, Lisa B., comes to the prenatal diagnostic center of a major hospital. She is intent on arranging for chorionic villus sampling (CVS) in order to determine the sex of the fetus she is carrying. A genetic counselor explains to her that the center has an established policy against making prenatal diagnosis (whether CVS or amniocentesis) available for purposes of sex selection. The genetic counselor, in defending the policy, tells her that there is a collective sense at the center that abortion purely on grounds of sex selection is both morally and socially problematic.
>
> Lisa B. proceeds to explain her situation. She and her husband already have three children, all of whom are girls. They want very much to have a male child but, for economic reasons, are determined to have no more than one more child. Indeed, if they had a boy among their three children, they would not even consider having a fourth. They feel so strongly about this fourth child being a boy that if they cannot gain assurance that it is a male they will elect abortion. Lisa B. insists that it is unfair for the center to deny her access to prenatal diagnosis. (Mappes and DeGrazia 1996, 641–42)

The sex-selection issue is quite complex in a case like that of Lisa B. Is it morally justified to abort a fetus simply because it is not a male or female? Is it morally appropriate to give patients information about a fetus's sex that may contribute to their aborting a fetus? Should Lisa B., and women in similar circumstance, be denied the information she seeks just because she has forthrightly expressed her intentions if she receives disappointing information? Currently, pregnant women are routinely offered knowledge of fetal sex within the context of their ordinary prenatal medical care. Women who receive this information are then in a position to use it as they wish.

In recent years a new preconception technique has become available. MicroSort is a commercial company that performs preconception sex selection.[2] A method known as flow cytometry is used to separate sperm into two groups. One group contains predominantly X-bearing sperm, and the other group contains predominantly Y-bearing sperm. The desired sperm sample is then inserted into a woman's body using artificial insemination. This method of sorting produces a success rate of 90 percent for achieving the birth of a girl and about 70 to 75 percent for achieving the birth of a boy.

Currently, MicroSort makes its techniques available to those who seek its services for two reasons only: (1) to avoid the conception of a child with a genetic sex-linked disease and (2) to facilitate the conception of a child whose sex achieves family balancing preferences. Significantly, MicroSort limits preconception sex selection for family balancing purposes to families who already have one or more child of a certain sex and desire a child of the other sex (Genetics and IVF Institute 2004). MicroSort claims that its services are not for use by those who have no children yet and by those who have no genetic disease issues.

The current fee for uncomplicated preconception sex selection (sperm sorting followed by artificial insemination) is about $2,500. In the United States, this fee, though significant, is affordable to high- and middle-income people intent on having a child of a particular sex. Moreover, even some low-income U.S. families may be able to afford preconception sex selection by making sacrifices elsewhere in their budget.

This is important to note because if sex preference were to become significantly stronger, MicroSort may be a very attainable method for many, possibly resulting in a considerable rise in the frequency of sex selection. For this reason, ethicists may want to direct attention toward this somewhat affordable, relatively easy to perform, and not overly invasive technique.

The technique entails procuring a sample of semen from a man by masturbation, sorting the sample using flow cytometry, and then inserting the sorted sample into a woman's body during the proper time in her menstrual cycle so that pregnancy can be achieved. This description is, of course, based on the simplest scenario where there are no added difficulties involving fertility or other issues.

A sex-selection decision made during the course of pregnancy and that involves an abortion seems more morally complex than a sex-selection decision made before one conceives a child. The former requires terminating the life of a developing fetus that some people view as a human person. The latter requires deliberately beginning the life of a child of a particular sex.

While some reasons for abortion may not seem permissible to some people, in my judgment the abortion decision is best made by the pregnant woman. A woman's freedom to abort if she so chooses constitutes a matter of basic autonomy. If a woman cannot control the use of her own body, she cannot be said to control her personal destiny. Many feminists may argue that having an abortion based solely on the sex of a female fetus is wrong and involves both sexual discrimination against women and the termination of the life of an otherwise desirable fetus. However, I claim that even if this is true, the abortion decision should remain in the hands of the pregnant woman. This is a key freedom. If we were to set up society so that abortions for certain reasons were not allowed, particular women would be deprived of a basic choice about what happens to their bodies. In my view, such a policy would violate feminist moral principles and result in a less morally desirable arrangement than the current system, under which perhaps some abortions are done for reasons that would be considered sexist or less than morally ideal.

Sex selection in the United States does not pose a grave moral danger at the present time. Most women or couples do not choose to terminate a pregnancy simply because the fetus is the "wrong" sex, nor do they take deliberate steps to conceive a child of a particular sex. Although some studies suggest that relatively high numbers of Americans (female as well as male) prefer that their first child be a boy (Williamson 1976, 29–65), this preference does not seem to translate into their taking any positive steps to secure their preference. In fact, overall, the sex ratio in the United States remains balanced (CIA World Factbook 2003). Restricting abortion rights of women to limit or eliminate sex selection that might in some cases be less than morally ideal would infringe significantly on women's most basic abilities to control their own bodies. Sex selection in the United States should continue to be monitored and analyzed by ethicists to guard against potential increasing moral problems. Any significant upsurge in the rate of sex selection merits investigation and analysis by ethicists.

Sex Selection in India

Although sex selection in the United States, where son preference is weak, is relatively unproblematic, sex selection where sons are strongly preferred is very worrisome (Williamson 1976, 1983, 129–45; Warren 1985, 12–16). In the developing world, sex selection is typically practiced after conception by the use of ultrasound or amniocentesis to detect the fetus's sex in utero, followed by abortion if the fetus is discovered to be the "wrong" sex. There is an abundance of data on sex-selection practices in India, where it is widespread. When discussing sex selection in India, it is important to stress that these techniques are used almost exclusively to select against female fetuses. For example, one study found that of 8,000 abortions performed in an Indian clinic, 7,997 (more than 99 percent) of the aborted fetuses were female (Rao 1986, 202). Additionally, in India and other developing countries, the continued survival of women and girls may be a challenge because their health care and nutrition are subpar when compared with that of men and boys (Sen 1990, 61–66).

It is often Indian women themselves who choose to sex select for males. The social backdrop in such scenarios is important to understand.[3] The traditional marital blessing for brides in India is "May you be the mother of a hundred sons," and this saying illustrates the general prevailing climate with regard to sex selection. Daughters are often viewed as a liability in India because of the economic costs of generating wedding dowries for them so that they can become members of their husbands' families (Kusum 1993). Traditionally, the dowry practice was only maintained among the higher castes, but it is now more extensive. Higher caste women were not allowed to work outside the family; their work at home was not recognized, and they were seen as a burden (Patel 1989, 114). The dowry is given to compensate the husband for having to bear the burden of the wife. A dowry can be equivalent in goods and cash to a year's income for a family (Jordan 2000). An Indian proverb says that raising a daughter is like watering your neighbor's plant (Jordan 2000; Kusum 1993).

While it is commonly known that the practice of a wedding dowry for daughters contributes to the desire for sons and hence sex selection for males, additional socioeconomic and religious causes foster Indians' strong son preference. A daughter is a burden in a variety of significant ways. Indian parents are responsible for maintaining their daughters' chastity before marriage. Tradition demands that Indian men marry virgins. Women with a sexual history are traditionally viewed as "damaged goods." In addition, Indian parents are responsible not only for providing a sizable dowry for their daughters but also for bestowing money and valuable gifts to their sons-in-law and their families after the marriage to ensure that their daughters are well treated. Another disadvantage of having a daughter in India is that she cannot continue the family name; without any son the family name dies. Furthermore, because women cannot maintain wealth or property, a family business will perish unless a son is available to take it over. Finally, it is not daughters but sons in India who take care of aging parents (Kusum 1993, 150–51). Another Hindu belief is that one goes to heaven only if a son lights the funeral pyre (Jordan 2000, 1).

Not only do parents perceive daughters as a liability, the tragic reality is that, within traditional Indian households, daughters are a liability. Parents may feel they need to abort female fetuses for a larger good. Their choice to do so is colored by the reality of daughters as a liability. Doctors as well believe they are providing a service that is a kinder solution than the alternatives, including female infanticide, which still takes place today among some very poor Indian villagers (Jordan 2000). Signs advertising sex determination services are numerous. They often read "Invest 500 rupees now and save 50,000 rupees later" (Kusum 1993, 152). Mothers or mothers-to-be may want a boy as much as their husbands, mothers-in-law, and fathers-in-law, or perhaps they are desperate to please those on whom they strongly depend for everyday existence (Dugger 2001, 1).

Theoretical Discussion

Women's choice to sex select for sons in this context can be understood in terms of relational autonomy. The social reality that structures women's lives and the choices available to them is a major determining factor of the decisions and desires that women actually make. Thus, the exercising of autonomy under a social reality that may limit the individual woman can be described as relational.

Autonomy in bioethics is, simply stated, a recognition of an individual's ability to make decisions about one's own body and one's own health care. Autonomy reflects the idea that people have the right to control what is done to their own bodies. A strong emphasis on autonomy can help guard against abuses or manipulation by the health care system and can foster patient choice in health care matters. When it comes to reproductive matters, a strong principle of, or strong commitment to, autonomy can help "increase the scope of personal control for women" (Sherwin 1998b, 23).

While certain interpretations of autonomy are associated with a conservative, nonfeminist viewpoint and may sometimes be regarded by feminist theorists with suspicion (Mackenzie and Stoljar 2000, 3), women have found other feminist interpretations of autonomy that are both more compatible with their understanding of what it means to be a fully human self and more empowering. Among these feminist interpretations of autonomy include the concepts developed by thinkers such as Diana Meyers (1989), Anne Donchin (2001; 2000, 213–35), and Susan Dodds (2000, 236–58). Sherwin's elucidation of relational autonomy is particularly useful with respect to the subject of the ethics of sex selection (Sherwin 1998a; Sherwin 1998b).

Sherwin makes a distinction between agency and autonomy; the two related concepts are sometimes confused with one another (Sherwin 1998a, 11). According to Sherwin, agency is demonstrated when women make decisions and choices about their health care; however, this decision making and choosing does not in and of itself constitute autonomy (Sherwin 1998b, 32–33). Autonomy, properly interpreted as relational autonomy, addresses the ways in which oppression limits the range of choices available and affects the weight individuals assign to each of their options (Sherwin 1998a, 12). Agency is simply the ability to make a reflective, informed choice from a limited range of options (Sherwin 1998a, 13). Autonomy, on the other hand, entails a more comprehensive notion of freedom: specifically, not only uncoerced choice among the limited options one happens to have but also the power to socially shape and create the quantity and quality of options available to oneself and others (Sherwin 1998a, 13). Full autonomy requires that we remove oppressive barriers that structure options in such a way as to further perpetuate oppression (Sherwin 1998a, 13). Sherwin calls this kind of autonomy relational autonomy (Sherwin 1998b, 19), and I find this interpretation of autonomy very useful in elucidating the apparent paradox of women who are seen as freely choosing options that reinforce oppression.

Although relational autonomy theorists show some variation in their accounts, they all share the conviction "that persons are socially embedded and that agents' identities are formed within the context of social relationships and shaped by a complex of intersecting social determinants, such as race, class, gender, and ethnicity" (Mackenzie and Stoljar 2000, 4). Sherwin's variation on the general relational autonomy theme lends itself particularly well to an analysis of the ethics of sex selection in India. Her work allows for a nuanced and culturally sensitive approach to sex selection that more accurately assesses the troubled moral terrain on which Indian women tread.

Indian women who select for sons may certainly be described as making a choice. However, their choice, and therefore their autonomy, is limited by the social and economic constraints and limitations that narrow Indian women's range of options. In a sad way, selecting for a son may be the best moral choice an Indian woman can make, for, in the context of India, men and families with boys may simply fare much better than women and families with girls given the social backdrop. Some feminists may view sex selection for the purpose of not having a girl as an act of femicide wherever and whenever it occurs—as a decision to reject all that women have to offer the world (Patel 1989). But such a view needs to be contextualized. If a woman has lived a limited and onerous life simply because she happens to be a woman who lives in a society that does not value women as much as men, her choice to have a son instead of a daughter, in order that her own child will have the best chance at a future possible life, is understandable. This choice may be made with the best intentions and out of love and care for her future child and the well-being of her current family.

Conclusion

Clearly, a strong moral tension exists between the importance of respecting the autonomy of women on the one hand and standing by as women choose to abort fetuses because they are female on the other hand. Strong support for the reproductive autonomy of women includes recognizing their right to abort for any reason they deem necessary, even if the reason is that the fetus's sex is female. As I see it, a consequence of a feminist commitment to women's reproductive freedom entails feminists allowing other women to abort for whatever reason they deem necessary, with no exceptions, not even excepting abortion of females per se. Nonetheless, feminists can and should work together to ameliorate women's circumstances under oppressive conditions, so that women and parents need not feel that the best thing they can do for their future child is to make sure that the child is not female.

Because some segments of the Indian population became concerned about the population's skewed sex ratio, laws were established in 1989 and 1996 in India banning sex-selective abortion. While enforcement of these laws may result in a reduction of sex-selective abortions in the short term, enforcement may also simply shift the problem of not wanting a daughter to a problem of increased cases of infanticide and of premature death resulting from neglect of women's nutritional and health needs throughout life. Thus, in my view, it is best to address sex selection at the heart of the matter, and that is the low level of status accorded women and girls.[4] Directly addressing the core of the problem may lead to a longer term and better solution than simply banning sex selection. In this way, the heart of women's oppression will be addressed and perhaps improved. Gender roles and beliefs about women and girls need to be changed. Education and public outreach messages can promote that girls and women are valuable members of society. Dowry practices could be fully abandoned or outlawed, with complete enforcement of the ban. Women's work could be publicly shown to have genuine value. Customs and traditions that are now performed only by males, such as lighting the parents' funeral pyre, maintaining property and the family business, and carrying on the family name, could be promoted as proper for women as well. Certainly, deeply held religious and cultural practices may take time to change. This is understandable. However, to evoke permanent positive change for women, it is crucial for women to have sufficient access to material resources meeting their basic needs and those of their children so that their choices regarding pregnancy and parenthood are less constrained by the threat of poverty and social isolation.

Notes

1. It is not the case that one may use any and all means to foster the health of one's child, however.

2. MicroSort has locations in Fairfax, Virginia, and Laguna Hills, California. The company's website is www.MicroSort.net.

3. While there of course exist significant professional educated women in India, I focus on the general climate of sex preference in India.

4. I agree with K. Shanthi's idea (chapter 7 in this volume) that if Indian women simultaneously refuse to abort female fetuses, son preference will be diminished. To give strength to Indian women so that they may reach the point at which they are empowered to actually do this, in my view the low level of status accorded to females must be addressed because it is the heart of the matter. Improving women's and girls' status will enhance their autonomy and will perhaps limit sex-selective abortion of females.

References

CIA World Factbook. 2003. "United States: Sex Ratio," at www.indexmundi.com/united_states/sex_ratio.html.

Dodds, Susan. 2000. "Choice and Control in Feminist Bioethics." In *Relational Autonomy: Feminist Perspectives on Autonomy, Agency and the Social Self*, edited by Catriona Mackenzie and Natalie Stoljar, 236–58. New York: Oxford University Press.

Donchin, Anne. 2000. "Autonomy and Interdependence: Quandaries in Genetic Decision Making." In *Relational Autonomy: Feminist Perspectives on Autonomy, Agency and the Social Self*, edited by Catriona Mackenzie and Natalie Stoljar, 213–35. New York: Oxford University Press.

———. 2001. "Understanding Autonomy Relationally: Toward a Reconfiguration of Bioethical Principles." *Journal of Medicine and Philosophy* 26, no. 4: 365–86.

Dugger, Celia W. 2001. "Abortion in India Is Tipping Scales Sharply Against Girls." *New York Times*, April 22, 1.

Genetics and IVF Institute. 2004. "MicroSort Clinical Trial," at www.microsort.net.html.

Jordan, Miriam. 2000. "Among Poor Villagers, Female Infanticide Still Flourishes in India." *Wall Street Journal*, May 9, 1.

Kusum. 1993. "The Use of Pre-Natal Diagnostic Techniques for Sex Selection: The Indian Scene." *Bioethics* 7, no. 2/3: 149–65.

Mackenzie, Catriona, and Natalie Stoljar. 2000. "Introduction: Autonomy Refigured." In *Relational Autonomy: Feminist Perspectives on Autonomy, Agency, and the Social Self*, edited by Catriona Mackenzie and Natalie Stoljar, 3–34. New York: Oxford University Press.

Mappes, Thomas A., and David DeGrazia. 1996. *Biomedical Ethics.* 4th ed. New York: McGraw Hill.

Meyers, Diana. 1989. *Self, Society and Personal Choice.* New York: Columbia University Press.

Patel, Vibhuti. 1989. "Sex-Determination and Sex Preselection Tests in India: Recent Techniques in Femicide." *Reproductive and Genetic Engineering* 2, no. 2: 114.

Rao, R. 1986. "Move to Stop Sex-Test Abortion." *Nature Magazine* November 20–26: 202.

Sen, Amartya. 1990. "More than 100 Million Women Are Missing." *New York Review of Books* 37 (December 20): 61–66.

Sherwin, Susan. 1998a. "Introduction." In the Feminist Health Care Ethics Research Network's *The Politics of Women's Health: Exploring Agency and Autonomy*, edited by Susan Sherwin. Philadelphia: Temple University Press.

———. 1998b. "A Relational Approach to Autonomy in Healthcare." In the Feminist Health Care Ethics Research Network's *The Politics of Women's Health: Exploring Agency and Autonomy*, edited by Susan Sherwin. Philadelphia: Temple University Press.

Warren, Mary Anne. 1985. *Gendercide: The Implications of Sex Selection*. Totowa, N.J.: Rowman & Allanheld.

Williamson, Nancy E. 1976. *Sons or Daughters: A Cross Cultural Survey of Parental Preferences*. Beverly Hills, Calif.: Sage Publications.

———. 1983. "Parental Sex Preferences and Sex Selection." In *Sex Selection of Children*, edited by Neil G. Bennett. New York: Academic Press.

Right-Making and Wrong-Making in Surrogate Motherhood
A Confucian Feminist Perspective

10

JULIA TAO LAI PO-WAH

> *Here the point lies not in any tangible quid pro quo but in the violability of family intimacy. If the most basic human relations cannot be respected and protected within the family where all virtue is nourished, if family members cannot trust one another, the whole fiduciary basis of society stands in jeopardy.*

—DE BARRY, *THE TROUBLE WITH CONFUCIANISM*

THIS CHAPTER EXAMINES two claims derived from liberal political theory about the liberatory potential of surrogate motherhood. These two claims support the view that certain features of surrogate motherhood ethically justify the practice of surrogacy. First, legal recognition of contracted motherhood enhances women's autonomy, understood as free choice, by creating the opportunity to choose to act as a surrogate mother or to contract the gestational services of another woman so that one can raise a child borne by another. Second, the practice of surrogacy enhances the subjectivity of women by creating greater opportunities to participate in reproductive relationships that do not involve essentialized understandings of pregnancy, reproduction, or motherhood. One clear debate underpinning the surrogacy controversy is the conflict between those who think it is right for women to make pregnancy contracts and to be paid for this use of their bodies because it enhances subjectivity and autonomous choice, and those who think it is wrong, not only because it commodifies human reproduction but also because it distorts significant human relations and undermines women's opportunity to become moral persons. Those who accept, to some degree, the liberal claims are likely to argue against prohibitions on legal recognition of surrogacy contracts or philanthropic surrogacy arrangements. Those who query the basis for those claims are likely to argue for legal limitations on any surrogacy arrangements or against any legal recognition of surrogacy arrangements.

In the first sections of this chapter, I analyze and evaluate the two liberal claims concerning autonomy and agency and Western feminist responses to them. Later in the chapter, I consider surrogacy in the context of the lived experience of Chinese women and Confucian ethics. These are used to develop a Confucian feminist perspective on the liberal claims concerning surrogacy, based on a reconstructed Confucian understanding of the notions of human virtues and agency, dignity, and autonomy. I argue, ultimately, that although surrogate motherhood arrangements can provide women with opportunities to express their autonomy and subjectivity in ways that have not previously been available, a Confucian feminist approach to surrogacy would urge the banning of surrogate motherhood, both contract and philanthropic, because it erodes family virtues, hurts women, and undermines motherhood.

Is Contract Motherhood Liberating or Oppressive?

Surrogate motherhood can take a number of forms: full or partial (gestational), commercial or noncommercial. In full surrogacy, women contract to gestate an embryo genetically related to them as a service for a commissioning party. In partial (gestational) surrogacy, no genetic relationship exists between the women serving as surrogates and the embryos they gestate. Commercial surrogacy done for the payment of a monetary fee is often referred to as "contract" motherhood. Noncommercial surrogacy, which may be done out of generosity or altruism, is referred to as "philanthropic" or "gift" motherhood. In general, the practice of gestational surrogacy has recently been on the rise, increasing from about 5 percent of contract pregnancies in 1988 to more than 50 percent in the United States in 1998 (Ragoné 2000, 57).

The argument that surrogacy has liberatory potential for enhancing women's autonomy and subjectivity could be thought of as grounding a feminist argument in favor of surrogacy. Such a position would argue that, where surrogacy arrangements are made on the basis of full disclosure and understanding, surrogacy contributes to women's autonomy, understood as the deliberate exercise of choice with respect to an individual's reproductive capacity. Surrogate motherhood could be seen as having a positive impact on women's liberation by promoting their autonomy through gaining greater control of their bodies, expanding choice, and exercising rights (Shalev 1989, 103). Furthermore, insofar as surrogacy breaks down essentialized understandings of women, reproduction, and motherhood, surrogate motherhood is to be welcomed because it emphasizes that not all women who bear children need to be thought of as "mothers," and it allows women who cannot bear children to assume the responsibilities of motherhood. Such a move could free up the oppressive understanding of women's subjectivity through which motherhood is viewed as women's preeminent, even defining, characteristic within patriarchal social arrangements. Because surrogacy separates the roles of biological parentage, gestation, and child rearing, it disrupts biologically essentialized or patriarchal assumptions about women and maternity and allows for greater diversity of subjectivities.

Feminist responses about the potential for surrogacy arrangements to enhance women's freedom of choice and self-determination focus on different aspects of this debate. The areas of focus include the relative merits of legal protection or prohibition of surrogacy arrangements, the ethical significance of women's capacity to gain a degree of economic freedom through participation in surrogacy contracts as compared with the ethical significance of the commodification of women's reproductive capacities or children through surrogacy, feminist retheorizations of autonomy and subjectivity, and considerations of the effects of surrogacy arrangements on the ways in which women and children are valued.

In assessing whether surrogacy agreements should be legally banned or enforceable, feminists have had to weigh the risk that legal enforcement of surrogacy agreements might force women to give up their children involuntarily against the risk that women's capacity to choose reproductive destiny would be subject to government interference. Lori Andrews, for example, emphasizes the importance of reaffirming a pregnant woman's right to make decisions about herself and the fetus during pregnancy; supporting a ban on contract motherhood amounts to letting governments dictate "the circumstances under which a woman should be allowed to have a child and under which families may be formed" (Andrews 1989, 365). Surrogate motherhood arrangements are, from this view, one means of resisting essentialism and its associated tendencies of exclusion and oppression for women.

Donna Dickenson offers a related argument. She is concerned that prohibition of surrogacy contracts limits women's capacity to be treated as self-owning subjects of property, holding property in their labor and reproductive capacities (Dickenson 1997, 160–63). Because women hold "property in the person," according to Dickenson, they have the right to contract their pain and suffering in labor to another. Surrogacy contracts are supported to protect the gestational mother for her labor and risk taking (Dickenson 2003, 130–32), rather than for merely "renting out a womb" or serving as a foster mother who cares for the child when the "true parents" are temporarily unavailable.

Arguments concerning the liberatory potential of surrogacy emphasize the point that in surrogate pregnancy, consent is given prior to conception. Where surrogacy arrangements are made as a matter of autonomous choice, the gestational mother's obligation to relinquish the child she bore for the commissioning party can be understood as a corollary of her freedom to undertake whatever work she chooses (Shalev 1989, 11–12, 96). Prohibiting surrogacy would, from this view, violate women's self-determination and would infringe on the commissioning parties' right to procreate. Such arguments also depend on distinguishing paid surrogacy from baby selling, that it is not the child or fetus for whom the woman receives payment, but her gestational services. Therefore, some feminists, despite reservations about the practice, support the recognition of pregnancy contracts under contract laws, avoiding differential approaches to men's and women's capacity to engage in employment contracts. These approaches emphasize the values of liberty, consent, and choice that underpin the conventional liberal individualistic notion of autonomy.

Surrogate Motherhood and Commodification of Women's Bodies

While Andrews's and Dickenson's positions provide some support for legal recognition of surrogacy arrangements, other feminists are concerned that recognition of surrogacy arrangements will reinforce views that women's bodies and capacities are subject to others' ownership, through the commodification of women's reproductive capacities. For these feminists, commodification of women's bodies poses a greater threat to women's autonomy than would prohibiting women from having legal protection for surrogacy agreements. Elizabeth Anderson, for example, challenges the claim that contract pregnancy promotes autonomy for women (Anderson 1993). Her view is that "when market norms are applied to the ways we treat and understand women's reproductive labor, women are reduced from subjects of respect and consideration to objects of use" (Anderson 1993, 198). The primary concern is that "contract pregnancy commodifies both women's labour and the child in ways that undermine the autonomy and dignity of women and the love parents owe their children" (Anderson 1993, 168). She concludes that "because the state has a legitimate interest in protecting the autonomy and dignity of women and the integrity of parental love for children, it is justified in prohibiting contract pregnancy" (Anderson 1993, 168).

Other feminists express similar concerns about the threat to women's freedom, in particular the freedom of women of color and women who are poor, from the commodification of women's bodies (see Gibson 1988; Corea 1985). The risk that surrogacy contracts will be oppressive is particularly acute in gestational surrogacy, where there may be a temptation to regard the child as a "product" wholly separate and distinct from the pregnant mother because of the lack of a genetic relationship between the surrogate and the child. Mary Shanley argues that due to women's biologically based experiences of pregnancy, payment for gestational services should be prohibited and pregnancy contracts should be nonenforceable (Shanley 2001, 102–23). Others suggest that surrogacy arrangements should be dealt with under modified adoption laws (Tong 1990, 40–56; 1995, 55–79). Concerns about the need to avoid replicating current hierarchies of race and class through surrogacy arrangements are expressed in these debates. They underscore the point that contractual freedom and human choice are not without limits; autonomy and human agency cannot be reduced to mere self-sufficiency or the exercise of choice.

Feminist Relational Autonomy and Human Agency

By questioning the conception that equates autonomy with choice, some feminist responses to surrogacy challenge the assumption that increased opportunities to make choices in the market will enhance autonomy. Ferdinand Schoeman argues that the crux of the problem arises from the liberal individualistic understanding of autonomy and human agency in terms of choice, rights, and self-determination. This has led to a predominance of rights talk that emphasizes "the appropriateness of seeing other persons as separate and autonomous agents," whereas the "relationship between parent and infant [or fetus] involves an awareness of a kind of union between people. . . . We share ourselves with those with whom we are intimate" (Schoeman 1999, 221). Feminists are rightly concerned that a legal rule enforcing a pregnancy contract would reinforce notions of human separateness and insularity, failing to recognize that the development of individuality and autonomy takes place through sustained and intimate relationships (Shanley 2001, 119).

A number of feminists have been working toward a reconceptualization of traditional notions of autonomy (see Meyers 1989; Sherwin 1998; Mackenzie and Stoljar 2000). As Susan Sherwin points out, "In the traditional view, individuals tend to be treated as interchangeable in that no attention is paid to the details of personal experience" (Sherwin 1998, 35). She argues, "If we are to effectively address these concerns, we need to move away from the familiar Western understanding of autonomy as self-defining, self-interested, and self-protecting, as if the self were simply some special kind of property to be preserved" (Sherwin 1998, 35). These writers share with care feminists (see Gilligan 1983; Held 1993) a critique of the common assumption that agents are single-mindedly self-interested, when so much of our experience is devoted to building or maintaining personal relationships and communities. Instead of an atomistic approach to the self, Meyers, Sherwin, and others advocate a "relational" alternative to our conception of the self (see, for example, Baier 1985; Held 1993) to build a relational interpretation of autonomy. Relational approaches thus challenge the liberal understanding of the individual rational chooser who is familiar to liberalism and protected by contract law. A relational approach to autonomy focuses attention on capacities for self-reflection, self-direction, and self-knowledge and analyzes the ways in which oppressive social environments can impair agents' autonomy at this level (Meyers 1989). Relational selves are inherently social beings that are significantly shaped and modified within a web of interconnected (and sometimes conflicting) relationships. They engage in activities that are constitutive of their identity and autonomy.

Relational approaches would question the purported enhancement of autonomy and agency offered by legal recognition of surrogacy arrangements, specifically the capacity of women to create meanings from those agreements that are not already embedded in broader social understandings. The relationships created and severed in these agreements are not fully chosen but may partly constitute a woman's subjectivity.

Contract Motherhood, Women's Self-Identity, and Subjectivity

Related to responses to surrogacy arrangements based on concerns about relational autonomy are those approaches that focus on the relations among embodiment, pregnancy, and women's self-identities. They emphasize that pregnant embodiment implicates a woman's self-identity (Mackenzie 1992). This shifts the debate from issues of rights and self-determination to issues of selfhood and identity of women. It brings realization that women's capacity for moral self-constitution needs protection in the demand for reproductive autonomy.

Surrogate Motherhood as Opportunity for Self-Constitution

Catriona Mackenzie argues that pregnancy is never simply a biological process. Instead, it is always an active process of shaping for oneself a bodily and moral perspective (Mackenzie 1992, 141–42). A pregnant woman must scrutinize her view of herself and attempt to arrive at an integrated self-understanding and to demonstrate compatible actions. The pregnant woman and the fetus are at one and the same time distinct and interrelated entities; they are linked as participants in a creative process of growth and change. The months of her pregnancy are the months she spends in relationship with a developing human being (Mackenzie 1992, 146). To the pregnant woman, the fetus is not simply an entity extrinsic to her that happens to be developing inside her body and that she desires either to remove or to allow to develop. It is a being, "both inseparable and yet separate from her, both part of and yet soon to be independent from her, whose existence calls into question her own present and future identity" (Mackenzie 1992, 148).

From this approach, surrogate arrangements threaten to undermine women's opportunity for self-constitution because such arrangements treat pregnancy as a merely "natural" event that just happens to women, in relation to which they are passive. Such a misunderstanding arises from the emphasis on the separability of the mother's body and the fetus and also on the strong analogy between the "work" of pregnancy and other forms of wage labor that underpin the demand for legal recognition of surrogate arrangements. These misunderstandings of both the relationship between the woman and child and the woman to her ongoing self deny the reality of the woman and fetus as beings in a relationship. They also misrepresent the experience of pregnancy as described by many women.

Representations of Women as Surrogate Mothers

Elizabeth Boetzkes argues against the practice of surrogacy because it limits rather than enhances women's opportunity for self-understanding and self-constitution through the reinforcement of degraded or stereotypical representations (Boetzkes 1999). Boetzkes argues that endorsing contract pregnancy perpetuates the symbolic relegation of women to reproductive labor, and also severely compromises the autonomy of the contracting surrogate, because the symbolism of contract pregnancy suggests that the surrogate mother's personal integration and autonomous agency can be traded away (Boetzkes 1999,129). Surrogacy also diminishes the possibility of full autonomy and moral agency for women in general. Whatever putative benefits of expanded options to be gained from contract pregnancy may be weighed against the harm of endorsing exaggerated female altruism or promoting reproductive labor as appropriate for women. When women as women are publicly devalued, their task of becoming persons is rendered problematic (Boetzkes 1999, 132).

Being devalued as female also jeopardizes self-esteem, which in turn undermines both personal individuation and possibilities for agency, understood as choosing a moral perspective and shaping one's life in accordance with it. This devaluing of the female is an impediment to the self-respect necessary for becoming a person. Drucilla Cornell notes that the demand for equality is the demand for an equal chance at becoming a person. Demands for equality include that citizens be recognized and that the basic conditions necessary for that recognition be provided. The state's role in protecting equality is twofold: (1) to protect bodily integrity and (2) to protect self-respect, which is instrumental to the possibility of personhood. This implies limiting the imposition of degrading images or exercising the degradation prohibition (Cornell 1995, 42). Banning surrogacy contracts is justified from this view because the gains to women's self-determination from surrogate motherhood are outweighed by the losses to self-respect and equality.

Surrogate Motherhood: Lived Experience of Chinese Women and the Potential for Confucian Feminism

The foregoing arguments concerning surrogate motherhood in response to the liberal claims for surrogacy are of particular interest to Chinese women trying to create a new self-understanding in the modern world.[1] Throughout Chinese history, women have been denied freedom and equality, have been subjected to patriarchal power and authority, and have been sequestered in the private sphere where they have been denied access to the ultimate in privacy, namely control over their own bodies. Women have been treated as social, economical, and legal unequals; they also have been denied autonomous control of their life choices through their exclusion from opportunities to exercise authority, to consent to treatment, and to make contracts, while having obligations and duties forced on them. Neither the socialist revolution nor recent market reforms have brought Chinese women true liberation. Thus, as victims of long-standing oppression and inequality, Chinese women might view surrogacy and, in particular, contract motherhood (commercial surrogacy) as a concrete means to help empower them.

But before surrogacy has any chance of becoming empowering for Chinese women, the deep structure of Chinese society must be freed of its sexist roots— a formidable task to say the least. One possible source of women's current situation in China is the role of Confucianism in Chinese society. Confucianism has meant many things over the centuries in China. One reading of Confucianism was that it sacrificed individuals for the sake of families and was particularly oppressive to women. Those who have defended Confucianism against charges of the oppression of women argued that core Confucian teachings had little to do with the oppression or denigration of women, especially the core ideas of the founders and leading thinkers of classical Confucianism, namely Confucius (551–479 B.C.E.) and Mencius (385–304? B.C.E.).

Without dismissing the connection between the gender system in China and Confucianism, I attempt to formulate a Chinese feminist perspective to evaluate the issue of surrogate motherhood, through extension and reinterpretation of Confucian notions of autonomy and human agency, human virtues, and human dignity. The reinterpretation I offer resonates with many of the feminist criticisms of surrogacy discussed in the first sections of this chapter. Such a reinterpretation and reconstruction entails a new reading of the original classical Confucianism, as distinguished from later Confucianism, which became the state-sponsored philosophy in China from the Han Dynasty (206 B.C.E. to 220 C.E.) until the Imperial years in China. What is being argued is that Confucian oppression of women is not a necessary implication of its general philosophy and that women in Confucian China had been able to participate in social and moral functions in society.

I am reminded in writing this chapter of recent observations made by historian Patricia Ebrey that "clearly it is time to discard the exaggerated stereotypes generated by the rhetoric of the New Culture Movement" in China at the beginning of this century (Ebrey 2000, xi). Ebrey points out that although Chinese society has been sexist, she and other historians over the years have produced increasing evidence that in virtually every period of Chinese history, there were women who had enough leeway to create productive and meaningful lives. She urges a proper analysis and explanation of the relationship between women's low status and Confucianism as the dominant social and political doctrine in China.

Lisa Raphals, a philosopher, linguist, and severe critic of Confucian patriarchy, also acknowledges that women in early China were often represented as intellectually adroit, politically astute, and ethically virtuous, directly countering the familiar image of Chinese women as always oppressed, powerless, passive, and silent (Raphals 1998). Sociologist Laurel Bossen further reminds us that

> the stereotype of women as domestic subordinates, politically powerless and economically burdensome, is increasingly modified by evidence that Chinese women were not easily restrained; they were productive, expressive, and found ways to pursue their own interests. Although historical studies do reveal recurrent patterns of patrilineal, patrilocal and patriarchal institutions, they are also shown to change over time. (Bossen 1999, 296)

These discussions suggest that the evolution of feminism in China should not be hindered by our attempts to explore, analyze, and evaluate the aspects of the Chinese culture that can account for the obstacles and opportunities facing Chinese women in their struggle to achieve and to be recognized in their achievements as moral persons. One approach is to examine the philosophical aspects of Confucianism and to assess whether conceptually Confucianism can accommodate women's equality and autonomy. In this regard, the chapter hopes to promote a more constructive engagement between Confucianism and feminism, through connecting their respective insights on the controversial issue of surrogate motherhood as a way to build a new relationship that may prove fruitful for the critical self-reflection and further development of the two philosophical systems.

Women's Status in the Traditional Chinese Family

Anthropologists who study the traditional Chinese family (Zang 1998) remind us of the relatively low status and limited power held by women. Their studies show that as an unmarried woman, the traditional Chinese woman had to obey her father; as a married woman, she had to obey her husband; and as a widow, she had to obey her adult sons. Even marriage did not bring traditional Chinese women a higher status in the family. If a traditional Chinese woman displeased her husband or her mother-in-law, or if there were economic hardships, she might be returned to her parents. Her position was weakest when she was still childless (sonless), stronger when she became a mother and bore a son, and even stronger when a daughter-in-law came under her direction. Her authority increased as she became advanced in age, and if her husband died earlier, she might come to command more respect as her son became the head of the family.

In his research on the contemporary Chinese family, American anthropologist William Jankowiak observed that even today mothers exercise tremendous psychological influence over their offspring and are the center of the familial communication network; they are the glue that binds families together (Jankowiak 1993). Within the traditional Chinese family, mothers command high respect because of their care for their children and their commitment to their family. Other studies also show how Chinese youth tend to confide in their mothers. Clearly, biological motherhood is an important power base for Chinese women.

Given Chinese mothers' lived experience, it is doubtful that surrogate motherhood would be good news for Chinese women. One of the consequences of splitting the function of motherhood into child begetting, childbearing, and child rearing is a reduction in power of the mother and her claim to a child. By reducing reproduction to a productive process with a fine and distinct division of labor, every stage of production and labor can easily be performed by replaceable, substitutable, totally unrelated, free and separate strangers. The segmentation of reproduction threatens to reduce motherhood to a thin concept and to yield a more impoverished status for women rather than enhance motherhood and empower Chinese women. In enabling more women to become mothers through technological interventions, surrogacy can also transform women into replaceable objects and substitutable parts in the child-production process.

The gendering of altruism through philanthropic motherhood should make Chinese feminists particularly nervous. In the Chinese context, it is highly probable that philanthropic motherhood would render women even more likely victims of exploitation than contract motherhood in that it asks women to provide their reproductive services for close relatives or senior family members without the hope of economic reward. Such appeals or requests are often even more oppressive and difficult to refuse than restrictive contracts sealed with impersonal strangers. In addition to the state and the market, relatives and friends intervene in women's private reproductive decisions, making Chinese women even more powerless and lacking in self-control. In a similar vein, Uma Narayan has also warned that in gift or altruistic surrogacy, relationships and emotional ties to the receiving parents may make the surrogate woman more vulnerable to emotional pressure and coercion concerning the conditions of pregnancy and childbirth (Narayan 1995, 178).

To conclude, this level of analysis indicates that the replacement of women's childbearing capacity by male-controlled technology may remove women's biological burden, but if the women who will raise children within a family no longer are the ones who give birth, they may end up having less power and less self-control. Since surrogate motherhood can imply less power and less capacity for agency for women, it seems unwise for Chinese women to give up what is for many of them the only power they could ever have—their power as mothers—if they were to claim subjectivity and autonomy as defined in the liberal perspective.

Locating Surrogate Motherhood within a Confucian Feminist Perspective

Surrogate motherhood can be further analyzed and evaluated from a Confucian feminist perspective. This section provides an analysis of the Confucian perspective on notions of autonomy and agency, caring and commitment, and family relationships and moral virtues, since these notions have been central to the feminist debate on surrogacy. I will then use these notions to identify precisely why surrogate motherhood is problematic from a Confucian feminist perspective, incorporating feminist ethical concerns about women's equal opportunity for self-development and moral personhood.

Autonomy and Human Agency in Confucian Moral Perspective

The Confucian perspective in this chapter is based on the early canons of Confucius and Mencius, who represent classical or ancient Confucianism. As Heiner Roetz points out: "Chinese moral philosophy in general, as well as Confucianism and the program of its founder in particular, cannot be understood unless one is aware of the problems of the epoch to which an answer had to be found" (Roetz 1999, 243). Often referred to as "the Warring States" period in Chinese philosophy (1111–249 B.C.E.), it was a period characterized on one hand by the decay of the central power of the Zhou king, the dissolution of the patriarchal feudal system, and the crisis of established conventional morality. On the other hand, it was also a period distinguished by many controversies of the age, made possible by the breakdown of traditions and received opinions, a period of regicide, patricide, genocide, extreme cruelty, and violence in Chinese history.

The challenge to find a new moral basis for rescuing ethical life in a disintegrating world was what prompted philosophical thought and systematic questioning by the Zhou philosophers in the first place (Roetz 1999, 243). It was a time when the traditional certainties disintegrated in the struggle of opinions and when the philosophers did not conform to their society. The unsettled life of these philosophers contrasted strongly with the embeddedness in tradition and community that dominated in former times. It is therefore no accident that the peak of Chinese philosophy fell into this period, also known as "the Hundred Schools" period, which built a "tradition of the critique of tradition" in Chinese philosophy (Roetz 1999, 239).

One of the important developments was the Confucian ethical vision that grounds ethics firmly in the moral life of the agent. From the point of view of Confucian virtue ethics, the way toward the interior as a means of finding the only solid basis for ethical life lies in the individual's inner self. But far from merely focusing on the inner life of an "interior self" or "inner entity" with a "private ego and will," Confucian emphasis on self-cultivation of the moral agent is both "self-directed" and "other-directed," exemplifying a moral perspective in which one's concern for oneself and one's concern for others are integrated as the direction of our ethical attention (Shun 2001, 230). From such a perspective of moral agency, understood as the integration of concern for oneself and concern for others, the human agent in Confucian ethics is always social and relational, not merely self-directed or self-interested.

Self-determination and autonomous action have moral value only insofar as they are based on ethical principles or are guided by moral virtues that integrate self-directed and other-directed concerns. Human agency is defined in terms of autonomous judgment and action to realize our potentials for moral virtues. According to Mencius, every human being is endowed with four potentials for moral virtues at birth (Mencius 1988): the seeds of compassion, righteousness, modesty, and right and wrong. These are also our "four beginnings" or "four moral possibilities" for achieving humaneness, righteousness, propriety, and wisdom. Because of these four moral seeds, the source of our human dignity, we all have the potential to achieve personhood. We humans have a moral obligation to develop these potentials and to uphold our dignity and self-respect. Autonomy in this sense deals more with not bending to power or wealth, not surrendering to poverty or adversity, and not conforming to selfish desires or social pressure as a way to preserve our self-respect and moral integrity in the process of self-development and self-cultivation. The notion does not emphasize self-interest, self-sufficiency, or self-control as in a liberal individualist understanding. Full humanity or personhood is defined by the cardinal virtue of *ren* (meaning love or benevolence), which emphasizes reciprocal relationships, empathetic understanding, and altruistic regard for others. The virtue of *ren* is to be achieved through cultivation of the moral self in the context of one's social relations. But there is no one single prescribed way to realize one's moral potentials. Mencius emphasized that there can be different paths to become a sage, although the goal of benevolence is the same for all (Mencius 1988).

From the Confucian perspective, it is clear that autonomous action and judgment are valued but not as ends in themselves. They are the necessary conditions for moral agency. The Confucian system emphasizes the development of autonomous agents as relational, interacting beings rather than the importance of autonomy as a property to be possessed by individual agents for protection of separateness and self-sufficiency. Similar to the feminist notion of relational autonomy, Confucian understanding of the self is also dynamic, engaged in an ongoing process of identity formation that involves relatedness to, and differentiation from, others. It posits a notion of autonomy that emphasizes self-respect grounded in a notion of inner human dignity possessed equally by all humans, not excluding women. Because of this inner dignity, all humans possess the moral potentials to achieve personhood, through the project of continuous self-cultivation and self-development.

But it would not be unfair to say that the Confucian notion of autonomy focuses on the moral nature of agents instead of on capacities for autonomy. It is not so concerned with the ways in which socialization and social relationships impede or enhance autonomy, a core concern in the feminist approach to autonomy. It is also true that Confucian literature pleads for the social differentiation of gender. This doubtlessly left more than enough scope for patriarchalism. A reconstructed Confucian ethics, based on a reinterpretation and expansion of its principles and values, can therefore be useful for refuting traditional stereotypes of women and for supporting expansion and recognition of women's participation in social and moral functions as beings with equal moral worth and dignity in contemporary Chinese society.

Caring and Commitment in Confucian Moral Perspective

As read through the lens of the Confucian and Mencian canon, classical Confucian ethics shares with feminist care ethics a keen insight into close relational ties and the humanizing role of caring and commitment in the development of human subjectivity and as the formation of self-identity or personhood (see, for example, Gilligan 1983; Chodorow 1978; Noddings 1984). For classical Confucians and feminists who emphasize an ethics of care, human connectedness is our moral starting point. Both traditions value relatedness instead of competitive individualism and emphasize a view of mutually self-creating individuals within intimate and caring relationships first experienced as family relationships (Li 1999; Tao 2000). There is no notion of human subjects as being distinct entities prior to, or independent of, experience in either classical Confucianism ethics or feminist care ethics.

Similar to feminist care ethics, Confucian ethics puts special emphasis on particularistic ties and family relationships, especially those between parents and children. Such intimate relationships are characterized by two important moral norms: commitment and care. Care, from the feminist understanding, is defined as "disinterested concern and the subsequent will/action/disposition to promote the welfare of the 'cared-for'" (Noddings 1984, 23–24). It denotes "a disinterested concern for the sake of the cared-for and not for one's exclusive prudential interests" (Noddings 1984, 23–24). Caring, from this understanding, means that one's attitude and the will or action to promote the welfare of the cared-for do not stem from one's consideration of the immediate or future benefits or gratifications one may gain through the promotion of the welfare of the cared-for. By definition, a calculation of one's own interests and self-regard cannot be the explanatory factor for caring attitudes and activities.

Commitment is another important defining norm of intimate relationships. An intimate relationship is "one in which one shares one's self with others" (Schoeman 1999, 220–27). In intimate relationships, one meets the other in himself or herself as a particular person. Particularity in this sense implies irreplaceability and nonsubstitutability. Such a conception of particularity has two goals. First, we see the person related to us as the irreplaceable particular. Second, we see the relationship as a unique particular good. In other words, when we perceive a person as a distinct particular, we mean that the person cannot be replaced or substituted without changing the nature of the relationship we have with the person. What is inimical to particularity in this type of intimate relationship are ulterior purposes defined independently of the person concerned. Each person in the caring relationship becomes the object of the other's emotions, not an object to fulfill one's purposes. It is in this sense that every parent and every child is irreplaceable, just as every mothering relationship is nonsubstitutable.

However, although parallels exist between Confucianism and feminist care ethics, there are also significant differences (Tao 2000). In addition to its strong care orientation, the Confucian moral ideal of *ren* requires the virtues of humaneness and righteousness for achieving caring and self-development. Humaneness stresses proper affective concern for other living things, while righteousness (*yi*) stresses "a strictness with oneself, involving a commitment to right conduct" (Shun 2001, 234). In other words, "the affective concern that is part of humaneness has to be regulated by a commitment to right conduct for the person to be truly humane" (Shun 2001, 236). Humaneness can lead to right conduct; but the affective concern of humaneness must also be regulated by a commitment to propriety and right conduct for the person to be truly humane. This emphasis on the link between humaneness and righteousness is the cornerstone of the Confucian ethical system. Because of this emphasis on humaneness and righteousness, a

Confucian agent can be justified to challenge and reject imposed caring or relationships that harm or threaten to harm self-respect and dignity. Likewise, he or she also has the duty to refrain from engaging in caring or relationships that harm the self-respect and dignity of the participants. Caring and commitment in human relationships are valuable, but they need to be governed by the virtues of humaneness and righteousness.

Family Relationships and Human Virtues in Confucian Moral Perspective

From a Confucian perspective, family relationships and motherhood derive their moral status and intrinsic value from deep commitment and caring. These commitments and caring define moral agency, although they do not and should not be confined and restricted to the family. But it is within the family context that human beings develop the kind of trust, bonding, and reciprocity that make possible these commitments and caring that constitute Confucian moral agency. This is a far cry from defining agency in terms of free choice, self-determination, and access to power.

It is not surprising that the Confucian discourse on the parent-child relationship is essentially virtue-based. In contrast to the dominant liberal rights-based discourse, which emphasizes concepts such as power, rights, duties, and benefits out of concern for the limit and scope of children's obligations and parental power, the key concepts in the Confucian discourse are virtues, affection, *hsiao* (filial piety), and reciprocity. From the Confucian perspective, the moral virtues of affection of the parent and filiality of the child stand at the heart of the parent-child relationship.

Chinese Confucian ethical tradition is known for its emphasis on the virtue of filial piety. For Mencius, children's filial obligation to provide dignified funerals for their dead parents is justified in this way:

> Presumably there must have been cases in ancient times of people not burying their parents. When the parents died, they were thrown in the gullies. Then one day the sons passed the place and there lay the bodies, eaten by foxes and sucked by flies. A sweat broke out on their brows, and they could not bear to look. The sweating was not put on for others to see. It was an outward expression of their innermost heart. They went home for baskets and spades. If it was truly right for them to bury the remains of their parents, then it must also be right for all dutiful sons and men of humanity to do likewise. (Mencius 1988, 5)

On this understanding, the Confucian notion of reciprocity is not conceived as a simple tit-for-tat notion. Confucian reciprocity prescribes returning good for good. Parental affection and filial piety are neither rights nor duties; they are moral virtues that constitute the parent-child relationship. Human agency, understood as achieving individuation and relatedness in our self-development, is possible because of the general certainty provided by the parent-child relationship, which enables human beings to handle the many uncertain features that are an essential characteristic of human existence. It is our embeddedness in these relationships of trust, care, and commitment that provides the basis for our security and autonomy, rather than the other way around.

Because of their emphasis that the family and family relations provide the initial starting point for the development of our moral agency, Confucians view the family as more than a mere social or a biological organization. The family is also a moral entity. Names for roles such as *father*, *mother*, *son*, and *daughter* are not just social categories. They are also moral categories governed by moral norms and infused with deep moral meanings. According to Confucius, a name serves not only an epistemological function (that is, reporting about or referring to something in reality) but also an operative one (Wang 1999, 246). Under the doctrine of Cheng Ming, or "rectification of names," developed by Confucius, naming (*ming*) cannot simply be a process of attaching appropriately corresponding labels to an already existing reality. To name something is to prompt it, to actualize it, "to cause certain possibilities to be realized" (Hall and Ames 1987). In other words, names carry within themselves some embedded normative request for action.

From the Confucian perspective, caring and commitment—and the intention of desiring such caring and commitment—constitute the moral virtues of parenthood. Therefore, names such as *father*, *son*, *mother*, and *daughter* not only report bare biological or social facts but also signal the obligatory norms of being a father, a son, a mother, or a daughter. Just as loving and taking good care of young children is implied in the name of *father* or *mother*, taking respectful care of aged parents is implied in the name of *son* or *daughter*. A Confucian perspective is therefore committed to the central value of the parent-child relationship as being the foundation of human virtues and morality.

In the Confucian moral tradition, humaneness, righteousness, trust, and reciprocity are nongendered virtues accessible to men and women, mothers and fathers, sons and daughters. The place of women in the Confucian tradition has always been a subject of great controversy between those who hold the view that women are, by nature, not capable of full self-cultivation but only of developing a limited number of wifely and maternal virtues, on the one hand, and those who insist that the original Confucian canon attributes to women the same moral and intellectual capacities as men, on the other hand (see, for example, Li 1999, 115–38; Goldin 2000, 133–62; Raphals 2000, 223–48). Under the ideal of filial morality, both Confucius and Mencius accorded the mother equal status with the father in relation to children. And for women who are not mothers, we learn in the story of Ti Ying about a young daughter, with the courage to challenge authority and to petition against the injustice of the laws of her time, who was responsible for bringing about the abolition of corporal tortures and for rescuing her father from imprisonment (c.167 B.C.E.) (Qian 1961, 300).

Although gender segregation in the Confucian tradition started early in its long history, it is not obvious that women were barred from participation in social and moral functions in society.[2] Moreover, even scholars who are very critical of Confucianism agree that evidence from *The Analects* through the Table of Ancient and Modern Persons in the Han history shows that at least "in Warring States and Han narratives, women were represented as possessing the same virtues valued in men: moral integrity, intellectual judgment, the ability to admonish a superior, courage, and chastity in the name of single-minded loyalty" (Raphals 2000, 236). In the Han history, the Table of Ancient and Modern Persons includes women in its named designations of Benevolent Persons and Wise Persons. It presents a ninefold classification of 1,955 individuals from legendary times to the Qin Dynasty, classified under four named categories: Sage Persons, Benevolent Persons, Wise Persons, and Stupid (or morally retarded) Persons (Shu 1962, 20). All these documents show that gendered virtue ethics are not inherent in Chinese culture, nor are women portrayed as necessarily of inferior moral and intellectual status, incapable of becoming a sage in the Confucian ethics. It is certainly true that "the tradition does not argue for the social equality of women—only their moral equality" (Goldin 2000, 149–50). The implication is that insufficient attention is given to the effects of oppressive social contexts on individual's capacities for autonomy and moral responsibility. A reconstructed Confucian ethical perspective should be committed to social and moral equality for women and should not stop at defending a principle of equal moral worth of all.

Why Surrogate Motherhood Is Problematic: A Confucian Feminist Perspective

Devaluing Women and Threatening Self-esteem

Given this discussion of Chinese family life and the insights of early Confucianism, from a Chinese feminist perspective, surrogate motherhood, whether commercial or philanthropic, is problematic because it undermines women's capacity for moral self-development by reducing human reproduction to a mere production process; the moral harm of surrogacy outbalances the moral good. In particular, surrogate motherhood negatively impacts the moral status of motherhood. It weakens the moral claims of mothers through segmenting the reproduction process and making biological, gestational, and social motherhood interchangeable and easily replaceable social roles and functions. Surrogate motherhood harms a woman's subjectivity and identity directly by depicting her either as a heartless woman who is not worthy of the name *mother* or as a passive "mother machine." Moreover, it reinforces a woman's low self-esteem and further distorts her subjectivity vis-à-vis men in society, making her appear less worthy of reciprocity of filial piety and reverence, thus impoverishing rather than enriching her moral identity. It limits rather than enhances women's opportunities for moral self-constitution, and it undermines women's self-esteem.

Fracturing of Trust and Degrading Care

In surrogacy arrangements, the relationship between the mother and the fetus is negotiated as a mere biological or productive relationship. Attention is focused on the contractual rights and obligations of the contracted mother and the commissioning couple and the technical procedures associated with the production process. The purpose of a contract is for the mutual gain and advantage of the contracting parties, which in this case are the commissioning couple and the contracted mother. Even where the contract imposes a requirement on the contracted mother to promote the interests and well-being of the fetus during the period of gestation, the requirement is derived from the primary objective of protecting the interests of the contracting couple as part and parcel of the terms of quality control and management in the production process: to make sure that there is value for the money.

In this sense, in emphasizing the obligations specified in the contract, contract motherhood undermines by omission the obligations based on care and commitment central to Confucian understandings of motherhood. Because the interests and well-being of the fetus have value only insofar as they have value for the contracting couple, the gestational mother's caring is driven by the conditions of the contract rather than by the fetus's well-being per se. The overall effect of a surrogacy contract is to absolve the contracted mother of her moral responsibility toward the fetus by replacing her personal moral responsibility owed directly to the fetus with a contractual moral obligation owed to the contracting couple. In this sense, caring in contract motherhood is not performed out of altruistic concern for the interest of the fetus, independent of any purpose other than the welfare of the fetus. The same problem applies to philanthropic motherhood where the pregnancy is motivated not by commitment to the fetus but by a commitment driven by altruism to the infertile couple. This commitment to the couple represents the primary purpose for pregnancy and for carrying the fetus to full term with the clear intention of transferring it after birth and terminating the relationship at will by the birth mother.

From a Confucian feminist perspective, surrogate motherhood undermines the trust and reciprocal relationship between the gestational mother and the child born through surrogacy. It fractures the fabric of trust of society. Moreover, it creates an impoverished subjectivity for mother and child since the surrogate motherhood arrangement makes it impossible for them to fully actualize the virtues of care and commitment inherent in the parent-child relationship. It is in this sense that surrogate motherhood undermines the development of identity and moral agency of both mother and child by fracturing trust and reciprocity.

Undermining Intimacy and Impoverishing Motherhood

A Confucian feminist point of view emphasizes intimacy as the moral basis of the family. In surrogate motherhood, however, there is no real intention on the part of the gestational mother to commit herself to an intimate relationship, which constitutes the mother's and fetus's mutual claim to each other's care and commitment. Surrogate motherhood, both contractual and philanthropic, is characterized by the total or partial absence of a commitment to personal intimacy. As a consequence, the surrogate mother has no moral obligation to act out of a disinterested concern to promote the welfare of the cared-for (in this case, the fetus), apart from the surrogate mother's own exclusive prudential interests. This absence of a moral commitment to intimacy and to caring means that the expectation for performance of the moral norms and responsibilities of motherhood cannot be applied. In other words, the norms and meanings with which *motherhood* is invested cannot be actualized or performed under surrogate motherhood. Instead, *surrogate motherhood* suggests an ambivalent view of gestational mothers as not properly "mothers." Furthermore, conceiving children to benefit another family, whether for economic or noneconomic reasons, is harmful to relationships within the surrogate mother's family because of its violation of family intimacy. The relationship has been initiated with the ulterior objective of benefiting someone else; in this case, the commissioning party. The pregnancy is not motivated by the value of motherhood for the woman herself. The purpose is to beget a child who can then be given away or handed over for adoption. A Confucian feminist perspective would object to surrogate motherhood, both contract and philanthropic, because of their wrong-making violations of motherhood itself.

Conclusion

It is important to note that on this second level of analysis, a Confucian feminist perspective objects to surrogate motherhood because of three wrong-making characteristics: (1) devaluing of women, (2) fracturing of trust, and (3) undermining of intimacy. Contrary to the views of surrogate motherhood advocates in the West, Confucian feminists would be unconvinced that contract motherhood can be a vehicle for the liberation of women by making them men's equal through putting an end to their propertylessness in reproductive labor. Unlike some feminist objections to surrogate motherhood in the West, the main objection raised by Confucian feminists to this arrangement is not based on its creation of inequality among women, or on concerns about harms to the interests of particular women and children. Rather, the major Confucian feminist objection to surrogate motherhood is based on violation of the moral norms of care and commitment in family relationships created by surrogacy, by the general harm it creates for mothering as a profound and fundamental relationship of trust and reciprocity essential for the development of human agency, and by the threat of impoverishing women's moral self-development. Surrogate motherhood threatens to remove the meanings of trust and reciprocity with which Chinese culture has invested the mothering relationship, undermining its moral status and ultimately reducing reproduction to a mere production process similar to that performed by other animal species, empty of any moral content. The mothering relationship, if regarded as no more than a biological or social relationship, will cease to be a source of meaning and value in human life and identity development.

One of the popular views held by some liberals in the West is that self-determination in pursuing life projects of one's own choice is an effective way to empower women and develop women's subjectivity. From a Confucian feminist point of view, however, embarking on a life project of one's own choice is only a necessary condition for developing women's subjectivity. It is not a sufficient condition for enhancing subjectivity if the life project lacks ethical content, even though it might have been chosen freely by women. As has been argued earlier, surrogate motherhood as a project for women can actually disempower women and harm women's subjectivity, even if chosen by women, because the project of surrogate motherhood involves fracturing the trust of the mother-child relationship and undermining women's integrity and moral agency.

It is of course important to recognize that mothering or motherhood is not the only, necessary, or inevitable way for women to acquire identity or to realize moral virtues. Mothering or motherhood does not have to constitute an essential aspect of woman's self-understanding and self-identity. The way to develop and achieve moral virtues and personhood can be different for different women, in the same way that the moral virtues to be developed and realized can vary for different women in different contexts. But it is important to recognize and underscore mothering as a moral activity, not just as a mere nurturing, natural, biologically determined activity that has functional values only and hence is easily replaceable and substitutable by other means or agents. Mothering is a moral relationship. We should not discredit it, or be ashamed of it, or degrade it. It is also important to recognize that there is no one single universal mothering experience for women.

A Confucian feminist perspective favors banning surrogate motherhood, both contract and philanthropic, because it erodes family virtues, hurts women, and undermines motherhood. The right-making conditions associated with surrogacy are outweighed by these wrong-making circumstances. A reconstructed Confucian ethics, based on the early canons of Confucius and Mencius, can lend support to the quest of contemporary feminists to build a new form of subjectivity, premised on connectedness and virtues, in which women can participate fully as moral agents.

Notes

1. In an opinion survey titled "Public Attitude towards Surrogate Mothering and Male Pregnancy in Hong Kong," conducted by Chan Ho-mun, Anthony Fung, and Julia Tao, City University of Hong Kong, March 1999, of the 1,013 respondents surveyed, 60 percent do not accept commercial surrogacy. Only one-third of the respondents do not object to it. Even in the case of noncommercial surrogacy arrangement, it is accepted by less than 40 percent and rejected by more than 50 percent of the respondents. The most common reasons against surrogacy are "unnatural" (commercial: 24.7 percent; noncommercial: 18.1 percent) and "immoral" (commercial: 27.9 percent; noncommercial: 30.2 percent). Other reasons for objection include the following: the presence of the surrogate mother would undermine family integrity (commercial: 5.9 percent; noncommercial: 11.7 percent), confusions and ambiguities in human relationships (commercial: 15.7 percent; noncommercial: 19.9 percent), and interests of the child not being protected (commercial: 2.9 percent; noncommercial: 6.4 percent). The total number of responses for these last three reasons equal the same number of responses for the first two. It is also no coincidence that the responses express a greater concern for the negative impact of noncommercial surrogacy on family integrity and human relationships than for commercial surrogacy. For further information, please see Chan and Tao 2000.

2. In fact, the only important statement Confucius made about women was the following remark: "Only women and petty men are difficult to nourish. If you are familiar with them, they become insubordinate; if you are distant from them, they complain" (Confucius 1979, 25). While Confucius may have considered women "difficult to nourish," he emphatically did not believe they were incapable of moral self-cultivation. Elsewhere in *The Analects*, he points out that an exceptional woman can be just as talented as an exceptional man (Confucius 1979, 20).

References

Anderson, Elizabeth. 1993. *Value in Ethics and Economics*. Cambridge, Mass: Harvard University Press.

Andrews, Lori. 1989. *Between Strangers: Surrogate Mothers, Expectant Fathers, and Brave New Babies*. New York: Harper & Row.

Baier, Annette. 1985. *Postures of the Mind: Essays on Mind and Morals*. Minneapolis: University of Minnesota Press.

Boetzkes, Elizabeth. 1999. "Autonomy, and Feminist Bioethics." In *Embodying Bioethics*, edited by Anne Donchin and Laura Purdy, 121–40. Baltimore: Rowman & Littlefield.

Bossen, Laurel. 1999. "Women and Development." In *Understanding Contemporary China*, edited by Robert Gamer, 293–320. Boulder, Colo.: Lynne Rienner.

Chan Ho-mun, and Julia Tao. 2000. "Should Hong Kong Ban Surrogacy? Public Opinion and Ethical Analysis." In *Global Bioethics*, edited by Yi Huifang, Liu Ciquan, and Qin Renzong, 246–61. Beijing: Higher Education Press.

Chodorow, Nancy. 1978. *The Reproduction of Mothering*. Berkeley: University of California Press.

Confucius. 1979. *The Analects*, translated by D. C. Lau. London: Penguin.

Corea, Gena. 1985. *The Mother Machine*. New York: Harper & Row.

Cornell, Drucilla. 1995. *The Imaginary Domain*. New York: Routledge.

Dickenson, Donna. 1997. *Property, Women and Politics: Subjects or Objects?* Cambridge, UK: Polity Press.

———. 2003. *Risk and Luck in Medical Ethics*. Cambridge, UK: Polity Press.

Ebrey, Patricia. 2000. "Foreword." In *The Sage and the Second Sex*, edited by Chenyang Li and Patricia Ebrey, ix–xiv. Chicago: Open Court.

Gibson, M. 1988. "The Moral and Legal Status of 'Surrogate' Motherhood." Invited address at the winter meeting of the American Philosophical Association, December.

Gilligan, Carol. 1983. *In a Different Voice*. Cambridge, Mass.: Harvard University Press.

Goldin, Paul Rakita. 2000. "The View of Women in Early Confucianism." In *The Sage and the Second Sex*, edited by Chenyang Li, 133–62. Chicago: Open Court.

Hall, David, and Ames, Roger. 1987. *Thinking through Confucius*. Albany: State University of New York Press.

Held, Virginia. 1993. *Feminist Morality: Transforming Culture, Society, and Politics*. Chicago: University of Chicago Press.

Jankowiak, William. 1993. *Sex, Death, and Hierarchy in a Chinese City*. New York: Columbia University Press.

Li, Chenyang. 1999. *The Tao Encounters the West*. Albany: State University of New York Press.

Mackenzie, Catriona. 1992. "Abortion and Embodiment." *Australasia Journal of Philosophy* 70, no. 2: 136–55.

Mackenzie, Catriona, and Stoljar, Natalie, eds. 2000. *Relational Autonomy: Feminist Perspectives on Autonomy, Agency and the Social Self*. New York: Oxford University Press.

Mencius. 1988. *Mencius*, translated by D. C. Lau. New York: Penguin.

Meyers, Diana. 1989. *Self, Society and Personal Choice*. New York: Columbia University Press.

Narayan, Uma. 1995. "The 'Gift' of a Child: Commercial Surrogacy, Gift Surrogacy, and Motherhood." In *Expecting Trouble*, edited by Patricia Boling, 177–202. Boulder, Colo.: Westview.

Noddings, Nel. 1984. *Caring: A Feminist Approach to Ethics and Moral Education*. Berkeley: University of California Press.

Qian, Sima. 1961. *Records of the Grand Historian: Han Dynasty I*, translated by Burton Watson. New York: Columbia University Press.

Ragoné, Heléna. 2000. "Of Likeness and Difference: How Race Is Being Transfigured by Gestational Surrogacy." In *Ideologies and Technologies of Motherhood: Race, Class, Sexuality, Nationalism*, edited by Heléna Ragoné, 56–75. New York: Routledge.

Raphals, Lisa. 1998. *Sharing the Light: Representations of Women and Virtue in Early China*. Albany: State University of New York Press.

———. 2000. "Gendered Virtue Reconsidered: Notes from the Warring States and Han." In *The Sage and the Second Sex*, edited by Chenyang Li, 223–48. Chicago: Open Court.

Roetz, Heiner. 1999. "The 'Dignity within Oneself': Chinese Tradition and Human Rights." In *Chinese Thought in a Global Context: A Dialogue between Chinese and Western Philosophical Approaches*, edited by Karl-Heinz Pohl, 236–62. Leiden, the Netherlands: Brill.

Schoeman, Ferdinand. 1999. "Rights of Children, of Parents, and the Moral Basis of the Family." In *Morals, Marriage, and Parenthood: An Introduction to Family Ethics*, edited by Laurence D. Houlgate, 220–27. Belmont, Calif.: Wadsworth.

Shalev, Carmel. 1989. *Birth Power: The Case for Surrogacy*. New Haven, Conn.: Yale University Press.

Shanley, Mary. 2001. *Making Babies, Making Families*. Boston: Beacon.

Sherwin, Susan. 1998. "A Relational Approach to Autonomy in Health-Care." In *The Politics of Women's Health: Exploring Agency and Autonomy*, edited by the Feminist Health Care Ethics Research Network, coordinated by Susan Sherwin, 19–47. Philadelphia: Temple University Press.

Shu, Han. 1962. *Table of Ancient and Modern Persons*. Beijing: Zhonghus Shuju.

Shun, Kwong-loi. 2001. "Self and Self-Cultivation in Early Confucian Thought." In *Two Roads to Wisdom: Chinese and Analytic Philosophical Traditions*, edited by Bo Mou, 229–44. Chicago: Open Court.

Tao, Julia. 2000. "Two Perspectives of Care: Confucian Ren and Feminist Care." *Journal of Chinese Philosophy* 27: 2.

Tong, Rosemarie. 1990. "The Overdue Death of a Feminist Chameleon: Taking a Stand on Surrogacy." *Journal of Social Philosophy* 2, no. 3: 40–56.

———. 1995. "Feminist Perspectives and Gestational Motherhood: The Search for a Unified Legal Focus." In *Reproduction, Ethics and the Law*, edited by Joan C. Callahan, 55–79. Bloomington: Indiana University Press.

Wang, Qingjie. 1999. "The Confucian Filial Obligation and Care for Aged Parents." In *Confucian Bioethics*, edited by Rui-Ping Fan, 235–56. Dordrecht: Kluwer Academic Publishers.

Zang, Xiawei. 1998. "Family and Marriage." In *Understanding Contemporary China*, edited by Robert E. Gamer, 267–92. Boulder, Colo.: Lynne Rienner.

RIGHTING GENETIC WRONGS: RESTORING RELATIONSHIPS

Patents on Genetic Material
A New Originary Accumulation

11

MARÍA JULIA BERTOMEU AND SUSANA E. SOMMER

T
HIS CHAPTER EXAMINES the ethico-legal significance of the extension of property rights, through patents, to genetic material. Recent and anticipated developments in patent law raise troubling issues for feminist bioethicists, many of whom are alarmed about the intensification of poverty in developing economies and the mounting effect of impoverishment on the health and well-being of vulnerable people. Women—the principal caregivers of children and the most impoverished group in virtually all economies—tend to suffer disproportionately from present trends toward the commodification of health-related resources. The increasing drive to permit patents on genetic material illustrates one dimension of this deepening threat to the fundamental human rights of many of the world's most vulnerable people.

Scientists, ethicists, and policy makers talk as if the human genome is "humanity's inheritance," when the reality is that it is in danger of being divided into pieces and becoming the possession of competing "discoverers." In this chapter, we argue in favor of keeping partial or total gene sequences in the public domain, and hence against patents over genetic material. Our position is based on concerns about how exclusive, legally protected genetic patents disadvantage developing nations, intensify the oppression of women in these countries, and bring about monopoly (or near monopoly) control over health research on the human genome. Specifically, we claim that any extension of exclusive property rights requires justification and that the old liberal political arguments that justified patents for traditional inventions do not apply to genetic material. Our view is that providing patents for inventing novel entities is very different from providing patents for discovering naturally occurring resources that, in a very profound sense, belong not to the individual discoverer but to the human community in general.[1]

Genetic Material in Patent Law

Patenting of genetic matter and living beings is a departure from traditional intellectual property laws. In fact, products of nature were not granted patent protection until the famous U.S. Supreme Court case *Diamond v. Chakrabarty*, 447 U.S. 303 (1980), in which the Court declared that the creation of a live, human-made organism is patentable. The U.S. Patent Office took this path-breaking decision further by making it possible for corporations to secure patents over plants formerly protected by plant breeders' rights. As if this commercial intrusion into nature was not enough, this same office decided in 1987 to extend patent protection to genetically modified animals and to associated research procedures and protocols for their development (Sommer 2001). These decisions paved the way for granting patents over all living organisms, including genetic material, as if they were industrial inventions.[2]

Large multinational firms vigorously sought such changes in patent laws. One of their strategies was to erase the distinction between discovery and invention—a traditional boundary in patent-rights law—and to claim patent rights over pre-existing microorganisms they "discovered" but in no way changed. Such patents have distorted scientific inquiry. Many projects are now chosen for their prospect of generating economic profit. Sponsors favor secrecy—until the project gets patent protection—as a way to guard eventual patent rights. As a result, publication of findings is often delayed, information is withheld from possible competitors, and samples are denied to other researchers to protect profits.[3] Introduced into international law under the rubric of intellectual property rights, such changes provide for exclusive commercial rights that permit a small number of multinational corporations to dominate major industries, including agriculture and health.

In the sphere of agriculture, developing countries have been required to pay royalties to use genetically modified (GM) seeds that have been patented by investors, who typically reside in developed countries. This system of royalties forces farmers to rely on fertilizers and herbicides produced by the same companies that sell GM crop seeds. Though the biotechnology companies may consider patents on GM crop seeds a just means of protecting their investment in research, we see them as unjustifiable devices to impose extortionate prices on vulnerable people (Sakakibara and Branstetter 1999).[4] We believe the development and recognition of patents on GM crop seeds creates a new sphere for capitalism, a new "originary accumulation" whereby agricultural laborers are forced to purchase seed to which they previously had free access (Juma 1989; Boyle 2003; Marx 1867/1976).[5]

Golden Rice, a genetically modified rice that produces provitamin A, a component usually not found in rice, is probably one of the best examples of the originary accumulation at work (Crouch 2001). The development of Golden Rice was part of a publicly funded project, the aim of which was to distribute the vitamin A–enriched rice to poor farmers in developing nations without charge or licensing restrictions. People in developing nations, where the staple food is regular rice, are usually seriously lacking in vitamin A. Absence of vitamin A leads to xerophthalmia (dryness of the skin, eye, or mucous membranes) and blindness. Golden Rice, which in theory would cost no more than regular rice, was meant to solve the vitamin A deficiency problem. If rice is the most common component of one's diet, then the more vitamins that can be packed into this food, the better.

The development of Golden Rice required the use of genes, DNA sequences, and other genetic components that correspond to more than seventy different patents owned by thirty-two companies and institutions (GRAIN 2001).[6] Ingo Potrykus (2000), the scientist who developed Golden Rice, believed humanitarian distribution of the product was feasible because some of the biotech companies involved were willing to make free licenses available to farmers in developing nations. However, new patent law may block these humanitarian impulses. On the basis of twelve patents that have been recognized by twenty-five countries where vitamin A deficiency exists, farmers' access to Golden Rice in poorer countries may be limited (GRAIN 2001). Due to the complexity of licensing arrangements, the inventors of Golden Rice ceded their rights to Greenovation, a biotech spin-off company from the University of Freiburg, Germany, which then struck a deal with AstraZeneca (now Syngenta).

According to GRAIN, the terms of the free license agreements are still unclear (GRAIN 2001). They appear to allow research but not release or commercialization. But in effect, private enterprise AstraZeneca acquired exclusive commercial control over a technology developed with public funding for humanitarian purposes (GRAIN 2001). According to one report (Tait and Wrong 2000), AstraZeneca will license noncommercial rights back to the inventors and help them improve the grain, deal with patent issues, and guide Golden Rice through the costly testing and regulatory process. The inventors will distribute the rice free to government-run breeding centers and agriculture institutes in China, India, and other rice-dependent Asian nations. Local farmers will each be allowed to earn $10,000 annually from the grain without paying royalties. In exchange, AstraZeneca will commercialize Golden Rice along with a range of "functional foods" that many analysts believe will appeal to increasingly age-obsessed and health-obsessed·people in developed nations (Tait and Wrong 2000). Because these kinds of foods contain many nutrients such as the antioxidant beta-carotene, which plays a preventive role in the fight against cancer and coronary disease, affluent people will probably want to eat them in an attempt to neutralize the bad effects of the fat- and sugar-loaded foods they ordinarily consume.

Is Golden Rice merely a benefit for the Gene Giants, or is it a real contribution to the poor, who are not generally their customers[7] (Rural Advancement Foundation International 2000)? We should not forget that the absorption of vitamin A depends on nourishment, and the majority of people in developing countries are undernourished and lack other micronutrients. Packing all the necessary nutrients into one food does not alleviate poverty and malnutrition. Nor does it prompt anyone to ask the right questions about the safety of enriched foods or the ways in which their growth and harvesting may negatively affect the environment.

The impact of the new originary accumulation is also evident in patent monopolies on genes BRCA1 and BRCA2. These genes, located on chromosomes 17 and 13, respectively, are implicated in some women's susceptibility to breast cancer (Sommer 1998). From 5 to 10 percent of breast and ovarian cancer is related to these genes, but their presence does not necessarily mean that a woman will develop cancer. Nevertheless, large pharmaceutical companies have been eager to secure patents on these genes. For example, researchers from the University of Utah reported their findings about the breast cancer genes to Myriad Genetics in 1994 (Nuffield Council 2002, 39). Myriad Genetics then filed patent applications that were granted in a number of jurisdictions. These applications asserted rights over the normal BRCA1 gene sequence and various mutations of it, as well as over diagnostic tests for detecting mutations in BRCA1 and methods for screening samples taken from tumors. The patents were awarded in 1997 (Nuffield Council 2002, 39).

Current Controversy Regarding Patents on Genetic Material

Monopoly control over the diagnostic use of BRCA1 is ethically contentious because it will likely hinder equitable access to screening tests and rational development of new diagnostic methods. Scientific societies, including some French organizations, the Belgian Human Genetics Society, and the Danish Medical Genetics Society, expressed their opposition to European patents of BRCA1 in 2001. They questioned the appropriateness of granting patent rights because BRCA1 is not an invention and the patent license is overly broad in the scope of diagnostic practices to which it may apply. In October 2001, the European Parliament resolved to oppose the patenting of gene BRCA1 on the grounds that such a monopoly is contrary to public health policies committed to the welfare and interests of high-risk patients (Nuffield Council 2002, 40).

The legitimacy of exclusive property rights over these genes, gene sequences, and diagnostic tests has also been challenged in the Canadian province of Ontario on similar grounds ("Ownership of Genes" 2003). Despite the fact that Myriad

Genetics threatens costly lawsuits against any other parties that develop tests using this genetic material without paying licensing or royalty fees, the Ontario Health Ministry has ignored this threat and developed tests based on the same gene, processed differently. In April 2003, this Canadian test became available. It now provides BRCAI test results faster and at a much lower cost than the Myriad Genetics test did. According to the Canadian Cancer Society, patent ownership of genes hinders research and prevents the development of better diagnostic and screening tests. These criticisms are not shared, however, by all Canadian cancer researchers. Some want gene patents to be recognized because they believe that the high costs and risks of genetic research can be offset only by the expectation of economic revenues ("Ownership of Genes" 2003).

Myriad Genetics has launched a media and advertising campaign to promote the BRCAI tests, which typically cost more than two thousand dollars, on radio and television. According to a *GeneWatch* article (Byravan 2003), the commercial promotes a number of misconceptions about the role of genetics in the development of cancer. A reductionist focus on genes dominates the advertisement and does not take into account the importance of environmental factors and their influence on breast cancer.

Women who can afford the test may be at risk of employment or insurance discrimination based on the results (Byravan 2003). In fact, the Council for Responsible Genetics (CRG) has already collected more than two hundred cases of discrimination based on genetic information (not specific to breast cancer). Research on 378 women previously diagnosed with breast cancer shows that women who did not disclose information about their cancer gave a variety of reasons for their decisions. About 13 percent said they worried about the stigma or embarrassment of cancer, and about 8 percent said they were concerned that talking about their cancer would affect personal or work relationships or their career prospects. Many women also reported difficulties in obtaining or continuing life insurance, extended health care coverage, or private disability insurance. In the European Union, an estimated 25 percent of patients with a history of cancer "experience disparate treatment in employment solely because of their medical stories" (Stewart et al. 2001).

The assignment of exclusive property rights over genetic material in the form of patents has been particularly damaging for people in developing nations where laws covering intellectual property rights are less stringent because of the countries' need to access essential medicines cheaply. Some countries, including South Africa and Brazil, have taken steps to increase access to inexpensive drugs in their countries by passing legislation that limits patent rights and makes reasonable licensing arrangements compulsory. These measures have allowed for the development of generic drugs for the treatment of HIV infection (Schoofs 2002, 14A).

Such moves, however, have met with significant reaction and threats from the U.S. government, which has an interest in protecting the patent rights of pharmaceutical companies (Gagnon 2002).

A communiqué by the Action Group on Erosion, Technology and Concentration (ETC Group) (2001) provides data on the concentration of corporate power with special reference to the "life sciences." The top ten pharmaceutical companies control more than 40 percent of the world market; the top ten veterinary pharmaceutical companies control 60 percent; and the top ten agrochemical corporations control 84 percent of the agrochemical market. Other figures show that 100 percent of transgenic seed production is controlled by five multinational enterprises. These five multinational companies also own 60 percent of the pesticide market (ETC Group 2001).

Millions of deaths in underdeveloped and developed countries could be prevented annually if all of humanity had better access to lifesaving drugs. Yet the World Health Organization (WHO) reports that, globally, only 0.2 percent of investment in health is devoted to diseases that routinely affect the poor, such as acute respiratory infections, diarrhea, and tuberculosis. Furthermore, only 0.1 percent of research funds are used in research on malaria, although expenses associated with malaria account for 10 percent of the health budget in sub-Saharan Africa. These diseases contribute to the death of billions of people who live on one dollar a day (Gates 2002). It is unlikely that the promise of patents would act as an incentive for pharmaceutical companies and other research institutions to develop affordable drugs for these conditions; few profits are to be made by providing affordable drugs to the poorest people or the poorest countries.

In short, the appropriation and patenting of genetic material has adverse effects on the development of scientific research, access to drugs, and development of agriculture in poorer countries. However, these negative effects are being brushed aside as "collateral damage" that is supposedly outweighed by the benefits that flow from expanded patent rights. We will show that this consequentialist argument favoring expanded patent rights is inconsistent with longstanding traditions in property law and political theory.

Private Property, Patents, and Genetic Material

Private property has been justified from a number of different political perspectives. Within classical liberalism, for example, property is understood as defining a sphere of private enjoyment, where owners exercise property rights. These rights must be duly protected against governmental interference. In this private sphere, individuals with certain capacities and wealth enter into agreements and exchange goods in a market that adjusts prices based on supply and demand. Socialism, by contrast, holds that the means of production should be owned by the state and controlled by its officials. Welfare liberalism, an alternative to classical liberalism, retains the notion of private property but also asserts and protects substantial basic rights for citizens, including rights of access to basic welfare goods. A fourth approach, democratic republicanism, considers private property to be a necessary condition for the autonomy and independence of citizens but limits property accumulation in order to preserve freedom and independence for everyone. The accumulation of private property is also limited to protect against exertion of unjust public influence by those who have amassed disproportional wealth (Simon 1991).

All these perspectives are represented in the arguments surrounding patents. First, those who oppose granting an absolute right of private property over the products of one's own intellectual work (see, for example, Radin 1996) must counter the arguments of those who claim an unrestricted natural right to the appropriation of the benefits accrued from one's own work and the initial investment required to develop an innovation. Second, those who affirm that patents favor unfair monopolies that conspire against the common good must rebut those who argue that monopolies arising from patents provide an efficient way to encourage technological research and development. We will discuss these two issues separately.

The Labor Theory of Value

One approach to justifying patent rights has been to apply the seventeenth-century labor theory of value according to which laborers have a natural right of ownership over the products of their labor. Some of the arguments used to defend the enclosure of land that had been held in common are noticeably similar to those used in debates about patenting genetic material. In the historical arguments, proponents claimed that allowing the private appropriation of common land would curb inefficient use of land, thereby benefiting everyone. They also argued that improvements to land, which would increase its potential for greater crop yields, would lead to efficiency in the use of common resources. Despite superficial similarities with the arguments for original appropriation found in Locke, important differences exist between the historical arguments concerning land and arguments used today to justify appropriation rights over the human genome.

According to this approach, intellectual labor must also be rewarded through exclusive property rights (Palmer 1990). In principle, this exclusivity is a legitimate recognition of the natural right of ownership that arises from one's own work. It is quite a stretch, however, to extend Locke's arguments in support of private property over land to today's granting of patent rights over gene sequences and proteins. In his chapter "Of Property," in the *Second Treatise of Government*, Locke explains how men [sic] can legitimately gain exclusive possession over several pieces of land from "the world" God has given to men "in common" (Locke 1689/1988, 25). Locke argues that land and everything within it was given to men by God for their support and comfort; the fruits of the land and the beasts that eat them belong to mankind in common. They are the spontaneous products of nature, and therefore nobody in the state of nature would have an exclusive private right over these things. However, these goods are there for men's use, and there must be a way to appropriate them from the common before they can be used to benefit any man in particular (Locke 1689/1988). Locke's argument for establishing private property is well known: each man owns the labor of his body and the work of his hands. By adding the labor of his body to that which is found in nature, he establishes exclusive rights of ownership over what was previously held in common, so long as enough and as good is reserved for the work of others. Thus, one's work determines what becomes one's own and what remains common property (Locke 1689/1988).

Arguments used to justify exclusive temporary ownership of DNA gene sequences partially follow Locke's arguments. First, in the European Union (EU) directive mentioned earlier, the appropriation of a natural element from the common requires justification. The EU directive draws on the idea of human intervention in nature for the technical procedures needed to isolate gene sequences from their natural environment or to reproduce these sequences through procedures considered equivalent to an "invention of a gene sequence" (*European Directive* 1988). Technical work and skill add something to the naturally occurring gene or gene sequence, and these efforts are deemed sufficient to justify exclusive appropriation in the form of intellectual property rights. This appropriation is justified in Lockean terms because "enough and as good is left in common for others." However, patents on gene sequences actually involve broader rights than Lockean rights. They assert significant rights over every aspect of genetic sequence reproduction, every possible use of the gene and protein, and all potential diagnostic and therapeutic applications of the gene sequence and related matter (Bergel 2002).

During the period of the patent, exclusive and unrestricted use extends to transfer, benefit, and income from isolated genes and gene sequences. The incentives afforded by monopolies trump any advantages that might result from governmentally imposed limits (Christman 1994). Here contemporary arguments clearly depart from Locke's. He attaches two clauses or conditions to his theory of appropriation: (1) the appropriation of a piece of land should be "for the benefit of human life" and (2) the situation of others should not be worsened by an individual's exclusive appropriation, which is the case when "enough and as good" is left in common. An appropriation from the common that is not used beneficially or whereby others are disadvantaged (as would be the case where not enough is left in common for others) is not permissible within Locke's theory. Locke justifies as a natural right only the private use of land for one's own subsistence and as a product of one's own work, but accumulation due to the introduction of money is legitimately constrained by government decisions. The person who submits to a government also accepts the authority of civil law (rather than natural right) to determine legal rights over one's present and future possessions.

As we stated initially, there is no evidence that genetic patenting benefits human life in general. Nor does the appropriation of gene sequences meet Locke's second restriction. For example, recall the Myriad Genetics case, where ownership was claimed over the BRCA1 and BRCA2 genes. Were Myriad Genetics granted patent rights over the breast cancer genes, it would be the only entity that is lawfully and rightfully allowed to develop breast cancer detection tests and the only enterprise allowed to market genetic therapies related to BRCA1 and BRCA2. Despite the fact that Myriad Genetics' exclusive patent rights would be of limited duration, it still cannot be demonstrated that patents on BRCA1 and BRCA2 genes would satisfy the Lockean provisos by benefiting human life and not worsening the situation of others. Specifically, patents that grant monopoly property rights over partial or total gene sequences, even for a finite period, may be viewed as a kind of "neofeudal" modification of the economy: a monopoly on certain natural resources granted to a handful of mega-enterprises that enables them to control the market and fix prices. Far from contributing to the commonwealth, such "rights" invite or intensify relationships of political domination and subordination.

Patents as Catalysts of Progress

During the nineteenth century, economists discussed the so-called natural right of the inventor to hold exclusive ownership of his inventions. Arguments favoring patents appealed to promotion of the public interest, avoidance of possible conflicts between justice for inventors and society's interest in the benefits of inventions, encouragement of monopolies as incentives to effect new innovations, and a "deserved" fair compensation for rendering society an original contribution (Machlup 2000). All these justifications are revisited in current debate over genetic patents. But something has changed. Now, as noted, not only *inventors* of novel techniques, processes, or products but also *discoverers* of preexisting entities can gain a monopoly on the use and exploitation of their discoveries. In other words, under current patent law someone may obtain exclusive property rights, for example, to a partial sequence of a naturally occurring human gene simply because no one previously discovered it.

Intellectual property rights—including patents, copyrights, trademarks, and trade secrets—possess certain characteristics that distinguish them from property rights over material goods. Nonetheless, the justification for recognition of intellectual property rights follows the same line of reasoning as the justification of property rights in general. Patents and other forms of intellectual property rights are known as nonrival goods. This means that different people in different corners of the earth can enjoy them without "exhausting" them, and the marginal cost of increasing the number of people using the property is close to zero (Stiglitz 1999). Beethoven's Fifth Symphony can be enjoyed by many of us simultaneously. Similarly, different researchers and pharmaceutical laboratories can use the same DNA sequence simultaneously for different studies without exhausting the supply of the genetic sequence. Certainly, the material support required for developing an idea or a skill has a cost in terms of time and resources, but ideas, concepts, knowledge, and other abstract entities are themselves nonrival.

Although resources are necessary to obtain knowledge, it does not follow that knowledge must have a price. Expenses are incurred, however, in acquiring the skills needed to obtain that knowledge and in transferring it, and for these the discoverer or inventor should be reimbursed. It has been argued that patents encourage financial investment in research and development because investors are granted the rights to use, sell, or obtain benefits from the initial investment or invention. The inventor also obtains financial benefits from the invention through royalties paid for permission to use the patent or by setting a monopoly price for use of the product. This argument, however persuasive with regard to inventions, does not readily apply to patents on the use of DNA gene sequences in research.[8] Indeed, patents on genetic material act as an impediment rather than an incentive to research for at least four reasons. First, research expenses may increase to the degree they include costs associated with securing a patent. Second, patents create difficulties for initiating research because of the need for prior negotiation to use patented genes and gene sequences. Third, patent owners may set outrageously high prices for royalties or licenses and may stipulate unreasonable limits on licenses. Fourth, and perhaps most significant, research institutions may be dissuaded from pursuing research on some therapeutic protein or diagnostic test after assessing the legal and financial burdens associated with negotiating access to patented genetic material (Nuffield Council 2002, 50).

Illustrations will clarify the connection between patent rights and research progress. In discussions of the distinction between discovery and invention, biotechnology companies argue that patentable gene sequences are not in their natural state, for research has created a novel complementary sequence (Duffield 2001a). However, patenting could hinder the development of therapeutic proteins—important new medicines based on naturally occurring DNA sequences that code for proteins such as erythropoietin, human growth hormone, or tissue plasminogen activator—or genetic diagnostic tests that require numerous gene fragments already patented by private corporations. As mentioned previously, Myriad Genetics holds a patent on the breast cancer gene, but other researchers have patented mutations of this gene. Significantly, any institution researching a breast cancer gene diagnostic test must obtain a license from all patent holders within that jurisdiction, thereby incurring costs that may stifle innovation—though the very goal of the patent system is to foster innovation (Nelkin 2002).

It is often argued that patents should be accepted when the benefits exceed the costs to society (Nuffield Council 2002). This might happen, for instance, with patents on therapeutic proteins that could bestow a right to appropriate the DNA sequence and the protein. For example, where information is encoded in DNA sequences that can be applied to produce certain molecules or proteins, some of these may be therapeutic, such as interferon (Nuffield Council 2002, 64). But what are society's benefits of sustaining monopolies on gene sequences and characterization of proteins that are essential to produce therapeutic proteins? If we take into account the view that genetic information is "humanity's inheritance" and not the exclusive property of any one group or society, the cost-benefit analysis for justifying exclusive appropriation via patents should be done on a global level.

The economics of contemporary capitalism utilizes variants of traditional cost-benefit analyses. At issue here is the difference between hypothetical and real competition. As economists have long argued, scientific and technological progress automatically provides an outlet for surplus in need of investment. While this can be true in a capitalistic model based on real competition, it is not true for monopolistic capitalism (Baran and Sweezy 1966). In a competitive system, some enterprises invest in innovation and reap financial benefits for the period of the patent, typically leading to increased supply and a consequent drop in prices. In monopolistic capitalism, major corporations introduce innovations to increase overall profit. They are not interested in the profits of the single product but in the net effect of that product on the profitability of the whole business. Thus, they will invest in innovation only when high financial returns are assured.

Generally, big corporations have an interest in patenting innovations to lead the market and, for a time, have an unchallenged monopoly. Medical innovations in particular usually produce high returns. This is not the case if these innovations are to be marketed to those with limited capacity to pay, as happens with certain medical developments related to diseases of the impoverished. This explains why there are many studies of diseases that affect elderly people in affluent societies, such as cancer and heart disease, while research on diseases such as malaria, which largely affects people in developing nations, is not well supported by private research organizations (Gates 2002). At the same time, the high profits to be gained from innovations explain why patents on scientific advances are demanded and granted daily. But is there a conflict between the concept of intellectual property and human rights (Duffield 2001b)? In August 2000, the Sub-Commission on the Promotion and Protection of Human Rights of the United Nations Commission on Human Rights adopted a resolution on intellectual property rights (IPRs) and human rights that stresses (1) impediments resulting from the application of IPRs to the transfer of technology in developing countries; (2) the consequences of plant breeders' rights and the patenting of genetically modified organisms for the enjoyment of the basic right to food; (3) the reduction of control by communities (especially indigenous communities) over their own genetic and natural resources and cultural values, leading to accusations of "biopiracy;" and (4) restrictions on access to patented pharmaceuticals and the implications for enjoyment of a basic right to health. The overall conclusion of the sub-commission (Duffield 2001b) is that human rights obligations should take priority over economic agreements.

Clearly, in assessing the net benefits of the patent system, costs resulting from legal protection of patent rights should be included. Property rights and freedom of contract involve public expenditures comparable to the expenses necessary for public welfare. To make rights effective, a legal system is necessary to enforce and protect these rights, a process that requires public funds. Monopolies operating domestically and internationally require public expenditures for policing and enforcing property rights, such as the Trade-Related Aspects of Intellectual Property Rights (TRIPS) resolution of the General Agreement on Tariffs and Trade (GATT). These agreements assume a bundle of rights and interdictions whose enforcement is clearly dependent on local law, supported by a public budget (Holmes and Sunstein 1999).

Conclusion

In this chapter, we first asserted that there are different kinds of property as well as different ways of characterizing different properties. Common property denotes legal protection with the intention of preserving rights of access and use for every member of society, or for humankind generally, where the resource extends beyond political boundaries. Common property allows for fair access to everyone and prevents use of the property or resource by some if it would hinder access to others (Waldron 2000). We have well-founded reasons for arguing that DNA sequences should be considered common property and that common access to genetic material should be protected at a universal level. Those who propose the privatization of gene sequences have not justified the exclusive rights claimed.

It is common in normative social theories to assess principles in light of our "shared moral intuitions" (Domènech 1998; Buchanan et al. 2000; Daniels 1980). John Rawls, in particular, employed the well-known method of reflective equilibrium to test the principles of justice that he proposed (Rawls 1971). Reflective equilibrium may also be applied to competing principles or policies where there are conflicts of values. Though many theorists working on ethically or politically contentious topics accept this method, feminist assessments vary. Diana Meyers views it critically (Meyers 1993). Susan Sherwin proposes a feminist version of it (Sherwin 1996, 191). Debate about patents over genetic material is just the kind of topic to which this method should apply. In reflective equilibrium, theories and moral intuitions are balanced through a process of working back and forth between moral intuitions about particular situations and general theories or principles. This equilibrium cannot be reached, however, if there is a radical difference of opinion regarding intuitions or principles (Domènech 1998). The key question here is, do we share basic moral intuitions on the subject of common or private property rights over gene sequences?

As we see it, among reflective equilibrium supporters there is widespread agreement that (1) neither the whole human body, in its different stages of constitution and development, nor the mere discovery of one of the body's elements, including its total or partial gene sequences, is amenable to patenting (*European Directive* 1988); (2) life forms should not be patented, as they are either naturally occurring entities or the biological expressions thereof; and (3) neither products nor substances in their natural state should be open to patent (*European Directive* 1988). These three moral intuitions about patenting genetic material have not been questioned by norms or national or international lawsuits to date. Nevertheless, courts have recognized patents on certain genetic material such as the BRCAI gene and the gene-based diagnostic test for hepatitis C (Nuffield Council 2002, 39).

One strategy used to permit patenting of such material has been to loosen the distinction between invention and discovery and to categorize as "inventions" human intervention into common natural resources. It is in this context that the labor argument for exclusive appropriation was adapted from Locke's justification for exclusive ownership of land. But as we understand Locke, uncultivated land had practically no value for him. Labor gave cultivated land 99 percent of its value. Thus, as we see it, no sensible person could argue that copying into another form the information comprised in a gene constitutes 99 percent of the value of the copied gene sequence. Why, then, should patents over genetic material be authorized where the human intervention does not meet the usual utility, novelty, and innovation requirements for patented inventions?

Additional approaches to justifying patents on genetic material have been based on a cost-benefit analysis that emphasizes the aggregate benefit to society that would follow from recognizing patents. But as we see it, a theory that seeks to justify its counterintuitive conclusion (that exclusive rights over genetic material will benefit society in general) must assume the burden of proof by showing that (1) the benefits obtained from patents by multinational corporations and trusts exceed the price of excluding others who are interested in conducting research and developing therapies; (2) the benefits of exclusion from the use of this common resource by the vast majority are greater than the cost generated by this exclusion (including costs to administer patents that are borne by taxpayers); and (3) the cost of transforming resources that are traditionally considered common property into exclusive possessions does not exceed the benefits of maintaining the property in common.

In our estimation, no literature considering this issue seriously analyzes costs and benefits in this manner. Proponents of patents on genetic material based on cost-benefit analyses need to refine their analyses or explain how their arguments fit the shared moral intuitions described previously. Those of us whose moral intuitions oppose patents on life forms and gene sequences should seek the adoption of national and international legislation that protects the common property of life forms and genetic material from exclusive ownership. A first step in this direction was the Human Genome Project, which created a consortium of research laboratories committed to public research and control of innovations that could be developed from research into human genetic material. But other equally well-motivated steps need to be taken—and soon.

The issues discussed in this chapter are not simply disputes among equals but the latest manifestation of the gross inequities dividing developed and developing economies and their populations. The richest 1 percent of the world population receives as much income as the poorest 57 percent (ETC Group 2001). The world's two hundred richest people more than doubled their net worth in the four years from 1995 to 1999, amounting to more than U.S.$1,000,000,000,000 for an average of U.S.$5,000,000,000 each. Their combined wealth equals the combined annual income of the world's poorest 2.5 billion people (Gates 2002). In 1960, the income gap between the fifth of the world's people living in the richest countries and the fifth living in the poorest countries was thirty to one. By 1990, the gap had widened to sixty to one. By 1998, it had grown to seventy-four to one (Gates 2002). In the midst of this situation, ten of the biggest multinational pharmaceutical corporations control more than 40 percent of the world's pharmaceutical market and five multinational enterprises control 100 percent of transgenic seed production (Shand 2001, 231). Rather than integrate the world economy, globalization divides people (both within and between nations), plunders natural resources, and imperils prosperity. Globally, coordinated rule-making resolutions such as TRIPS could ensure that global capital flows in directions that advance the social, economic, and environmental dimensions of fundamental human rights. But presently, those whose lives are adversely affected by global economic policies have no voice because they lack property-based rights (Gates 2002). Meanwhile, millions of people die because they lack access to life-saving drugs.

Trade talks between countries within the World Trade Organization have failed to agree on rules allowing poor countries to import expensive medicines at cheap prices. Without a settlement, global trade rules will not permit people in the poorest countries to buy cheap generic versions of recently developed, patented, and therefore expensive drugs. Even if multinational companies cut prices to local firms (for example, as the Indian firm Cipla did for generic HIV/AIDS drugs) ("Cipla to Apply" 2001), there is no guarantee that such drugs would be cheaper than generics because it is difficult to establish what the lowest prices might be. Before TRIPS, poor countries using alternative processes were able to develop a local industry and cheaper medicines (Oxfam 2001). TRIPS allows compulsory licenses under national emergencies, but this approach can only be used by countries that have a domestic pharmaceutical industry. Unfortunately, countries that cannot *produce* drugs must *import* them.

Proponents of free enterprise tend to ignore the ways that government, industry, and foundation funding shape and direct scientific research. Property interests have skewed research toward biotechnological cures rather than toward conventional therapies and determination of the underlying social and environmental causes of disease. If biotechnology is to play a significant role in meeting the health and nutrition needs of the poor, the terms and conditions of that interaction must be based on the needs of the poor rather than on patent law. Outstanding issues remain unresolved: Who will be the beneficiaries of the new technologies? What obligations will the winners have to compensate the losers?

To secure the fundamental human rights of millions of the world's most vulnerable people, it is essential that we analyze and reduce the perverse effects of property rights that have contributed to a new originary accumulation of the means of production. Control of patent rights by the United States, Western Europe, Australia, and Japan has reduced the purchasing power of developing countries lacking rights over human genetic material to lives dependent on "consent from others." The concentration of wealth and control among owners of life patents violates the Lockean proviso and fails to respect our common human inheritance on which the foundation of universal human rights rests.

Notes

The authors express their thanks, for the editing and helpful suggestions, to the editors: Rosemarie Tong, Anne Donchin, and Susan Dodds. We are grateful to Arleen Salles and

Salvador Bergel for their useful comments on an earlier version of this paper. We appreciate the solidary remittance to this forlorn place of essential articles either by post or by e-mail from Susan Sherwin, Susan Dodds, and Anne Donchin.

1. This research is framed within a research project financed by the Spanish Ministry (BFF 2002-C02-01), directed by Dr. Antoni Domènech of Barcelona. We have also received funds from the Victor Grifols i Lucas Foundation.

2. Changes in patent law turned commercial attention toward research in genetics. In 1984 there was a growing tendency toward the commodification of the body. There was a collision between commercial claims for body tissue and individual interests or cultural values. This development reflects that turning bodily tissue, DNA, and the like into commodities may seriously violate bodily integrity, exploits powerless people, and distorts research agendas (Nelkin and Andrews 1998; Radin 1996).

3. According to the law, patented living matter must be stored in a qualified institution in order to be available to whomever asks for it (Budapest Convention).

4. The European Directive 44/98, in its eleventh article, allows the use of collected seed without the need to pay new royalties.

5. "Originary accumulation," or "primitive accumulation," is a term from Marx that captures the starting point of capitalist production: the historical process whereby producers are separated from the means of production, leading to the creation of two distinct groups: wage-laborers and the owners of capital (Marx 1867/1976).

6. No established empirical evidence demonstrates a direct relationship between patents, research, and development. For example, a recent econometric study of the impact of a 1988 reform on the patent system in Japan shows that the allure of patents does not strongly motivate Japanese scientists to do certain kinds of research (Sakakibara and Branstetter 1999). Moreover, a study by U.S. researchers shows that fear of liability or lawsuits has been more of a deterrent to work with specific DNA sequences than lack of patenting rights (Schissel, Merz, and Cho 1999).

7. The Gene Giants are the top seven agrochemical corporations, which are also the world's top seed corporations (ETC Group 2001).

8. Some DNA sequences applications include diagnostic tests to determine if an individual has a particular genetic variant that can make him or her more prone to certain illnesses; research to identify potential targets for which new drugs or vaccines can be designed or developed; gene therapy to replace faulty genes with normal ones; and therapeutic proteins, such as interferon or insulin, to be used as medicines.

References

Action Group on Erosion, Technology and Concentration (ETC Group). 2001. "Globalization, Inc. Concentration in Global Power: The Unmentioned Agenda." *Communique* 71 (July/August): 1–11.

———. 2003. "Adwatch Myriad Genetics." *Gene Watch* 16, no. 1: 14.

Baran, Paul, and Paul M. Sweezy. 1966. *Monopoly Capital: An Essay on the American Economic and Social Order*. New York: Monthly Review Press.

Bergel, Salvador. 2002. "Entre la Dignidad y el Mercado. Una Sentencia Objetable del Tribunal de Justicia de las Comunidades Europeas, Que Toca Aspectos de Interés Jurídicos y Bioético" ("Between Dignity and the Market: An Objectionable Verdict"). *Revista de Derecho y Genoma Humano* 157–80.

Boyle, James. 2003. "The Second Enclosure Movement and the Construction of the Public Domain," at www.law.duke.edu/pd/papers/boyle.pdf.

Buchanan, Allen, Dan Brock, Norman Daniels, and Daniel Wikler. 2000. *From Chance to Choice: Genetics and Justice.* Cambridge, UK: Cambridge University Press.

Byravan, Sujatha. 2003. "Can Genetics Provide Better Treatment for Breast Cancer?" *GeneWatch* 16, no. 1 (January/February): 13–14.

Christman, John. 1994. *The Myth of Property: Toward an Egalitarian Theory of Ownership.* Oxford, UK: Oxford University Press.

"Cipla to Apply for a Compulsory License to Manufacture HIV/Aids Drugs Locally." 2001. *Business Report,* at www.busrep.co.za.

Crouch, Martha L. 2001. "From Golden Rice to Terminator Technology: Agricultural Biotechnology Will Not Feed the World or Save the Environment." In *Redesigning Life?* edited by Brian Toker, 22–39. London: Zed Books.

Daniels, Norman. 1980. "Reflective Equilibrium and Archimedian Points." *Canadian Journal of Philosophy* 10, no. 1: 83–103.

Domènech, Antoni. 1998. "Los Ocho Desiderata de las Ciencias Sociales Normativas" ("The Eight Methodological Criteria of Normative Social Sciences"). *Isegoría,* Revista de Filosofía Moral y Política, Madrid: 18.

Duffield, Graham. 2001a. "Intellectual Property and Basic Research: Discovery vs. Invention." *Intellectual Property Dossier,* at www.scidev.net.

———. 2001b. "IPR Rules and Human Rights: Is There a Conflict?" *Intellectual Property Dossier,* at www.scidev.net.

European Directive. 1988. 98/44/EC, at europa.eu.int/smartapi/cgi/sga.

Gagnon, Marc André. 2002. "TRIPS and Pharmaceuticals Inquiry into the Foundations of the International Political Economy of Intellectual Property Rights." *Cahiers de Recherche CEIM* 02–03, Montreal.

Gates, Jeff. 2002. "Ownership Statistics: Why a Shared Capitalism Is Needed." *Shared Capitalism Institute,* at www.sharedcapitalism.org/scfats.html.

GRAIN 2001. "Grains of Delusion: Golden Rice Seen from the Ground," at www.grain.org/publications.

Holmes, Stephen, and Cass R. Sunstein. 1999. *The Cost of Rights.* New York: Norton.

Juma, Calestous. 1989. *The Gene Hunters.* London: Zed Books

Locke, John. 1689/1988. *Two Treatises of Government.* Cambridge, UK: Cambridge University Press.

Machlup, Fritz. 2000. "Die wirtschaftlichen Grundlagen des Patentrechts." *Patentrecht in der Kritik. Fragen der Freiheit,* Heft 255, at www.sffo.de/machlup1.htm.

Marx, Karl. 1867/1976. "The So-Called Original Accumulation." *Capital I.* Middlesex, UK: Harmondsworth.

Meyers, Diana Tietjens. 1993. "Moral Reflection: Beyond Impartial Reason." *Hypatia* 8, no. 3 (Summer): 21–47.

Nelkin, Dorothy. 2002. "Patenting Genes and the Public Interest." *American Journal of Bioethics* 2, no. 3: 13–15.

Nelkin, Dorothy, and Lori Andrews. 1998. "Homo Economicus: The Commercialization of Body Tissue in the Age of Biotechnology." *Hastings Center Report* 28, no. 5: 30–39.

Nuffield Council. 2002. "The Ethics of Patenting DNA." Discussion paper. London: Nuffield Council on Bioethics, at www.nuffieldbioethics.org.

"Ownership of Genes at Stake in Potential Lawsuit." 2003. *Christian Science Monitor*, at www.csmonitor.com.

Oxfam Policy Papers. 2001. "Patent Injustice," at www.oxfam.org.uk/cutthcost/indepth.htm.

Palmer, Richard. 1990. "Are Patents and Copyrights Morally Justified? The Philosophy of Property Rights and Ideal Objects." *Harvard Journal of Law and Public Policy* 13: 819.

Potrykus, Ingo. 2000. "The Golden Rice Tale." *AgBioView* (October 23), at www.mindfully.org/GE/Golden-Rice-Ingo-Potrykus.htm.

Psycho-Oncology. 2001. 10: 259–63, at www.cancerpage.com/cancernews.

Radin, Margaret Jane. 1996. *Contested Commodities.* Cambridge, Mass.: Harvard University Press.

Rawls, John. 1971. *A Theory of Justice.* New York: Cambridge University Press.

Rural Advancement Foundation International (RAFI). 2000. www.rafi.org.

Sakakibara, Mariko, and Lee Branstetter. 1999. "Do Stronger Patents Induce More Innovation? Evidence from the 1988 Japanese Patent Law Reforms." Working Paper 7066, National Bureau of Economic Research.

Schissel, Anna, Jon F. Merz, and Mildred K. Cho. 1999. "Survey Confirms Fears about Licensing of Genetic Tests." *Nature* 402, no. 6758: 118.

Schoofs, Mark. 2002. "Doctor Group Defies South Africa AIDS Policy: Importing Brazilian Generics to Expand Treatment, Physicians Risk Lawsuit," *Wall Street Journal,* January 30, 14A.

Shand, Hope. 2001. "Gene Giants: Understanding the Life Industry." In *Redesigning Life?* edited by Brian Toker, 222–37. London: Zed Books.

Sherwin, Susan. 1996. "Theory Versus Practice in Ethics: A Feminist Perspective on Justice in Health Care." In *Philosophical Perspectives in Bioethics,* edited by L. W. W. Sumner, 187–209. Toronto: University of Toronto Press.

Simon, William. 1991. "Social-Republican Property." *UCLA Law Review* 38: 1335–413.

Sommer, Susana E. 1998. *Genética, Clonación y Bioética. Cómo Afecta la Ciencia Nuestras Vidas? (Genetics, Clonation and Bioethics: How Are Our Lives Affected by Science?).* Buenos Aires: Editorial Biblos.

———. 2001. *Porqué las Vacas Se Volvieron Locas (Why the Cows Went Mad).* Buenos Aires: Editorial Biblos.

Stewart, Donna E. E., A. M. Cheung, S. Duff, Chung F. Wong, M. McQuestion, T. Cheng, Laura Purdy, and T. Bunston. 2001. "Long-Term Breast Cancer Survivors: Confidentiality, Disclosure, Effects on Work and Insurance." *Psycho-Oncology* 10 (May/June): 259–63.

Stiglitz, Joseph. 1999. *Public Policy for a Knowledge Economy*. London: World Bank Department for Trade and Industry and Center for Economic Policy Research.

Tait, Nikki, and Michela Wrong. 2000. "Third World to Receive GM Rice." *Financial Times* (London), May 16, 14.

Waldron, Jeremy. 2000. "Property Law." In *A Companion to Philosophy of Law and Legal Theory*, edited by Dennis Patterson, 3–23. Oxford, UK: Blackwell.

Genetic Restitution?
DNA, Compensation, and Biological Families

12

MICHELE HARVEY-BLANKENSHIP AND BARBARA ANN HOCKING

IN THIS CHAPTER, WE EXPLORE feminist ways to remediate the harms done to children, mothers, and families when children are forcibly removed from their mothers. Specifically, we analyze whether it is morally appropriate for human rights organizations to demand that the state use DNA analysis to identify children kidnapped or stolen from their biological parents during periods of internal conflict (Durbach 2002). Our conclusion is that DNA analysis should be used to help reconnect or reconstruct broken biological families provided it is in the best interest of the *child* that such a reunion be attempted. We base our conclusion on our conviction that destroying an intake family is a violation of its members' rights (UN Declaration of Human Rights, Article 16, Section 3) and on feminist concerns about children who have more than one family.

Psychological Effects of Child Separation

According to Stephen Wolking and Michael Rutter (1984), the quality of an individual's future relationships is profoundly affected by his or her first experiences as a child. Separating an infant from the biological mother or primary caregiver is correlated "with a substantially increased likelihood of both emotional disturbance and personality disorders in adult life" (Wolking and Rutter 1984, 45). In addition, John Bowlby describes the relationship between an infant and his or her biological mother as a "secure base from which to explore and learn about the world and to which the individual can 'retreat' when such threatening situations as illness, fatigue or distress are experienced" (Bowlby 1988, 23). He argues that the biological "purpose" of an infant's instinct to form an attachment is "to provide emotional security and social autonomy" (Bowlby 1988, 23). As Sara Ruddick and other exponents of maternal ethics have effectively argued, the bond that children develop with their mothers and other family members in the early years is the foundation for future relationships with others and their own physical, social, and psychological development (Ruddick 1989). Mothers—whether male or female—help their children survive, grow, and gain acceptance into society.

Juliet Mitchell and Jack Goody, as well as Ruddick and other feminist maternal thinkers, point out that this parenting role need not rest on a biological base; it may be performed equally well by adoptive parents. Although we agree with this point, we also think that adoptive parents face challenges that biological parents are generally spared. Initially, adoptive parents need to help their child forge new family relationships to replace the ones that have just been disrupted (Mitchell and Goody 1999). From the child's perspective, separation from his or her biological parents is not risk free, particularly when the separation is forced or coerced by state authorities or profiteering kidnappers. The literature establishes that attachment occurs in infancy and, furthermore, that disruption to the process of attachment at this early stage of development is most damaging and must be carefully and appropriately remedied.

Institutional Separation: The Cruelest Cut?

Among the children who have suffered the most from what may be termed "biological disruption" are Australian Aboriginal children (McGregor 1997). As a result of mainstream ("white") policies, Australian Aboriginal children were often wrenched from their biological families. Civil authorities claimed the children would be better off in white Australian families or white-run institutions than in the supposedly "uncivilized" Aboriginal families (Australian Law Reform Commission 2003, 912). The Human Rights and Equal Opportunity Inquiry into the "stolen generation" of Australian Aboriginal children focused on the devastating effects such forcible separations typically had on the children (Human Rights and Equal Opportunity Commission 1997). The Inquiry found that

> when a severe disturbance occurs in the organization of attachment behaviour, it is likely to lead to learning difficulties, poor ego integration and serious control battles with the care giving adults. . . .When the infant's attachment must be transferred to a large number of ever-changing adults on the staff of an institution or because of multiple foster placements, the objective of attachment behaviour is defeated. (Human Rights and Equal Opportunity Commission 1997, 7)

Separation from their biological parents often causes children trauma and grief, making them particularly vulnerable to loss of self-esteem and self-determination. Such children may grow into depressed adolescents and adults, unable to sustain strong emotional bonds with others because their feelings of caring and being cared for were somehow "numbed" or otherwise distorted in their early childhood (Raphael, Swan, and Martinek 1996; Noddings 1984).

Psychological Effects of Reunification

However traumatic forcibly separating a child from his or her biological mother or primary caregiver may be, reunification with the child's biological mother or primary caregiver at a later date may be equally distressing and problematic. When reunified with the biological, or natural, mother, a child may initially feel sadness and anger, wondering how his or her biological mother could have let the initial separation happen and suspecting, down deep, that his or her biological mother may have actually wanted to get rid of him or her (Parking 1987). Such a child may have significant behavioral and learning problems. For example, in the course of trying to treat a child, named Destiny, who was reunified with her biological mother after being in foster care for some time, Dr. Akhter Rahmann observed that Destiny displayed difficulties "understanding social mores," showed poor skills of "visual discrimination and perceptual organization," "exhibited 'highly aggressive' behaviour," and manifested significant "attention and thought problems" (Rahmann 1999). Rahmann also noted that on being returned to her biological mother, and forcibly separated from her adoptive mother, Destiny tended to "be more demanding of attention" by "throwing tantrums, and whingeing about being bored, and being deliberately rough" (Rahmann 1999, 8). Worse, Destiny "exhibited confusion as to where she belonged, splitting herself in half, pretending there were two Destinys—one in each home" (Rahmann 1999, 8). Clearly, having two families may be worse than having one, when placement in one family is bought at the price of forcible displacement from the other (Chandra-Shekeran 1998, 107). Feminists who work in the area of relational ethics probe the benefits and harms to children of adoption, divorce, separation, and biological custody by a parent or parents (Mahoney 1995; Donchin 2000).

Should We Search?

Clearly, given the previous commentary, the search for a child's biological origins is not without its hazards. Proposals to use DNA technologies to reunite children with their "real" (that is, biological) parents affect multiple parties—the biological family, the imposed adoptive family, and the child. The biological family's interest lies mainly in knowing that their missing child is alive and safe. Additionally, there is the hope that the child will accept them and perhaps even become an active member of the family. The imposed adoptive family, on the other hand, is probably threatened by the process, fearing that a positive identification will destroy the relationship they have established with the child. Even more threatening to them is the chance that the child may want to join his or her biological family. The child's interests are complex. Children may benefit from knowing the history of their biological families and how they had been forcibly removed from their biological mothers or primary caregivers. Yet there is always the chance this knowledge may actually bring harm to a child rather than benefit.

One can imagine the stress that the biological family and the imposed adoptive family experience once they are made aware that DNA technologies are being used to establish conclusively the biological identity of the child they both regard as theirs. In the event that the child's biological identity is conclusively established, there is the problem of deciding how each family—the biological one and the imposed adoptive one—should be involved in the child's life. Often these stresses and problems are decreased with the help of psychologists, psychiatrists, lawyers, and social workers who work with the families as well as the child. But sometimes, even such help fails to handle the complex relational issues that are triggered between parents and children when no one is quite sure whether or to what degree they will be loved in the future. Although genetic technology gives us the power to reunite biological parents with their kidnapped, trafficked, or state authority–removed children, we must bear in mind that the knowledge DNA technology offers is not an unalloyed blessing. In fact, "like human words [DNA words have] the power to hurt, and that power is the greater because, given the right conditions, DNA words can dictate with stronger predictability than most human imperatives" (Burley 1998, vi).

The Grandmothers of the Plaza de Mayo:
A Case Study in Human Rights Violation

Over and above the issue of whether it is in the best interests of biological children to be reunited with their biological parents is the issue of whether biological parents unfairly deprived of their children have a right to be reunited with their biological children. In reflecting on this matter, it is useful to focus on the harm that is done to women when the children they have gestated, birthed, and nursed are ripped from their arms by political authorities who use cruel tactics to maintain their power. In 1975, Argentina entered a dark period when the Peron government was overthrown and a military junta seized power. The junta, which remained in power from 1976 to 1988, immediately resorted to oppressive measures to control the population. Cleverly and systematically, they began to remove anyone who would oppose them. They were explicit in their goals: "First we will kill all the subversives; then we will kill their collaborators; then . . . their sympathizers; then . . . those who remain indifferent; and finally, we will kill the timid" (General Iberico Saint Jean, Governor of Buenos Aires Province, in a May 1976 speech).

They were also effective in their goals. Journalists were silenced, students disappeared from their dormitories, families were removed from their houses, and professionals vanished from the streets. Bodies washed up along riverbanks and ocean beaches and filled unmarked graves. Secret detention centers (more than three hundred) sprang up throughout Argentina, but especially in the province concentrated primarily around Buenos Aires (Penchaszadeh 1997). Victims were taken to the detention centers and tortured. Children who were old enough to talk were generally killed with their parents. In addition, at least five hundred and probably many more young children, infants, and newborns were given away to childless couples connected to the military or police (Herrerra and Tenenbaum 1990).

As we know, biological mothers who give up their children for adoption voluntarily often feel a profound sense of loss, even when they rationally know they have made the best choice for themselves and their child. But this sense of loss is not anything like the anguish, depression, and emptiness biological mothers deprived of their children involuntarily feel. Yet despite their feelings and the fact that they knew protest could result in great junta-inflicted harm to themselves, many aggrieved mothers in Argentina refused to be victims of the "system." They summoned their inner strength to organize themselves against a culture of violence and to protest the harm that had been inflicted on them (Worral 2001). In accord with many feminist thinkers, including Sarah Lucia Hoagland, they tried to *affect* their situation even though they knew they could not totally control it. Rather than being paralyzed by their plight, they moved in the ways they could, joining together to resist those who would reduce them to purely passive victims (Hoagland 1991).

Initially, a small group of mothers looking for their children met at the Ministry of the Interior, where an office was devoted to the documentation of their cases (Werbner 2001, 140). One of the mothers, Azucena de Villaflor de Vincente, stood out because of her drive and energy. She slowly gathered more mothers around her, and within months, a small group began to become politically involved for the first time in their lives. Prior to being deprived of their children, most of these mothers had maintained traditional societal roles, caring for their children or teaching primary school. But in their drive to find their children, they united to contest political power and demand justice. Meetings were called that fueled their camaraderie. Petitions were signed demanding full disclosure about the whereabouts of their missing children. Marches in the Plaza de Mayo—the park in front of the presidential palace and governmental offices—became their signature, along with the white scarves that symbolized their maternity and their loss (the names of their missing children are still embroidered on their scarves).

Within a year, the group of mothers grew significantly as their feminist consciousness deepened and their feelings of power increased. They challenged the
view that as "housewives" they lacked political power, social significance, or
voice. They found solidarity in standing together as mothers, publicly shaming
the authorities for their inaction. They formalized their organization and named
it Madres de la Plaza de Mayo (Valente 2002, 1). Then a new group sprang up,
the Abuelas de la Plaza de Mayo, composed of older women whose grandchildren or daughters were missing. The two organizations supported each other in
their demand that those who caused their grief be brought to justice, but their
emphasis was different. Whereas the Madres wanted to know what had happened to their children—whether they were alive and well—the Abuelas wanted
to know what had happened to their daughters as well as their grandchildren.

Significantly, the grandmothers were even more vocal than the mothers about
the harm the junta had inflicted on them. Occasionally, one of their missing
daughters or grandchildren surfaced. Their daughters were generally in very poor
physical and psychological shape, having survived months or even years of prison
confinement. The stories they told were truly shocking. They had been routinely
beaten and raped, and they had seen pregnant women kept alive solely for the purpose of snatching their babies from their wombs (Robert 2002). Having delivered
this valuable "property," they were killed or left imprisoned. But with their horri-
fying tales, the released or escaped women also brought information. They knew
what had happened to some of the children, and in some instances, where they
had been taken and by whom.

The children surfaced in the homes of military or police personnel, some of
whom had been directly involved in the torture and murder of their adopted children's biological parents, a fact that weakened any rightful, legal claim they had to
the children. Under such circumstances, using DNA tools to identify the biological identity of an adopted child seems to outweigh possible harms to him or her.
After all, if adoptive parents are capable of torturing and even killing innocent human beings, their fitness as parents is questionable.

The Abuelas also gleaned information from documents anonymously sent to
them. They received copies of obviously falsified birth certificates used to enroll
children in grade school. They also received copies of falsified birth certificates
signed by physicians known to be complicit with the army or even known tortur-
ers (King 1989). To further gather information regarding the disappearances of
their daughters and grandchildren, the grandmothers used ingenious investigative
techniques. They dressed up as vacuum cleaner saleswomen and visited houses
where kidnapped children were suspected of being harbored. Clandestinely, they
would peak into backyards to watch children (de Carlotto 1996).

Although these documents and testimonies provided a basis for investigations and hypotheses, the grandmothers realized this was not enough. Early on, they recognized that more precise scientific techniques would be required to identify their children and grandchildren conclusively (Oren 2001). They approached many governments and human rights groups and described the extent and devastation of the disappearances. The American Academy for the Advancement of Science sent a team of international geneticists to Buenos Aires. They used scientific techniques to resolve the issue King Solomon resolved in a nonscientific way in the Old Testament, namely, who is the "real" mother of a child. Specifically, they used mitochondrial DNA to provide positive proof of a child's biological mother or grandmother (Ginther, Issel-Tarver, and King 1992; King 1991; Penchaszedah 1992).

Mitochondrial DNA

Mitochondrial DNA is maternally inherited; the father plays no role in its transmission. All the children of a biological mother will have precisely the same mitochondrial DNA sequence. Additionally, these children will also have the same mitochondrial DNA as their *maternal* grandmother and all her siblings. All individuals in a family with the same biological mother can be compared for identification purposes through mitochondrial DNA analysis.

The use of mitochondrial DNA as a tool for identification began with the need for more accurate techniques to identify the children of the disappeared in Argentina and elsewhere, including El Salvador. Specifically, Mary-Claire King, a geneticist from Berkeley, developed the use of mitochondrial DNA as a precise tool of identification. To this end, a genetic database was established of the mitochondrial DNA sequences of all those relatives looking for their missing children. As a child is identified using classical investigative techniques, his or her blood sample is sent to the laboratory and the mitochondrial DNA sequence is compared with the database. If there is a match in the database, further investigations are undertaken to ensure the match is correct. If there is no match, the sequence is placed in the database with the hope that the DNA of a relative will eventually be submitted. To more clearly illustrate the steps in this complex genetic identification process, we discuss the case of Odir, a kidnapped child from El Salvador.

The Children in El Salvador

Four years after the tragedy in Argentina, which resulted in the unjust breaking up of biological families, a civil war in El Salvador resulted in that country's loss of thousands of its people. From 1979 to 1991, the civil war in El Salvador claimed seventy-five thousand lives, approximately 20 percent of the country's population (Rohter 1996; Rosenberg 1999). Thousands more disappeared, among them an estimated five hundred children (Rohter 1996; Rosenberg 1999). Initially collected in *Chiapas* (refugee camps), personal statements about kidnapped children were so numerous that an organization, Asociación Pro-Busqueda de Niñas y Niños Desaparecidos (Association for the Search of Disappeared Children), was formed to document kidnappings and to search for missing children, in many instances with the help of mitochondrial DNA tests.

A particularly poignant case involved a child named Odir. In 1982, when Odir was three months old, his mother, Maria, was shot during a military sweep in the small village El Salvador of El Higueral (Rosenberg 1999). The military were on a campaign to "remove the water from the fish"—that is, to remove support from the guerrillas. Since Odir's village was in the middle of a guerrilla stronghold, it was suspected of supporting guerrilla activity. The military swept through with the intent to destroy the community. Much of the village had fled by the time the military arrived. But because of her partial deafness, Maria did not hear either the military enter the village or her neighbors fleeing. Odir's older brother, Cristobal, who was three years old at the time, was visiting his grandmother and fled with her to a nearby village (unfortunately, his grandmother died soon afterward and he spent the next three years in an orphanage). Thankfully, an aunt found him and he was brought back to the village, where he was surrounded by those who most loved him. Odir was not as lucky. The military shot his mother, plucked him from her side, and put him in a helicopter with other children from the village (de Carlotto 1996).

Twenty miles away, at the military barracks, an announcement was made to the local community that children were available for those who wanted them. They were "given out like chickens," remembers Ricardo, another boy who was kidnapped. The Hernandez family took Odir. They had two daughters and wanted a son. Odir grew up in their household thinking that his biological family was dead. But then, after many years, Asociación tracked him down, equipped with the mitochondrial DNA tests that would resurrect his biological family for him.

Odir's DNA

The sequence from Odir's blood sample proved to be identically matched to one from his putative brother, Cristobal. Still, from this information alone, it could not be conclusively established that these two young men were from the same biological family. Odir's DNA sequence had to be compared with that of a whole family population to ensure that his particular DNA sequence was indeed unique. But establishing uniqueness was not easy in Odir's case because he lacked a large number of distant relatives—a family population—whose DNA could be compared with his. Although his putative mother, Maria, had survived her bullet wounds, she had died of natural causes during the initial course of the investigation. Odir's father was not known, and all his grandparents were dead. Fortunately, besides his putative brother Cristobal, Odir had a younger sister. Apparently, four years after Odir was kidnapped, his mother had a daughter, Maria Lucia. The scientific team added Maria Lucia's DNA to their analysis. Maria Lucia's mitochondrial DNA was identical to Odir's. This was expected as all of these children were from the same biological mother even though Maria Lucia did not have the same biological father. Fifteen different nuclear DNA markers from different chromosomes were then analyzed. At the completion of the analysis, there was enough similarity between Odir's, Cristobal's, and Maria Lucia's maternal mitochondrial DNA to overwhelmingly prove they were maternal siblings. In fact, the odds that the three individuals were not from the same biological family was one in twenty million.

Soon after the news was received, a meeting between the biological and imposed adoptive families was planned. After a two-hour hike through a butterfly-filled jungle, surrounded by their neighbors, seventeen-year-old Odir met his sister for the first time in his life and his brother for the first time since his kidnapping. Their shy smiles were identical. Within hours of meeting, the siblings decided to spend time with both families. By the end of the day, Odir's imposed adoptive family and his brother and sister headed down the mountain on horseback to spend time at the place where Odir was raised, with the family with whom Odir grew up. One can only begin to speculate as to the complexity of emotions and tensions of each party.

Rights of the Child

Under the UN Convention on the Rights of the Child, a child has a right to know his or her biological identity. This is particularly the case, as it was in Argentina, El Salvador, and to a certain degree, Australia, when children were literally stolen from their families. Commenting on the "disappeared" children in Argentina, Dr. Norberto Liwski states that

> people take children and reduce them to war booty, appropriating them like commodities, falsifying their identity, raising them amid lies and falsification, stealing a part of their past, after directly or indirectly being implicated in the deaths of their parents. This kind of emotion is merely the desire to possess a coveted object, not the true love that requires respect for the other, for the truth of her identity. Nothing was more important for the stability of a child than this truth. (Oren 2001)

We realize that some of the imposed adoptive families in Argentina, El Salvador, and Australia were not part of the horrendous processes that led to their receiving a child. We also realize that, in many instances, they provided their adopted children with loving homes. Still, these children have, upon reaching adulthood, a right to know (or not know) their biological identity. Indeed, the lesson to be learned from Odir's case—a feminist lesson—is that biological parents do not have to view children as property and can, under the right circumstances (which may have something to do with the age of their children), create relationships with adoptive parents—even imposed adoptive parents—that result in flexible and salutary familial relationships.

Conclusion

According to Roy S. Lee, "today's conflicts are often rooted in the failure to repair yesterday's injury" (Lee 1999, 1). But the problem of how to repair the injuries done to children through war and oppression continues to elude legal authorities and policy makers. The situations we outline in this chapter throw into sharp relief the clear dilemma as to whether it is always good to reunite biological families, and if so, when. They also cause us to reflect on how difficult it is to negotiate relationships between biological and adoptive families when the children were wrongfully separated from their biological parents. Finally, they make us reconsider the full implications of the UN Convention on the Rights of the Child statement that children have the right to know their biological identity upon reaching adulthood. The question is whether such knowledge can assuage the harm that has been done to so many people, and how we can sanction state authorities and criminal elements who inflict such misery. They are the ultimate source of the human rights violations of which we speak, and so we invite feminists in particular, because of their concern for women and children, to join in the effort to help people in oppressive societies overturn regimes that would stoop so low as to dole out children as if they were nothing more than the booty of war.

Note

Michele and Barbara would like to extend their heartfelt appreciation to Scott Guy and to the editors of this volume, whose assistance they are most grateful for.

References

Australian Law Reform Commission. 2003. *Essentially Yours*. Report 96 (March).
Bowlby, John. 1988. *A Secure Base: Parent-Child Attachment and Healthy Human Development*. New York: Basic.
Burley, Justine. 1998. *The Genetic Revolution and Human Rights*. Oxford, UK: Oxford University Press.
Chandra-Shekeran, Sangeetha. 1998. "Challenging the Fiction of the Nation in the 'Reconciliation' Texts of *Mabo* and *Bringing Them Home*." *Australian Feminist Law Journal* 107, no. 11: 107–33.

de Carlotto, Estella. 1996. Personal communication. (MHB)

Donchin, Anne. 2000. "Autonomy and Interdependence: Quandaries in Genetic Decision Making." In *Relational Autonomy: Feminist Perspectives on Autonomy, Agency and the Social Self*, edited by Catriona MacKenzie and Natalie Stoljar, 236–38. New York: Oxford University Press.

Durbach, Andrea. 2002. "Repairing the Damage: Achieving Reparations for the Stolen Generations." *Alternative Law Journal* 27, no. 6: 262.

Ginther, Charles, Laura Issel-Tarver, and Mary-Claire King. 1992. "Identifying Individuals by Sequencing Mitochondrial DNA from Teeth." *Nature Genetics* 2: 135–38.

Herrera, Matilde, and Ernesto Tenenbaum. 1990. *Identidad: Despojo y Restitucion*. Abuelas de Plaza de Mayo.

Hoagland, Sarah Lucia. 1991. "Some Thoughts about *Caring*." In *Feminist Ethics*, edited by Claudia Card, 250. Lawrence: University Press of Kansas.

Human Rights and Equal Opportunity Commission. 1997. "National Inquiry into the Separation of Aboriginal and Torres Strait Islander Children from Their Families." Sydney: Human Rights and Equal Opportunity Commission.

King, Mary-Claire. 1989. "Genetic Testing of Identity and Relationship." *American Journal of Human Genetics* 44, no. 2: 179–81.

———. 1991. "An Application of DNA Sequencing to a Human Rights Problem." *Molecular Genetic Medicine* I: 117–31.

Lee, Roy S. 1999. *The International Criminal Court: The Making of the Rome Statute*. Amsterdam: Kluwer Law International.

Mahoney, Joan. 1995. "Adoption as a Feminist Alternative to Reproductive Technology." In *Reproduction, Ethics and the Law: Feminist Perspectives*, edited by Joan C. Callahan, 35–54. Bloominton: Indiana University Press.

McGregor, Russell. 1997. *Imagined Destinies: Aboriginal Australians and the Doomed Race Theory, 1880–1939*. Melbourne: Melbourne University Press.

Mitchell, Juliet, and Jack Goody. 1999. "Family or Familiarity?" In *What Is a Parent?* edited by Andrew Bainham, Shelley Day Sclater, and Martin Richards, 107–17. Oxford, UK: Richard Hart.

Noddings, Nel. 1984. *Caring: A Feminine Approach to Ethics and Moral Education*. Berkeley: University of California Press.

Oren, Laura. 2001. "Righting Child Custody Wrongs: The Children of the 'Disappeared' in Argentina." *Harvard Human Rights Journal* 14: 1–72.

Parking, Roger. 1987. *Child Psychology*. Sydney: McGraw-Hill.

Penchaszadeh, Victor. 1992. "Abduction of Children of Political Dissidents in Argentina and the Role of Human Genetics in Their Restitution." *Journal of Public Health Policy* 13, no. 3: 291–305.

———. 1997. "Genetic Identification of Children of the Disappeared in Argentina." *JAMWA* 52: 16–21.

Rahmann, Akhter. 1999. "Early Intervention or Resilience: A Case Study." Paper presented to the 1999 Department of Human Services Conference on "Early Intervention: Risk, Resilience and Results." Adelaide: South Australian Department of Human Services.

Raphael, Beverly, Pat Swan, and Nada Martinek. 1996. "Intergenerational Aspects of Trauma for Australian Aboriginal People." In *An Intergenerational Handbook of Multi-Generational Legacies of Trauma*, edited by Yael Danieli, 327–40. St. Lucia: University of Queensland Press.

Robert, Hannah. 2002. "'Unwanted Advances': Applying Critiques of Consent in Rape to *Cubillo v. Commonwealth*." *Australian Feminist Law Journal* 16: 1–23.

Rohter, Larry. 1996. "El Salvador's Stolen Children Face a War's Darkest Secret." *New York Times*, August 5, A1.

Rosenberg, Tina. 1999. "What Did You Do in the War, Mama?" *New York Times Magazine*, February 7, 52–93.

Ruddick, Sara. 1989. *Maternal Thinking: Toward a Politics of Peace*. Boston: Beacon.

Valente, Marcela. 2002. "The Mothers of Civil Resistance." *Global Information Network* (May 2): 1.

Werbner, Phillip. 2001. "Searching for Life: The Grandmothers of the Plaza de Mayo and the Disappeared Children of Argentina." *Sociological Review* 49, no. 1: 140.

Wolking, Stephen, and Michael Rutter. 1984. "Separation, Loss and Family Relationships." In *Child and Adolescent Psychiatry*, edited by Michael Rutter and Lionel Hersov, 34–57. London: Blackwell.

Worral, Janet. 2001. "From Human Rights to Citizenship Rights: Recent Trends in Latin American Social Movements." *Latin America Review* 136, no. 2: 163.

VIEWING HIV POLICIES THROUGH A HUMAN RIGHTS FRAMEWORK IV

Global Migrants, Gendered Tradition, and Human Rights
Black Africans and HIV in the United Kingdom

13

EILEEN O'KEEFE AND MARTHA CHINOUYA

MIGRATION IS ONE OF THE KEY FACETS of globalization. Much discussion of human rights and bioethics treats the social world as divided into a developed and a developing world (Nuffield Council on Bioethics 2002). This division needs to be revised in light of the demographic profile of developed countries where migrants from developing countries increasingly constitute a significant proportion of the population.

Black-African migrants enter the United Kingdom (UK), pushed by social and economic circumstances in their home countries that contribute to their contracting HIV at an extraordinarily high rate. Their vulnerability to contracting HIV is reinforced by aspects of gendered tradition. By gendered tradition, we mean an array of social roles, norms, and practices differentially assigned to females and males. Gendered tradition has its roots in African rural societies but has been profoundly reshaped by colonial experiences, as well as postcolonial contact with global organizations such as the World Bank. Such gendered tradition continues to shape the health of Black-African migrants in developed countries, not least their risk for acquiring HIV infection. In the UK, more than half of new infections in 2001 occurred in the Black-African migrant communities, and most of them were the result of sex between men and women. Women in both developed and developing societies "are often unable . . . to avoid HIV-related consequences of the sexual practices of their husbands or partners as a result of social and sexual subordination, economic dependence on a relationship and cultural attitudes" (Office of the United Nations High Commissioner for Human Rights and the Joint United Nations Programme on HIV/AIDS 1998, 41). We believe that the high prevalence of HIV/AIDS among Black-African migrant women is a feminist human rights issue. Crucial to this is women's right to information about threats to their health. Women are often unable to access this information because sexual partners do not disclose that they are HIV-positive. The Black-African migrant community must address this issue. In so doing, they should be supported by UK health planners.

UK health planners now focus on so-called cultural issues to stem the spread of HIV among the Black-African migrant populations. But this objective can have only limited success for two reasons. First, the health planners highlight sexual practices without examining how those practices are shaped by factors operating at the global level. Treating lack of disclosure as stemming from traditional culture, they have not identified other powerful motivations that hamper disclosure. Second, and more important, health planners have not identified how Black-African tradition might provide positive resources to reduce the spread of HIV. This chapter aims to help UK health planners gain a better understanding of traditional and transformed cultural relations in the Black-African communities so that they can better support those communities in addressing the health problems they face. First, Black-African feminists in the developing countries are contesting traditional gendered norms. Second, Black-African communities affected by HIV in developed countries are using traditional materials to confront the impact of gendered practices on their health. Both of these movements find that gendered tradition is linked causally to social and economic circumstances initially shaped by colonial experience and now shaped by circumstances operating at global levels. Specifically, we consider Black-African feminists' insights regarding gendered tradition, in the context of the African Charter on Human and Peoples' Rights and economic and social marginalization associated with globalization. This background enables us to discuss attempts by Black-African migrant communities in the UK to use and transform traditional materials in community-based research and health promotion. This involves building up community capacity—the skills and knowledge base within a given population that enable them to work together to take an active role in identifying and solving the problems they face. We describe how communities affected by HIV/AIDS are taking steps to make disclosure easier.

Our argument is grounded in our understanding of human rights. We take the view that human beings have rights because we are embodied persons who have the capacities as individuals to engage critically with our beliefs and values and to guide our behavior in accord with them. Our capacities as individuals are shaped and sustained through interaction with others. This interaction involves interdependence due to the universality of human vulnerability. Interdependence or mutual encumbrance is part of the human condition. De facto interdependence gives rise to our responsibilities or duties. Our capacities as individuals to engage critically with our health-related beliefs and values are hampered or promoted by economic and social factors operating at the global level. Therefore, our approach amounts to a recommendation: those who wish to draw on the universalizing value of human rights need to recognize that rights to health involve duties or responsibilities that we bear to one another, locally and globally, and that human rights need to be contextualized, that is, to be prioritized, protected, and respected in ways that are attentive to the circumstances of the ordinary lives of the groups whose rights are under discussion—for example, HIV-infected Black-African women in the UK.

HIV Trends: Africa, Europe, and the United Kingdom

People at risk of heterosexual transmission of HIV bear the heaviest burden of infection worldwide. Data on new diagnoses of sexually acquired HIV in ten countries in Western Europe show a 20 percent increase in new cases between 1995 and 2000 (Nicoll and Hamers 2002), half of them heterosexually transmitted. Of these infections, 64 percent occurred in migrants from high-prevalence countries, most notably from sub-Saharan Africa, where 35 percent of the population is already infected with HIV/AIDS and the situation shows no signs of improving. Specifically, 3.5 million new cases of HIV/AIDS were reported in 2000 alone (Walker et al. 2003).

Not surprisingly, migrants from sub-Saharan Africa and other African nations bring their health problems with them to their new place of residence. In the UK, where Black-African migrants are the key group affected by heterosexually transmitted HIV infection, two-thirds of the infected are women (Unlinked Anonymous 2002).

Thus, it is absolutely crucial that women's potential sexual partners know their seropositive status and be willing to disclose it. But this is unlikely to occur in the UK because Black-African migrants have less than optimal contact with health services. Few Black-African migrants come forward voluntarily for sexual health tests. Many find out about their own diagnosis at a late stage of the condition or after a sexual partner has died, thus missing out on opportunities for prevention. Many women discover they are HIV-positive when they are tested in prenatal clinics (Chinouya, Musoro, and O'Keefe 2003). Traditional taboos regarding discussion of sex between partners make it difficult for Black-African migrants, preoccupied with immigration concerns, to find out and disclose their health status to their intimates, although they know they should do so and may even want to do so. Fears about deportation back to their home countries, where opportunities for employment and education are few or even nonexistent, serve as an impediment to accessing UK health services (Chinouya 2002).

Black-African Migrants in a Globalizing Labor Market

Among the circumstances that profoundly affect migrants is the nature of the labor market in wealthy developed countries, which generally need more workers than their immigration laws are willing to accommodate. Wealthy developed countries are committed to providing services to both their aging, ill, and disabled populations and their young, healthy, able-bodied populations. Yet they are unwilling to pay more than minimum wages for these services, wages so low that they fail to attract an adequate supply of native workers since they can get jobs that pay more elsewhere. Global migrants, however, are willing to work for low wages to support themselves and their families. Thus, they tend to work in the informal economy, where documentation is not required and it is dangerous to disclose health problems, including HIV/AIDS.

Nowhere in the world is the use of migrant workers in the service industry more obvious than in the UK. Dire shortages in the health care delivery system have occasioned the importation of large numbers of skilled, affordable health care workers. As of 2002, 42,000 of the UK's 350,400 nurses were trained overseas, and five-year government health plan projections envision that before 2010 one-third of all UK nurses will be members of one or another migrant population. The key sources are expected to be Africa, Philippines, India, and Eastern Europe (Buchan 2003; Butler 2003). Likewise, acute shortages of social workers have led to reliance on imported workers: one-fourth of new social workers in 2002 were trained abroad. As of 2002, one-half of qualified Zimbabwean social workers were employed in the UK. Further extensive overseas active recruitment is planned (Batty 2003).

Those accepted as professional workers in the public sector, such as the National Health Service, are in the more fortunate section of the migrant workforce. Pay and conditions are more transparent and more closely regulated. Employers take steps to secure these valued employees' immigration status. However, a high percentage of foreign nationals in the UK workforce are employed while their immigration status is under review or as thoroughly undocumented workers (Trades Union Congress 2002). A significant proportion of these workers hold professional or other higher education qualifications from their home countries. These migrants supply the needs of low-paid occupations, many of them in the informal economy. They are particularly likely to be poorly paid and to have little job security; they have few employment benefits such as sick pay, maternity leave, training opportunities, or pension entitlements; and they fear complaining about pay or work conditions because they know that they are at risk of being reported to immigration authorities. Hence, these migrant workers are easily exploited. This is particularly the case for Black-African migrants who tend to work as caregivers for people with long-term mental health problems and age-related physical disabilities,

as cleaners in commercial establishments, as security guards, and as domestic workers in private homes. They may have entered the UK originally as asylum seekers,
but their refugee status has been denied; or they may have entered as university students but have overstayed their student visa entitlement. These migrant workers fear
that exercising rights to health care may expose them and their families to deportation. In particular, they worry that revealing their HIV status to government authorities may reduce their chances of obtaining permanent residency or citizenship
for themselves or their children. Their employment and immigration circumstances
reinforce traditional cultural inhibitions about disclosure of positive HIV status.

Human Rights to Health, Globalization, and HIV

The World Health Organization (WHO) treats Article 12 of the International
Covenant on Economic, Social and Cultural Rights (ICESCR) as setting out the
most authoritative interpretation of the human right to health (World Health Organization 2002, 9). This includes "timely and appropriate health care" and "the
underlying determinants of health" (WHO 2002, 10). WHO asserts that economic and political trends associated with globalization, including privatization,
deregulation, and reduction of public sector spending, constrain the ability of
governments to protect vulnerable groups. WHO notes that "the globalization
process has contributed to the greater marginalization of people and countries
that have been denied access to . . . essential goods such as new life-saving drugs"
(WHO 2002, 24). Residents of sub-Saharan African countries do not have access to timely and appropriate medication for HIV infection despite a UN resolution stating that all nations should provide such access to the extent they are able
(United Nations General Assembly 2001). Patent law, which protects the market
position of pharmaceutical companies, is assiduously defended by wealthy countries in global trade negotiations.

In addition, the World Bank policy of encouraging states to adopt markets in
goods, services, and labor negatively impacts poor people's health as the governments are obliged to prioritize global markets over local needs for health service
provision (WHO 2002). Critics argue that the World Bank's macroeconomic policy has worsened inequality (O'Keefe 2003). Feminists in Africa present evidence
that World Bank–led structural adjustment has been damaging to the population
generally, but especially to women (Mupedziswa and Gumbo 2001). Hence, lack
of affordable health care along with the economic and social destabilization that
accompanies globalization encourages migration from Africa to developed countries. We have seen already how important this immigration is to the UK health
and social care labor force. WHO singles out migrants and refugees, especially
women, as vulnerable to the negative consequences of globalization.

In the United Kingdom, human rights requirements are interpreted to mean that all refugees and asylum seekers and their dependents are entitled to subsidized health care from the National Health Service (Burnett and Fassil 2002). They have the same eligibility to health care as citizens and legally accepted immigrants. The British Medical Association (BMA) notes that successive governments have become more restrictive on asylum policy as well as immigration policy generally and have tried to require doctors to report suspected illegal immigrants (BMA 2001, 398). This association takes the view that requiring health care workers to report suspected illegal immigrants in their patient population undermines trust between health care workers and service users and puts public health at risk. The BMA believes that public health and human rights are mutually reinforcing. Fear of being deported following a failed immigration application leads many to opt for life in the UK as illegal immigrants. If one's immigration status is experienced as an impediment to disclosing one's HIV status, and hence is an impediment to treatment and prevention of infection, then there are significant connections between rights of migrants and rights to health care.

Human rights discourse has been successfully deployed in relation to gay men infected with HIV in developed nations. Already subject to discrimination because of their sexuality, HIV-infected gay men have been further stigmatized on account of their health status. However, because a relatively large number of HIV-infected gay men in developed nations are well educated and fairly affluent (physicians, public health analysts, lawyers, government officials, journalists, and media figures), the activists among them have been able to argue convincingly that protecting gay men's human rights goes hand in hand with enlightened HIV public health strategies. In addition, they have been able to convince the gay community that in order to protect themselves from the spread of HIV, they need to build community capacity, that is, the ability to work together to carry out research about their needs and develop service models that meet these needs. To remain healthy it is not enough for gay men to contest traditional taboos against homosexuality in the larger society. They must exercise control over the health services available to them.

In contrast to the situation of gay men, the application of human rights discourse to women affected by heterosexually transmitted HIV has been slower. So far, there is no critical mass of HIV-infected women either in developing or developed countries in sufficiently powerful positions to shape services to meet their needs. Nonetheless, some progress has been made. Recent international guidelines on human rights as applied to HIV-infected or HIV-infectible women recognize the following:

- Discrimination puts women disproportionately at risk for HIV infection.
- Women's gendered position within the family and public life is one of the prime causes of the increased incidence of HIV among women.

- Gender discrimination "impairs women's ability to deal with the consequences of their own infection and/or infection in the family, in social, economic and personal terms" (Office of the United Nations High Commissioner for Human Rights and the Joint United Nations Programme on HIV/AIDS 1998, 41).

For women to exercise health-related rights, they must be able to engage critically with their community's beliefs and values about gender. Women must be able to form and act on their own views about the extent to which gender constructs promote or fail to promote their health. More important, women need to be able to speak in their own voices. They need to be free to reject discourse that promotes individualism and to embrace discourse that promotes the informal cooperation and intergenerational solidarity that underpins community capacity.

Disputes about Rights

Recently, significant interventions have been made by powerful actors treating rights, especially for women, as a Western cultural invention of questionable value, the outcome of parochial European struggles. For instance, "at the 1994 United Nations Population Conference in Cairo, the Vatican joined with several Muslim governments to condemn what they viewed as the imposition of western norms of . . . individual autonomy on the rest of the world" (Higgins 1996, 405). By contrast, in his examination of the evolution of health and human rights, Stephen Marks begins with "the Ashoka adopting tolerance and individual freedom as state policy and abolishing torture in the third century B.C.E." (Marks 2002, 739). In addition, John Strawson asserts that "without the action of colonised people, women, ethnic minorities, lesbians and gays . . . there would be no international human rights law today" (Strawson 2003, viii). Moreover, there is no reason to think that just because one tradition does not use rights discourse presently, it is wrong for another tradition to introduce rights discourse to it. Traditions are not Platonic forms incapable of or in no way in need of change and transformation. Martha Nussbaum notes that the culture of our origin is accidental, that "real cultures contain plurality and conflict, tradition and subversion," and that the human potential to engage in critical reflection means that no culture or tradition should be above judgment (Nussbaum 1999, 37). Tradition has been constructed and can be reconstructed (Jones 1999).

Universal human rights language is not without serious problems. It can be misused. For example, Eurocentric rights have sometimes masqueraded as universal human rights. However, such misuses of the concept of universal human rights do not invalidate it as a concept. Many feminists have attempted to shape nonprivileging versions of human rights. In general, feminist versions of human rights demonstrate how fundamental women's economic and social circumstances are in shaping whether women can exercise political and civil rights as individuals (Fraser 1989). They also emphasize that universal human rights language is not an atomistic language that pits individual against individual but a relational language that can create community. Feminist work on relational autonomy is particularly helpful in developing this last point. It is significant that Anne Donchin's view that "social relations provide the ground for the development of autonomy capacities" is congruent with Black-African feminists' emphasis on the contingent connections between colonial and postcolonial economic and political conditions and the gendered practices sanctioned by tradition (Donchin 2000, 239).

Nonfeminist Eurocentric focus on civil and political rights, highlighting the entitlements of atomistic (male) individuals, typically unencumbered by children or noneconomically active elders, continues to be dominant, despite the burgeoning of feminist developments in philosophy resulting in a deeper and richer canvas for understanding what it is to be a bearer of human rights (O'Keefe and Scott-Samuel 2002). Human rights discourse is still shaped by profoundly unequal power relations between wealthy capitalist nations and developing countries; it continues to be used in a misguided way in real political and economic struggles carried out with regard to processes of globalization (O'Keefe 2003).

We think that a better conceptualization that can challenge that dominant understanding is desirable and achievable. This takes duty or responsibility to be as important as entitlement, mutual interdependence to be a more sound basis for autonomy than atomistic individualism, and social and economic rights to be crucial to the exercise of all rights, including those to health. The African Charter on Human and Peoples' Rights (ACHPR) goes some way in this direction.

The African Charter on Human and Peoples' Rights (1981)

The starting point of the ACHPR is the need for a continuing struggle for independence against neocolonialism and the importance of the universality and indivisibility of the full range of human rights. The ACHPR treats the family as the "natural unit and basis of society" and the "custodian of morals and traditional values" (ACHPR 1981, 1449). Consistent with Nussbaum's earlier point, the charter does not treat tradition as fixed or unproblematic. It identifies social relationships needing change, stressing the importance of addressing problems faced by women and children. Hence, Article 18 asserts that the "state shall ensure the elimination of every discrimination against women and ensure the protection of the rights of the woman and the child as stipulated in international declarations and conventions" (ACHPR 1981, 1452). As a rights instrument, the ACHPR is distinctive in the way it simultaneously emphasizes duties. In particular, it foregrounds the duty "to preserve harmonious development of the family and to work for the cohesion and respect of the family" (ACHPR 2000, 1554). The ACHPR gives us a picture of people embedded in a network of duties as well as entitlements, where kinship is the primary focus.

For many African feminists, rights discourse is rife with tensions insofar as African gender and family relations typically involve inequity. For instance, land ownership in Africa is overwhelmingly in male hands, with only 7 percent of land in Uganda owned by women. Florence Butegwe notes that women "increasingly realize that lack of access to land is the major determinant of poverty and social status both in rural and urban areas" (Butegwe 2002, 110). If women owned their own property—especially farmland—it would be easier for them to support themselves and their children. They would be less dependent on male power and less the victims of cultural practices that put their health at risk. Discussing Nigeria, Hussaina Abdullah argues that "due to the patriarchal character of the family, male members are favored over women in the construction of rights" (Abdullah 2002, 174). Analyzing gender relations in Zimbabwe, commentators assert that women "bear a disproportionate share of the burdens of economic and social deprivation both as breadwinners and caretakers" (Moyo and Kawewe 2002, 169). Commitment to cohesion within the family can mask real differences of interest, and respect for the family can prevent people from being honest about the presence of stigmatizing conditions or behavior that puts others at risk of contracting HIV.

Gendered tradition damages women in Africa. Within popular culture in Zimbabwe, women have been implicated as the chief cause of the spread of HIV/AIDS, and negative images of black women in popular culture are on the increase (Vambe and Mawadza 2001). Women are urged to maintain fidelity within marriage and chastity before it. Their lapses from the path of purity and obedience to male kin through "loose" and "dangerous" behavior are blamed for the spread of HIV/AIDS. In popular oral culture, female identity is presented as legitimately defined by men with a focus on male-controlled motherhood. At the same time, popular culture does not consider multiple partners and unsafe sex by men a problem. Thus, pressure to seal marriage with childbearing puts women's health at risk. The construction of women as needing to be tamed into the respectability of marriage and motherhood through men's sexual control over them is part of a "new moral discourse" about African women nourished by "the role of colonialism in collusion with African patriarchy" (Vambe and Mawadza 2001, 57). All of the feminist African writers cited concur that we need to struggle for rights against a complex background in which economic factors operating at the global level impact on what passes for tradition.

Gendered Family Relations

Gwendolyn Mikell depicts African feminism as differing from Western forms of feminism by being "distinctly heterosexual, pro-natal, and concerned with many 'bread, butter, culture and power' issues" (Mikell 1997, 4). Gendered relations are marked by exchange among families. Marriage is understood as a contract between families rather than individuals. Taking kinship to be central to African tradition, Welshman Ncube and associates depict the kin structure as involving complex networks of obligation based on consanguinity and affinity through marriage, re- sulting in diverse forms of household formation wider than the nuclear family (Ncube et al. 1997). They also find the Zimbabwean family to involve a complex of demanding reciprocal obligations. The most distinctive aspect of African fam- ily life, as opposed to Western family life, is that the African family is not con- fined to a single residence. Rather, it extends over a variety of residences, and individual family members often range over residences inhabited by other family members. Within African families, parenting duties are not restricted to biologi- cal mothers and fathers but are shared by aunts, uncles, grandparents, and older siblings. For these extended family structures to function economically, the shar- ing of family income among different households within the family is required. Therefore, family life requires the obligatory circulation of remittances, funds sent by those working in developed countries to support kin in developing coun- tries. Family members are duty-bound to share income and housing, as well as car- ing responsibilities. Significantly, this form of family life is not the exclusive product of unchanging tradition. Rather, it is distinctively marked by the colonial experience. Many African feminists share the perception that women's problems are accentuated by the legacy of colonial rule reinforced by an unjust global eco- nomic order that damages sons, lovers, husbands, and fathers.

African Feminists' Views on Socially Constructed Traditions

Otude Moyo and Saliwe Kawewe are critical of the view that we can treat the gen- dered nature of Zimbabwean society as derived from pristine tradition (Moyo and Kawewe 2002). Colonial rule, lasting ninety years until 1980, involved the loss of land by indigenous communities and the strengthening of gender inequality by mak- ing women the legal "wards of their male relatives and husbands. . . . As minors for life women could not own property and make decisions that affected their liveli- hoods" (Moyo and Kawewe 2002, 166). Males were recruited into waged work in cities, on commercial farms, and in mines. They lived in all-male hostels and were controlled through passbooks. However, women were not incorporated into the for- mal economy. Married women who stayed in the rural areas worked in the informal economy as agricultural workers and caregivers within the households they headed; single women who left the rural areas were expected to work as domestics for Whites, largely because they could not get documents to work in the formal economy. Polygyny—including informal procreational and sexual relationships—was strengthened through the enforced separate habitation of husbands and wives. Moyo and Kawewe's account of the gendered nature of economic and social deprivation is echoed by accounts in many African societies.

African women's circumstances have not turned them into passive victims. Many have taken steps to ensure they are not economically dependent on a male sexual partner. In particular, they have learned not to rely on men to support them and their children. Whether in a rural or urban environment, women have learned how to survive through informal and "diverse work strategies, including self-provisioning, self-employment, use of social networks in saving strategies, migration, cross-border trading" (Moyo and Kawewe 2002, 172). To be sure, it has not been easy for women to provide for themselves and their extended families. To make matters worse, structural adjustment programs imposed by the International Monetary Fund and World Bank have made it even harder for African women. In Zimbabwe, women have been particularly hard hit. Some with employed husbands have left their children with others to secure work far from home, only to discover that higher and higher user fees for their children's health care and schooling consume most of their earnings (Mupedziswa and Gumbo 2001). Women with unemployed husbands have left their children with their fathers, only to expose their children to economic hardship or health risk because some husbands used monies meant for their children for themselves or introduced HIV into the household as a result of their extramarital sexual activity (Mupedziswa and Gumbo 2001, 103–4).

Although gendered culture, circumstances, and opportunities are unequal, Black-African women have clearly taken active steps to secure livelihoods for themselves and their families. Motherhood is rarely considered a sufficient reason not to engage in economic production. Women often embark on enterprises that require the development and exercise of considerable problem-solving and negotiating skills in public spaces, such as informal trading or migration. African migrants in developed countries bring with them traditional norms that were forged in the vortex of colonialism. These norms are then further modified within the countries to which they migrate. We saw earlier that African family members do not confine themselves to a single residence; they expect to be accommodated in a number of households. The experience of global migrants in developed countries extends the distances over which a family distributes itself in these households. Hence, a Black-African woman living in London may have her sister and her sister's children living with her, while one or more of her own children are living with her aunt in Zimbabwe, and her husband, a resident in London, makes frequent trips back to Zimbabwe. These women's central priority is to organize their economic situation so they can discharge their demanding family obligations that range across continents. Unfortunately, as a result they accord their health a low priority. In the context of family dispersal, women are at particular risk for HIV infection because of its prevalence and because of cultural inhibition regarding disclosure of HIV status among sexual intimates, as well as inhibition regarding disclosure of HIV status due to fear of the immigration authorities.

Researching Sexual Health and Promoting Sexual Health

Within the UK, HIV prevention and treatment strategies with respect to Black-African communities focus narrowly on sexual behavior. This emphasis is reflected strongly in standard epidemiological research (Chinouya, Fenton, and Davidson 1999). Researchers working on conventional epidemiological projects, designed to quantify HIV infection among Black-African migrant communities, were encouraged to identify sexual beliefs, values, and behavior that put these populations at risk of contracting or passing on HIV infection. Such research is carried out within a biomedical paradigm and funded largely by service providers or pharmaceutical companies. Its primary objective is to quantitatively map the pattern of disease, which involves carrying out extensive work among those who are already in contact with health services. This in fact gives a distorted picture of the underlying risks. It does not engage the population at large who have reason to avoid contact with health services. Not grounded in the social sciences, this research does not focus on the economic and social conditions African migrants face, either in the developing country from which they came or the developed country in which they currently reside, that lead them to avoid early or any contact with health services. Moreover, such research is not grounded in an understanding of the historical conditions that have forged the "tradition" that shapes beliefs, values, and behavior, nor does it consider the global context that makes migration so desirable—even when it means living as illegal residents and working in the informal economy.

An investigation comparing problems experienced by Black-Africans infected with HIV with their White British counterparts found dramatic differences. African residents in the UK identified two kinds of issues presenting difficulties for HIV health promotion. The first group of issues, centered around immigration status, constituted an overriding problem for Black-African migrants but presented no problem for their White British counterparts. The second group posed problems for both, but Black-Africans experienced more severe difficulties by several orders of magnitude. These issues included inadequate income, housing, and living conditions; discrimination; and poor knowledge about anti-HIV treatments (Weatherburn et al. 2003). Such issues give Black-Africans reasons to stay away from health services altogether, to present late, and (for men) to not disclose to female sexual partners that they are HIV-positive.

Epidemiological studies increasingly employ Black-Africans as part of the research team to recruit subjects for further research about sexual beliefs, attitudes, and behavior among the Black-African population at large and to estimate the prevalence and incidence of HIV/AIDS. Some Black-Africans have become increasingly restive about their position as handmaidens recruiting members of their community to research programs. They were concerned that programs had little or no input from those communities themselves regarding research design and method. These programs did not explore the place of HIV/AIDS in relation to the economic and social conditions in their ordinary lives that migrants saw as threatening their health.

Studies monitoring and evaluating HIV/AIDS health promotion interventions in the UK convinced Black-African researchers that information and condom distribution campaigns were bound to be ineffective (Chinouya 2001). Conventional epidemiological and health promotion research on HIV in the UK discomforts and exposes the population under surveillance. It raises fear among research subjects about the consequences to them personally and to their community should the results "get out" to the population at large. Furthermore, such a climate of fear does not promote the community's capacity to engage critically with traditional beliefs and values and to challenge them when they promote the spread of HIV/AIDS. There is a better way for health researchers to carry out health-promoting research in comparison with the standard research narrowly focused on sexual beliefs, attitudes, and behavior. This starts from the social and economic problems that Black-Africans themselves prioritize in their ordinary lives rather than the risk factors that health planners focus on. It offers opportunities for capacity building, most especially by providing safe spaces in which communities can foster a culture that makes it easier for groups to discuss sex and gender more openly as well as for intimates to disclose compromised health status.

Reconstructing Tradition through Community-Based Action Research

Health planners have typically treated epidemiological research and health promotion as emphasizing sexual behavior in isolation from the totality of people's lives. Interventions have focused on providing information to help people engage in safer sex by promoting the use of condoms. In fact, sexual health can be more effectively promoted by mobilizing resources so that marginalized groups can take responsibility for their own learning about health. Black-African communities affected by HIV are developing community-led, bottom-up research and health promotion strategies. These collective self-help initiatives draw on, challenge, and reconstruct tradition. Tradition needs to be challenged regarding prohibitions on open discussion about sexual matters between partners and within communities more broadly. Repeatedly, it has been found that concerns about immigration and economic problems reinforced the harms already present in the health-damaging gender tradition of Black-African migrants.

One of us, in the course of writing her PhD dissertation, discovered that an effective way to determine the prevalence of HIV-positive Black-African immigrants in the UK was not to rely on narrowly defined epidemiological research but instead to use anthropological research methods informed by social science literature (Chinouya 2002). Significantly, this methodology supported initiatives of Black-African communities in developing their own capacity for action research and health promotion. These initiatives involved convincing public health planners and their partners that mapping health trends requires using community development methods and providing health promotion interventions that are meaningful and acceptable to the population. Conventional research and health promotion with Black-African migrants has been overwhelmingly confined to people who are already service users. Community development–based initiatives involve achieving trust among hard-to-reach migrants affected by HIV and AIDS. It requires establishing effective contact with refugees, asylum seekers, and undocumented migrants who are fleeing humanitarian crises in Africa, many of whom work in the informal economy.

One example of community development action research that engages undocumented migrants and transforms tradition is taken from work by and with Black-African communities in the UK. It involves the development and implementation of culturally sensitive consciousness raising, reworking the traditional practice of *Padare* (Chinouya and Davidson 2003). The *Padare* is a spatial location in Zimbabwean communal areas where men meet separately from the rest of the community to discuss their sexual activities. Information disclosed in this space is privileged and not available for gossip outside. Hence, it provides a possible opening to allow discussion of the importance of disclosure. A *Padare* was created in London for creative problem solving and for sharing the experience of living with HIV. However, the reconstructed *Padare* is not confined to men. It is available to both men and women for both single-sex and mixed-sex discussion and social activities, peer-led by members of the communities living with HIV. This confidential social space for disclosure of sensitive information has made it possible for participants to explore gendered traditional norms. In light of the emphasis on heterosexual sexuality within what passes for African tradition, it is significant that of 178 *Padare* participants, 20 percent of men reported having only same-sex partners in the previous twelve months, while 5 percent of women reported same-sex partners and 2 percent of women reported both male and female partners. The *Padare* starts from tradition but opens up novel opportunities for learning, disclosure, and consciousness raising about gendered norms and activities. Crucially, it involves addressing participants' economic and social priorities, including housing and legal issues, not just their health care problems. *Padare* has also provided opportunities for training as researchers and community development workers, offering personal validation as well as much needed pay for unemployed or underemployed people.

Much action-based research, especially with marginalized communities, is carried out by enthusiastic activists who are severely underpowered in their research training and resources. Black-Africans typically function as assistants, carrying out research designed by Europeans who have little cultural capital regarding these communities. Capacity building within the community itself is crucial for research that enables Africans affected by HIV to set the questions that matter to them. This needs to be linked to action research protocols resulting in evidence-based interventions. It is not enough to carry out creative research that imaginatively engages research populations as objects of research and policy formation. They may still remain subordinate. Key to this enterprise is negotiation of management change in partner agencies to ensure that Black-African migrant communities are empowered to carry out their own research that can feed into the planning of policy and service provision. These efforts are bearing some fruit. The National AIDS Trust, the umbrella body for HIV-related civil society groups, has produced a national policy framework document on HIV prevention and Black-African communities in England (National AIDS Trust 2001). Furthermore, the Department of Health has undertaken to cooperate with the African HIV Policy Network to plan a work program informed by this framework.

Conclusion

Poised in precarious spaces, global migrants are subject to transboundary threats to their health while global work opportunities, which might offer some safety, are increasingly policed to exclude migrants with HIV. Skilled adult migrants are recognized as essential to the health, education, and social care labor force, but preferably without making claims on public welfare. In the heartlands of the developed world, especially in urban areas, African women and their families live as global denizens: with enormous ingenuity, they negotiate their first world and developing country identities and obligations. They simultaneously experience

HIV/AIDS in the first and developing worlds, grounded in a gendered tradition: dispersal of their closest kin between metropolis and home, internationally based intergenerational caring arrangements, and internationally based obligatory economic transfer arrangements. The future is global. Major cities and their metropolitan surroundings are home to populations pushed to migrate by the economic and social consequences of the global order shaped by the disproportionate power of developed countries. Developed societies rely on global migrants as a crucial source of labor in the international care chain. Moyo and Kawewe ask, "Are policies of receiving countries supportive of women trying to survive shifts in the global economy by emigrating to centers of wealth to support their families back home?" (Moyo and Kawewe 2002, 175) Feminists in Africa and African feminists in the UK have produced insights for understanding and strategies for engaging in traditional discourse to contest gender inequities that promote the spread of HIV infection. In so doing, they are producing some of the policies that can empower women, not only to survive shifts in the global economy but also to create a world in which the theory and practice of global migrants enrich human rights discourse through emphasis on responsibilities grounded in interdependence.

References

Abdullah, Hussaina. 2002. "Religious Revivalism, Human Rights Activism and the Struggle for Women's Rights in Nigeria." In *Cultural Transformation and Human Rights in Africa*, edited by Abdullahi An-Naim, 151–91. London: Zed Books.

ACHPR. 1981/2000. "African Charter on Human and Peoples' Rights." In *International Human Rights in Context*, edited by Henry Steiner and Philip Alston, 1449–57. Oxford, UK: Oxford University Press.

Batty, David. 2003. "Crippled by Ambition." *Guardian Society*, February 19, 3.

British Medical Association (BMA). 2001. *The Medical Profession and Human Rights: Handbook for a Changing Agenda*. London: Zed Books.

Buchan, James. 2003. *Here to Stay?* London: Royal College of Nursing.

Burnett, Angela, and Yohannes Fassil. 2002. *Meeting the Health Needs of Refugee and Asylum Seekers in the UK*. London: National Health Service.

Butegwe, Florence. 2002. "Mediating Culture and Human Rights in Favour of Land Rights for Women in Africa: A Framework for Community-Level Action." In *Cultural Transformation and Human Rights in Africa*, edited by Abdullahi An-Naim, 108–25. London: Zed Books.

Butler, Peter. 2003. "Image of the Future." *Guardian Society*, February 19, 2–4.

Chinouya, Martha. 2001. *HIV Prevention in African Communities Living in England: A Study of the Challenges in Service Provision*. London: National AIDS Trust.

———. 2002. "HIV Disclosure Patterns amongst African Families Affected by HIV and AIDS in London." PhD dissertation, University of North London.

Chinouya, Martha, and Oliver Davidson. 2003. *The Padare Project*. London: Camden and Islington Primary Care Trust.

Chinouya, Martha, Kevin Fenton, and Oliver Davidson. 1999. *The Mayisha Study: The Social Mapping Report*. Horsham, UK: AVERT.

Chinouya, Martha, Livingstone Musoro, and Eileen O'Keefe. 2003. *Ubuntu-Hunhu in Hertfordshire: Black Africans in Hertfordshire, Health and Social Care Issues*. St. Albans: Crescent Support Group.

Donchin, Anne. 2000. "Autonomy and Interdependence: Quandaries in Genetic Decision Making." In *Relational Autonomy*, edited by Catriona Mackenzie and Natalie Stoljar, 236–58. Oxford, UK: Oxford University Press.

Fraser, Nancy. 1989. *Unruly Practices: Power, Discourse and Gender in Contemporary Social Theory*. Cambridge, UK: Polity Press.

Higgins, Tracy. 1996. "Anti-Essentialism, Relativism, and Human Rights." In *International Human Rights in Context*, edited by Henry Steiner and Philip Alston, 405–09. Oxford, UK: Oxford University Press.

Jones, Nikki. 1999. "Culture and Reproductive Health: Challenges to Feminist Philanthropy." In *Embodying Bioethics*, edited by Anne Donchin and Laura M. Purdy, 223–37. Oxford, UK: Rowman & Littlefield.

Marks, Stephen. 2002. "The Evolving Field of Health and Human Rights: Issues and Methods." *Journal of Law, Medicine & Ethics* 30, no. 4: 739–54.

Mikell, Gwendolyn. 1997. "Introduction." In *African Feminism: The Politics of Survival in Sub-Saharan Africa*, edited by Gwendolyn Mikell, 1–49. Philadelphia: University of Pennsylvania Press.

Moyo, Otude, and Saliwe Kawewe. 2002. "Dynamics of a Racialized, Gendered, Ethnicized and Economically Stratified Society." *Feminist Economics* 8, no. 2: 163–81.

Mupedziswa, Rodreck, and Perpetua Gumbo. 2001. *Women, Informal Traders, and the Struggle for Survival in an Environment of Economic Reforms*. Uppsala, Sweden: Nordiska Afrikaintsitut.

National AIDS Trust. 2001. *HIV Prevention and African Communities Living in England: A Framework for Action*. London: National AIDS Trust.

Ncube, Welshman, Julie Stewart, Joyce Kazembe, Beatrice Donzwa, Elizabeth Gwaunza, Tsitsi Nzira, and Kebokile Dengu-Zvobgo. 1997. *Continuity and Change: The Family in Zimbabwe*. Harare, Zimbabwe: Women & Law in Southern Africa Research Trust.

Nicoll, Angus, and Francoise Hamers. 2002. "Are Trends in HIV, Gonorrhea and Syphilis Worsening in Western Europe?" *British Medical Journal* 324: 1324–27.

Nuffield Council on Bioethics. 2002. *The Ethics of Research Related to Healthcare in Developing Countries*. London: Nuffield Council on Bioethics.

Nussbaum, Martha. *Sex and Social Justice*. 1999. Oxford, UK: Oxford University Press.

Office of the United Nations High Commissioner for Human Rights and the Joint United Nations Programme on HIV/AIDS. 1998. *HIV/AIDS and Human Rights: International Guidelines*. New York: United Nations.

O'Keefe, Eileen. 2003. "Contested Macro-Economic Policy as Health Policy: The World Bank in Ukraine." In *The Social Significance of Health Promotion*, edited by Theodore Macdonald, 122–38. London: Routledge.

O'Keefe, Eileen, and Alex Scott-Samuel. 2002. "Human Rights & Wrongs: Could Health Impact Assessment Help?" *Journal of Law, Medicine & Ethics* 30, no. 4: 734–38.

Strawson, John. 2003. "Strife Is Swept Under the Carpet." *Times Higher,* May 30, viii.

Trades Union Congress. 2002. *Migrant Workers.* London: Trades Union Congress.

United Nations General Assembly Special Session on AIDS. 2001. "Declaration of Commitment on HIV/AIDS: Global Crisis—Global Action." In "25 Questions & Answers on Health & Human Rights," WHO. *Health & Human Rights Series* no. 1 (July): 32.

Unlinked Anonymous Surveys Steering Group/Department of Health. 2002. *Prevalence of HIV & Hepatitis Infections in the United Kingdom: Annual Report of the Unlinked Anonymous Prevalence Monitoring Programme, 2001.* London: Department of Health.

Vambe, Maurice, and Aquilina Mawadza. 2001. "Images of Black Women in Popular Songs and Some Poems on AIDS in Post-Independence Zimbabwe." In *Orality and Cultural Identities in Zimbabwe,* edited by Maurice Vambe, 57–72. Gweru, Zimbabwe: Mambo Press.

Walker, Polly, Michael Worobey, Andrew Rambaut, Edward Holmes, and Oliver Pybus. 2003. "Sexual Transmission of HIV in Africa." *Nature* 422 (April 17): 679.

Weatherburn, Peter, Winnie Ssanyu-Sseruma, Ford Hickson, Susie McLean, and David Reid. 2003. *Project Nasah: An Investigation into the HIV Treatment Information and Other Needs of African People with HIV Resident in England.* London: Sigma Research.

World Health Organization. 2002. "25 Questions & Answers on Health & Human Rights." *Health & Human Rights Series* no. 1 (July).

HIV/AIDS Policies
Compromising the Human Rights of Women

14

LAURA DUHAN KAPLAN

THE CENTER FOR REPRODUCTIVE RIGHTS (CRR) is an international legal advocacy fund dedicated to helping women win legal and legislative victories on reproductive issues. Its activities include advocacy, policy analysis, legal research, international litigation, and public education, with particular attention to ten issues, including sexual violence, family planning, and HIV/AIDS. In the area of HIV/AIDS, the CRR's public education efforts include research reports and analyses on international practices for treating women with HIV/AIDS.

In one such report, published in December 2002 under the title "HIV/AIDS: Reproductive Rights on the Line," the CRR "urges governments to accept their international legal obligations to protect the sexual and reproductive rights of HIV-positive women and girls" (Center for Reproductive Rights 2002).

With this urgent call, the CRR implies two allegations. First, the "sexual and reproductive rights of HIV-positive women and girls" are being violated by governments around the world. Second, the "international and legal obligations to protect" these rights are being ignored. In the report, the allegations are supported primarily with statistical and anecdotal examples of challenges faced by HIV-positive women around the globe. The examples portray a heavy-handed, inconsistent, and poorly thought-out local and international response to a public health crisis. The CRR does not explicitly argue in the report that the inadequate response constitutes a violation of women's rights. In another publication, however, the CRR cites relevant sections of eleven different international treaties and conventions to show that the international community has identified reproductive rights as human rights since the 1940s (Center for Reproductive Law and Policy 2001).

In this chapter, I support the CRR's call for systematic attention to the reproductive rights of women. After conceptually organizing the center's allegations
of rights violations, I place the allegations in a philosophical context by focusing
on two specific international human rights conventions. These two conventions,
the United Nations Declaration of Human Rights in 1948 and CEDAW, the
Convention on the Elimination of All Forms of Discrimination against Women
in 1979, offer two different but related theories about the nature of human rights.
According to both sets of theories, international HIV/AIDS policies clearly violate the human rights of women.

Facts and Claims about Rights Violations

The CRR's report begins by citing statistics showing that heterosexual women and
adolescent girls in Africa, the Caribbean, and the United States are more likely to be
infected with HIV than are their male counterparts. Nonetheless, the report notes,
the health concerns of females themselves have been overlooked in favor of the role
they can play in preventing transmission of HIV to their children. The report then
lists a variety of difficult situations for women and girls with HIV/AIDS, specifically naming sixteen different countries in North America, South America, Europe,
Asia, and Africa. The challenges, listed in the following order, include

- poor research on the risks and benefits of breastfeeding versus formula
  feeding
- limitations on the right to marry
- restrictive abortion laws
- poor counseling on abortion and family planning
- placing all the responsibility for preventing premarital sex on girls
- mandatory HIV testing or reporting requirements that expose women to
  ostracism and violence
- the availability of antiretroviral drugs to pregnant women only

At first glance, it seems as though the center's goals for HIV-positive women
and girls might not be clear and consistent. For example, when issues are understood using the polarities that frame political discourse in the United States, some
of the complaints seem to contradict one another. On the one hand, the CRR
criticizes restrictive abortion policies. This would imply that the center would like
to see abortion—and thus the option not to reproduce—readily available to HIV-
positive women. On the other hand, the CRR complains about restrictions on
marriage rights. This would imply that the center would like to see unrestricted
marriage rights—and thus the option to reproduce with legal support—available
to HIV-positive women.

Other complaints could seem to be at odds with the goals of women's health advocacy. Surely the CRR staff wants women to know if they have HIV and thus be eligible for care. Yet they complain about policies designed to encourage testing. And surely the staff wants to see improved care for pregnant and nursing women. Yet they criticize initiatives targeted to the specific needs of pregnant and nursing women.

A deeper and more careful look, however, can reveal that the CRR's criticism of global HIV/AIDS policy is informed by a clear definition of human rights and reproductive rights. Later, I will take that more careful look by organizing the complaints thematically and relating the themes to philosophical literature about ethics and human rights.

The complaints offered by the Center for Reproductive Rights can be grouped into two categories. The first category includes practices that overemphasize mothering at the expense of women's other needs, interests, and functions. These practices may privilege mothers over nonmothers or ignore nonreproductive dimensions of women's lives. The U.S.-sponsored initiative announced in 2001 that would make antiretroviral drugs available in Africa only to pregnant women privileges mothers over nonmothers, excluding nonmothers from receiving up-to-date care. Restriction of the rights of HIV-positive women in India and China to marry ignores nonreproductive dimensions of women's lives. Women unable to marry may lose opportunities for economic protection, increased social status, and family companionship. Similarly, mandatory testing and result reporting as practiced in Romania and in some states in the northeastern United States may lessen the likelihood of mother-to-child transmission but increase the risk to women of violence and ostracism. Studies of women in Kenya and Tanzania show that the risk is real in at least some communities: these women report abuse, violence, and abandonment by partners who learn about their HIV-positive status.

The second category of complaint includes practices that show a poor regard for mothers or a lack of understanding for their needs. In Zimbabwe and Swaziland, for example, girls, but not men and boys, have been asked to take responsibility for abstaining from sex. The likely result of this one-sided emphasis is not less sexual activity but more blaming and shaming of women for their pregnancies. Once women are pregnant, some countries' laws and practices allow health care providers to deliberately give incomplete information to pregnant women. In South Africa, for example, health care providers are not required to discuss the option of abortion with HIV-positive pregnant women, while in India women report coercion by physicians to undergo abortions. Finally, studies on the impact of breastfeeding on the health of HIV-positive mothers have been poorly coordinated with one another. Many studies have left out obvious variables such as local water quality for formula preparation and the physical demands of breastfeeding. Poor information makes it difficult for HIV-positive mothers to make informed decisions.

Each of these categories of complaints leads to a specific allegation of a human rights violation:

1. The majority of health care policy makers view HIV-infected women solely in terms of their reproductive roles. Treating women *only* as reproductive agents violates their human rights.
2. In their roles as mothers, women with HIV/AIDS do not receive adequate research support, counseling, or health care services. Providing poor health care to HIV-positive women violates their human rights.

A next step in understanding philosophically the allegations made by the Center for Reproductive Rights is to explain in what way each of these practices—treating women solely as reproductive agents and providing them with poor health care—constitutes a violation of human rights. The explanations will be grounded in the theories of human rights provided by the UN Declaration of Human Rights and CEDAW.

Declaration of Human Rights:
A Theory of the Subjects of Human Rights

The UN Universal Declaration of Human Rights provides a clear and useful set of concepts for understanding these two violations. According to Brian Orend, the declaration systematically specifies first the *subjects* and then the *objects* of human rights. In Orend's language, the *subjects* of rights are rights holders. The *objects* of rights are the particular goods due to rights holders (Orend 2002, 117–19). An understanding of the *subjects* of human rights, as specified by the declaration, can be useful in understanding how treating women as reproductive agents violates their human rights. An understanding of the *objects* of human rights can be useful in understanding how providing poor health care can be seen as a violation of human rights.

The Declaration of Human Rights begins with a specification of the subjects of human rights and the ultimate reasons why human rights must be protected. The declaration recognizes that these reasons are both consequentialist, that is, dependent on the consequences that flow from rights protection, and deontological, that is, rooted in the nature of human beings. Nonetheless, Article I emphasizes deontological reasons for the protection of human rights, stating, "All human beings are born free and equal in dignity and rights. They are endowed with reason and conscience and should act toward one another in a spirit of brotherhood" (Orend 2002, 244–50).

Using a sketch of the moral philosophy of Immanuel Kant, I can show how the language of Article I evokes Kant's *Grounding for the Metaphysics of Morals* (1785) (Kant 1977, 925–76). Like Kant, the article recognizes the role that reason plays in enabling human beings to respect the dignity of all members of the human family. Kant begins the presentation of his moral philosophy by trying to understand the role of reason in moral decision making. Speaking universally on behalf of all rational beings, he notes that by the time we reach maturity we have many types of instructions installed in our minds. Kant calls these instructions "imperatives" and notes that most of them can be called "hypothetical imperatives." Hypothetical imperatives are "if-then" statements explaining the means to various ends. A hypothetical imperative tells us that if we want to achieve particular end *x*, we should take particular step *y*. Hypothetical imperatives help us deal with practical problems and also guide us in our efforts to attain happiness.

A very small handful of our imperatives, however, take a different form. Moral imperatives are not instructions about how to reach a particular end. Moral imperatives are not "if-then" statements. Rather, they are categorical imperatives of the form, "Do *x*." They simply tell us what is the right thing to do. To use Kant's language, they express the moral law. The moral law is, so to speak, larger than life; its instructions are not relative to anyone's personal aims or concerns. The pure form of the moral law is, according to Kant, expressed in the following principle: "Act only on that maxim whereby you can at the same time will that it should become a universal law." In other words, act on categorical rather than hypothetical imperatives; act so as to do your duty, not to fulfill your personal aims. Because the only end of the moral law is to do a good action, it requires that we do not use others as a means to an end. Thus, all human beings exist as ends in themselves. Their worth is not relative to the use we can make of them in carrying out our ends. According to Kant, moral law is also expressed in this principle: "Act as to treat humanity, whether in your own person or in that of any other, in every case as an end in itself and never as a means only."

When health policy makers overemphasize mothering at the expense of women's other needs, interests, and functions, women are seen as a means to an end. From this view, women are no more than a necessary tool for supplying the next generation. Their social worth, that is, their eligibility for public and humanitarian funds, is calculated in terms of their reproductive capacity. As the Center for Reproductive Rights notes, when mother-to-child transmission of HIV/AIDS is a risk, women receive attention; when it is not, the attention ceases. Women are not targeted for health care because they are economic producers, politicians, advisors, or companions but because they are mothers. Even though the targeting may have its roots in the generous motive of protecting children, a motive that many women share, it nonetheless reduces the interests of women to that single motive.

Susan Bordo, in an analysis of the erosion of the legal rights of pregnant women in the United States, gives an elegant philosophical description of this reduction. For more than one hundred years, the U. S. Supreme Court regarded the right to bodily integrity as a fundamental right. A person's body was not to be understood as a series of objective processes but as the house of a psyche. The body was to be seen as an expression of the life of a subject with a history, a projected future, a sense of meaning. The subject living within the body was to be in control of it. However, legal decisions concerning (female) obstetrical patients have increasingly set aside this principle. In these decisions, the pregnant woman is viewed only as a life-support system for her fetus. Her subjectivity, informed consent, views of medicine, bodily integrity, religious beliefs, and ideas about how to spend her time are irrelevant. She is not viewed as a body that expresses the life of a subject but as a series of objective processes that might at some point bring forth another subject (Bordo 1993, 71–93). While Bordo speaks of pregnant women, her analysis applies to the situation of nonpregnant women with HIV/AIDS as described by the Center for Reproductive Rights. When a woman is valued only as a body that brings forth a child, a woman who is not involved in childbearing has no status at all.

Although the UN Declaration of Human Rights clearly states that "all human beings" are "equal in dignity," global AIDS policy does not acknowledge this. Women, it turns out, are not equal in dignity because they are treated as means and not as ends in themselves. Although women are named as *subjects* of human rights, they are not so treated. On the most fundamental philosophical understanding of the nature of human rights, then, the human rights of women are violated by global AIDS policy.

UN Declaration of Human Rights:
A Theory of the Objects of Human Rights

Examining the human rights *objects* that appear in the UN Declaration of Human Rights can also be useful, in two ways. First, they provide an additional argument to the conclusion that global AIDS policies violate the human rights of women who are not necessarily mothers. Second, they are helpful in understanding why providing poor health care to mothers can be seen as a violation of human rights.

Articles 2 through 6 of the declaration provide what Orend calls a "first level specification of human rights objects" (Orend 2002, 117–19). These are the objects required to secure the freedom and dignity described in Article I of the declaration. The Declaration of Human Rights recognizes five specific objects: security, subsistence, liberty, equality, and recognition as a person before the law, recommending that these objects be protected by national laws. The rest of the declaration offers what Orend calls a "second level" enumeration of the specific human rights commitments that follow from the first level (Orend 2002, 117–19). Several of these specific commitments are particularly relevant to the needs of women with HIV/AIDS. Article 12 prohibits "interference with . . . privacy [and] family"; article 16 guarantees the right "to marry and to found a family"; article 25 announces the right to "medical care and necessary social services," stating that "motherhood and childhood are entitled to special care and assistance."

In its report, the Center for Reproductive Rights implies that these specific first- and second-level rights objects of women with HIV/AIDS are being violated. Some of the same practices that violate women's right to be treated as ends in themselves also compromise women's right to security and subsistence. When the right to marriage is restricted, women lose access to security and subsistence. When the privacy of women's health records is not maintained, their security is compromised. When medical care is withheld from women who are not pregnant, their very subsistence is threatened.

In the case of pregnant and nursing mothers with HIV/AIDS, the CRR implies that the rights to privacy, necessary social services, and medical care are violated. Health care providers interfere with the right to privacy and family planning when they give only information in keeping with the national bias for or against abortion. They fail to provide necessary social services when the counseling they offer is incomplete, one-sided, or filled with pressure. They also fail when they offer sexuality education to women only and not to men. Medical care is compromised when research on infant feeding, research that affects every baby on the planet, lags far behind the well-known standards of good research. Poor health care counseling and medical research compromise the human right to subsistence, understood both as the opportunity to produce future generations and to live in good health. Thus, these violations of second-level rights objects also constitute violations of first-level rights objects. (One could also argue that lack of respect for the rights of mothers also violates the basic principles of dignity and equality, following Bordo's argument. The CRR, however, emphasizes that line of thinking in its discussion of the treatment of nonmothers.)

Upon analysis, it turns out, the CRR's list of challenges for women with HIV/AIDS is consistent with the theory of what constitutes human rights and their violations found in the UN Declaration of Human Rights. Global policies toward women with HIV/AIDS thus include three levels of human rights violations: violations of the specification of human rights subjects, of first-level human rights objects, and of second-level human rights objects.

CEDAW: A Theory of the Environmental Conditions of Human Rights

The 1979 Convention on the Elimination of All Forms of Discrimination against Women (CEDAW) offers a radical update to the 1948 UN Declaration of Human Rights. Whereas the declaration grounds the existence of human rights in human reason, CEDAW asserts that pure reason is not a powerful enough tool to establish human rights. In actual fact, people cannot implement human rights under certain conditions of social disruption. Disruptive conditions listed in the preamble to CEDAW include "all forms of racism . . . colonialism . . . aggression . . . [and] domination." Under certain conditions, CEDAW argues, people cannot even envision human rights. Specifically, a society lacking the full participation of women cannot develop a vision of human flourishing (Convention on the Elimination of All Forms of Discrimination against Women 1979).

Discrimination against women, according to CEDAW, initiates a damaging cycle. The lack of full participation by women—half the human race—stunts the growth of any society. In a stunted society, women as well as men cannot develop as fully flourishing human beings. Thus, the society is denied the nourishing impact of their participation. Thus, by implication, the society exists in a permanent state of disruption, instability, and inequality, making it difficult to imagine and implement appropriate human rights protections.

The cycle of disruption can only be broken, as CEDAW asserts in Article 5, by widespread change in the "social and cultural patterns of conduct of men and women, . . . which are based on the idea of inferiority or superiority of either of the sexes or on stereotyped roles for men and women." One of the first areas of intervention must be an understanding of "the social significance of maternity." Maternity should not ever constitute grounds for discrimination against women. Instead, as the preamble states, all societies should recognize that raising children "requires a sharing of responsibility between men and women and society as a whole."

To use Kantian language, CEDAW does not ground its guarantee of human rights in a categorical imperative. The categorical imperative alone is judged insufficient. CEDAW thus supplements it with a series of hypothetical imperatives. If you want to guarantee human rights, you must create a stable, flourishing society. If you want to create a stable society, you must abolish all forms of discrimination. If you want to abolish all forms of discrimination, you must change patterns of thought and practice that legitimate discrimination.

CEDAW thus offers an answer to some feminist philosophers who are skeptical about the use of rights language grounded in Kant's categorical imperative. Some feminist critics of Kant suggest that Kant's limitations and biases make his philosophy, at least without significant emendation, a poor foundation for moral argument. Genevieve Lloyd (1984) and Sally Sedgwick (1977, 77–100) argue that Kant's emphasis on reason excludes from moral relevance categories of inner experience relegated to the feminine. Robin May Schott explains that Kant's ethics actually reflect a devaluation of human worth. By privileging reason that yields universal rules over the needs of human bodies in specific situations, Kant "reflects the reified social relations that characterized the emerging capitalist order in which persons . . . became reduced to objects of exchange in the marketplace" (Schott 1988, x). Finally, Onora O'Neill notes the lack of emphasis on community in the pure form of Kantian ethics. Even purely rational agents, she asserts, "need support from others if they are to remain agents" (O'Neill 1989, 354).

CEDAW is a product of the same vision that inspired this feminist philosophical critique of Kant. Its discussion of the *subjects* of human rights presents the vision of a gender-integrated society where male and female categories of experience inform public policy. When CEDAW begins to specify human rights *objects*, it calls for attention to the needs of gendered individuals in their specific social locations, so that these real needs can play a role in policy formation. And CEDAW calls for a revisioning of community in terms of equality, inviting human beings to join in a shared enterprise of cultural evolution. Instead of simply showing the irrelevance of Kant's concept of the categorical imperative, CEDAW shows that Kant's concept of the hypothetical imperative can be creatively used to sharpen the international vision of universal human rights.

CEDAW: Avoiding Discrimination in Human Rights Subjects and Objects

Because of CEDAW's insistence on creating conditions of nondiscrimination in which the human rights of women can flourish, its description of the subjects and objects of human rights is connected. For women to fully be subjects of human rights, Article 3 asserts, changes must be made in the "political, social, economic, and cultural fields." Political, social, economic and cultural equality are the first-level rights specified in CEDAW.

Clearly, international HIV/AIDS policies violate the human rights of women according to CEDAW's understanding of the basic principles of human rights *subjects*. When health policy makers overemphasize mothering at the expense of other dimensions of women's lives, they are guided only by ideas of "stereotyped roles for men and women." When policy makers place the burden of controlling sex and reproductive health squarely on women and girls, they are ignoring the "sharing of responsibility" that makes a new generation possible. At the same time, they are bypassing gender equality in the four spheres of first-level rights objects identified by CEDAW.

244 LAURA DUHAN KAPLAN

CEDAW's enumeration of second-level rights objects reflects ideals for a society free of sexism and other forms of discrimination. Thus, Articles 7 through 16 include at least ten areas of practice in which women have a right to equality and autonomy, including health care, housing, legal rights, and marriage rights. CEDAW is careful to give specific instructions for implementing these rights without discrimination. For example, the right to health care includes family planning, the right to housing includes adequate sanitation facilities, and the right to economic participation includes attention to the roles of rural as well as urban women.

The application of this list of second-level rights objects to the allegations made by the Center for Reproductive Rights is obvious. For example, when pregnant mothers with HIV/AIDS are given incomplete information about family planning, their rights to education and health care are violated. When research studies into infant feeding fail to take into account obvious variables such as local water quality, the rights of rural women to equal health care and sanitation are ignored. In these ways, CEDAW's specification of rights objects strengthens the CRR's claims that international HIV/AIDS policies violate the human rights of women.

Conclusion

Clearly, the Center for Reproductive Rights is justified in its allegations that the human rights of women are violated by global HIV/AIDS policies. It is possible, however, to question the wisdom of criticizing these policies on human rights grounds. Here I offer three possible questions and answer each of them.

The first question deals with the issue of cultural differences. In some countries, majority opinion favors abortion, and in others it does not. Some traditional societies honor abstinence and hold individuals strongly to social norms, while more modern societies value the dissemination of objective information so that individuals can make informed decisions. Is it really right to hold all of these societies to the same standards when evaluating the ways that the human rights of women with HIV/AIDS are compromised?

The answer to this question is simple. Any country that has signed on to an international human rights convention is bound by its articles. While there may be room for interpretation on certain points, such as the nature of good counseling, the Declaration of Human Rights, for example, is quite clear on other points. The security and subsistence of women may not be compromised by poorly designed and implemented health care policies. This is particularly true in cases where well-designed policies cost no more than poorly designed ones.

The second question comes from noting the severity of the global AIDS crisis. Many rights theorists note that human rights can be suspended in certain emergencies. For example, when self-defense is required, one person may be excused from murdering another. In the case of a defensive war, a country may be excused from lessening civil liberties to restrict an enemy's ability to infiltrate public organizations. Could not the AIDS crisis be seen as an event that demands self-defense? Might it not be appropriate to restrict rights to reproduction, marriage, and equal distribution of health care benefits?

My response to this question is twofold. First, even if one could construct an argument about the limitation of certain rights, this argument would not defend practices that limit the access women with HIV/AIDS have to good health care, research, and counseling. These limitations are not based in reasoned self-defense but in other political and social currents. Second, the AIDS crisis is not analogous to a violent situation that requires short-term acts of self-defense. The spread of AIDS can be slowed through education that leads to gradual changes in behavior. Practices that interfere with this education are counterproductive. Because education requires recognition of the subjectivity of the persons being educated, practices that ignore the subjectivity of women with HIV/AIDS are also counterproductive.

The third question recognizes that, when resources are limited, difficult choices must be made. For example, the UN declaration states that "motherhood and childhood are entitled to special care and assistance." In some cases, providing that special care might entail limiting the access nonmothers have to health care. Is this hard reality not simply a pitfall in the implementation of human rights commitments?

My response is to note that yes, this is a pitfall, and even the declaration itself recognizes it. Articles 29 and 30 give voice to the difficulties of honoring all human rights commitments. Article 29 notes that nations may enact laws that limit the rights of some people to secure the rights and freedoms of an ordered society, while Article 30 notes that nothing in the declaration gives people the right to compromise any human rights. Thus, any decision made to advance the rights of some by limiting the rights of others must be carefully thought out so as to cause the least damage possible. One way of deciding how to distribute a second-level human rights object is to refer to higher principles. If a second-level right is compromised, it should be done in a way that increases access to a first-level right. Thus, if nonpregnant women cannot receive antiretroviral drugs, the aim and result should be to increase their overall access to subsistence, security, dignity, or equality. If this is not a likely outcome, the policy choice is not a good one. Many of the policy choices described by the Center for Reproductive Rights fail precisely this test. In addition to placing obstacles in the way of pregnant and nursing women, these policies diminish the social importance of women in their many other roles.

Thus, the appeal to human rights presented by the Center for Reproductive Rights is appropriate as well as powerful. As Patricia Williams argues, academic discourse about the limitations of rights theory sometimes emerges from a situation in which rights are already established. But for those treated as if they have no rights, the recognition of rights represents a huge step forward (Williams 1992). In its report "HIV/AIDS: Reproductive Rights on the Line" (2002), the CRR appeals to an internationally accepted political language, grounded in human rights treaties and conventions. This language expresses some of the higher social and moral ideals that should inform a feminist critique of global AIDS policies.

References

Bordo, Susan. 1993. *Unbearable Weight: Feminism, Western Culture, and the Body*. Berkeley: University of California Press.

Center for Reproductive Law and Policy. 2001. *Reproductive Rights Are Human Rights* (July): 5–6, at www.crlp.org.

Center for Reproductive Rights. 2002. "HIV/AIDS: Reproductive Rights on the Line," at www.crlp.org.

"Convention on the Elimination of All Forms of Discrimination against Women." 1979. At www.unhchr.ch/html/menu3/b/e1cedaw.htm (Accessed September 2003).

Kant, Immanuel. 1977. "Grounding for the Metaphysics of Morals." In *Classics of Western Philosophy*, 2nd ed., edited by Steven M. Cahn, 925–76. Indianapolis, Ind.: Hackett.

Lloyd, Genevieve. 1984. *The Man of Reason: "Male" and "Female" in Western Philosophy*. Minneapolis: University of Minnesota Press.

O'Neill, Onora. 1989. "Universal Laws and Ends-in-Themselves." *Monist* 1022: 354.

Orend, Brian. 2002. *Human Rights: Concept and Context*. Orchard Park, N.Y.: Broadview.

Schott, Robin May. 1988. *Cognition and Eros: A Critique of the Kantian Paradigm*. Boston: Beacon.

Sedgwick, Sally. 1977. "Can Kant's Ethics Survive the Feminist Critique?" In *Feminist Interpretations of Kant*, edited by Robin May Schott, 77–100. University Park: Pennsylvania State University Press.

Williams, Patricia. 1992. *The Alchemy of Race and Rights*. Cambridge, Mass.: Harvard University Press.

Index

About the Editors and Contributors

Karen L. Baird, PhD, is associate professor of political science at Purchase College, State University of New York. Her research focuses on the politics of women's health, and she is currently completing a book on women's health policy and activism in the United States in the 1990s. Other research interests include women's health and women's health activism in Africa. She previously published *Gender Justice and the Health Care System* (1998).

María Julia Bertomeu holds a PhD in philosophy from the Universidad Nacional de La Plata in Argentina. She is full professor of ethics in the philosophy department and a research member of CONICET (National Research and Technological Council). Her publications include *Bioethics: Latin American Perspectives*, coedited by Arleen Salles and María Julia Bertomeu (2002); and *Republicanismo y Democracia* (*Republicanism and Democracy*), coedited by Andrés De Francisco, Antoni Domènech, and María Julia Bertomeu (2002).

Martha Chinouya is director of Ubuntu-Hunhu, which she founded. This organization has invented community development methods for carrying out action research with African communities in the United Kingdom. Her research has provided much of the evidence base for policy development in respect to health promotion with African communities affected by HIV in the UK. She is postdoctoral research fellow at London Metropolitan University.

Donna L. Dickenson is the John Ferguson Professor of Global Ethics at the University of Birmingham (UK) and the author of *Property, Women and Politics* (1997), along with many journal articles and books in the field of bioethics. She was formerly Reader in Medical Ethics and Law at Imperial College School of

Medicine, London. Her particular interests include global commodification, trade, and property in tissue, gametes, and the human genome; she is currently directing a European Commission project on those themes, together with another on European women's rights as human rights.

Susan Dodds, PhD, is associate professor in philosophy at the University of Wollongong, New South Wales, Australia, where she teaches feminism, bioethics, and political philosophy. She is the current co-coordinator of the International Network on Feminist Approaches to Bioethics. Her research publications include work on research ethics, feminist bioethical responses to reproductive technology, and aged care policy and the political theory of postcolonialism. Her current work examines theories of democratic decision making as they apply to bioethics policy and regulation.

Anne Donchin is Emerita Professor of Philosophy and Women's Studies at Indiana University-Purdue University, Indianapolis. A founding "mother" of FAB, her research focus is bioethics and feminist philosophy. She has published numerous articles at the intersection of biomedical ethics and feminism and is coeditor (with Laura Purdy) of *Embodying Bioethics: Recent Feminist Advances* (Rowman & Littlefield, 1999), based on presentations at FAB's first international conference. She is currently completing a manuscript tentatively titled *Procreation, Power, and Personal Autonomy: A Feminist Critique*.

Michele Harvey-Blankenship, MD, PhD, is research associate at the Centre for International Health at the University of Toronto. Her use of genetics for the identification of disappeared and trafficked persons began in the laboratory of Mary-Claire King at the University of Washington in Seattle. She is continuing this work at the Genome Core Facility at the Hospital for Sick Children in Toronto.

Barbara Ann Hocking, PhD, LLM, is senior lecturer in the School of Justice at Queensland University of Technology Faculty of Law, Brisbane, Australia. She is the author of *Liability for Negligent Words* (1999) and is particularly interested in comparative human rights law. She is a visiting teacher and researcher at the Raoul Wallenberg Institute of Human Rights and Humanitarian Law in Lund, Sweden; vice president of the Association of Canadian Studies in Australia and New Zealand (ACSANZ); and a member of the International Commission of Jurists (ICJ) Queensland Chapter.

Laura Duhan Kaplan is professor and chair of philosophy at the University of North Carolina at Charlotte. Her publications, which include *Family Pictures: A*

Philosopher Explores the Familiar (1998) and *Philosophy and Everyday Life* (2002), address issues in peace studies, Jewish studies, and applied phenomenology. In 2002, she was named a U.S. Professor of the Year by the Carnegie Foundation and CASE.

Jing-Bao Nie, MD (tcm), PhD, was trained in traditional Chinese medicine in China and the medical humanities and social sciences in North America. He is senior lecturer at the Bioethics Centre of Otago University in New Zealand and holds adjunct or visiting professorship in several universities in China. He has published nearly sixty articles and book chapters on medical ethics and the history of medicine in Chinese and English, with a forthcoming book titled *Voices Behind the Silence: Chinese Views and Experiences of Abortion.*

Eileen O'Keefe is senior lecturer in philosophy and health policy at London Metropolitan University. She manages a health project in Ukraine, is consultant to the Commonwealth Secretariat, and is a member of the management committee of Consumers for Ethics in Research (CERES). Her books and other publications are devoted to inequalities in London, management of community health services, health impact assessment, and the role of multilateral bodies in globalization.

Carol Quinn, PhD, is assistant professor in the Department of Philosophy at the University of North Carolina at Charlotte. She is the UNC Charlotte Center for Professional and Applied Ethics Area Leader in Environmental Ethics. Her areas of specialization include philosophy of trauma, medical ethics, feminist ethics, ethics and the Holocaust, and the philosophy of sex. She is currently newsletter editor for the International Society of Lesbian and Gay Philosophy and the American Philosophical Association's Committee on the Status of Lesbian, Gay, Bisexual, and Transgendered Studies.

Arleen L. F. Salles, PhD, teaches philosophy at John Jay College of Criminal Justice (CUNY) and is a docent in the master's program in applied ethics at the University of Buenos Aires, Argentina. Her research interests include ethical theory, moral psychology, bioethics, and political philosophy. Recent publications center on emotions in ethical theory, particularism in bioethics, and autonomy and cultural differences. She is coeditor of *Bioethics: Latin American Perspectives* (2002), *Decisiones de vida y muerte* (1995), and *Bioética* (1998). She is an advisory board member of the Feminist Approaches to Bioethics network.

K. Shanthi, PhD, professor in the Department of Econometrics, University of Madras, India, also heads the university's Center for Gender Studies. She has published approximately thirty-five articles in various journals of national and international repute and guided scholars for their doctorate program. She was a recipient of a Fulbright Senior Postdoctoral Fellowship, an Indo-Canadian visiting lectureship, and UGC and ICSSR fellowships. India's FAB representative, she has traveled widely and participated in many international conferences.

Susana E. Sommer is a biologist at the Universidad de Buenos Aires, Argentina. A FAB board member since 1998, her recent publications include *Porqué las Vacas Se Volvieron Locas* (*Why the Cows Went Mad*) (2001); "Women's Reproductive Rights and Public Policy in Argentina," with M. V. Costa, in *Bioethics: Latin American Perspectives*, edited by Arleen Salles and M. J. Bertomeu (2002); "Prenatal Diagnosis, Women, and Bioethics," in *Bioetica Feminista Contemporánea*, edited by Debora Diniz (2003); "Transgenic Animals and Other Issues," in *Redes*; and "From Watson and Crick to Dolly," in *DNA: Fifty Years After. From the Double Helix to Biotechnology.*

Julia Tao Lai Po-Wah, PhD, is associate professor in the Department of Public and Social Administration at the City University of Hong Kong. She is currently the director of the Governance in Asia Research Centre. Her main research interests include the areas of applied ethics; comparative ethics with an emphasis on liberal, feminist, and Confucian ethics; and values of public policy.

Rosemarie Tong, PhD, is Distinguished Professor of Health Care Ethics at the University of North Carolina at Charlotte. In 1986, she was named National Professor of the Year by the Carnegie Foundation and Council for the Advancement and Support of Education. She is the author of fourteen books including *Globalizing Feminist Bioethics* (with Aida Santos and Gwen Anderson; 2001). She is immediate past co-coordinator of the International Network on Feminist Approaches to Bioethics, current chair of the National Committee for the Status of Women for the American Philosophical Association, and a member of the Executive Board of the International Association for Bioethics. Her research interests include global bioethics, genetic and reproductive technology, health care reform, biomedical research (insofar as it involves vulnerable or underrepresented populations), and foundations of feminist thought.

Julie M. Zilberberg is Ethics Fellow at Mount Sinai School of Medicine in New York, where she teaches biomedical ethics. Her recent academic activities include presenting papers at Oxford University and Vassar College and publishing an article in *American Journal of Bioethics*. She is currently writing her dissertation on *The Ethics of Sex Selection* in the philosophy department at the Graduate Center of the City University of New York.